10 0197952 7

Author GEOLOGY

Classmark QE 261.5

Book No. 1001979527

UNIVERSITY
OF NOTTINGHAM

*George Green Library
of Science and Engineering*

# Geology of the Cirencester district

The Cirencester district, covered by 1:50 000 Geological Sheet 235, lies in the eastern part of Gloucestershire, in the heart of the Cotswolds Hills, a designated Area of Outstanding Natural Beauty. The Cotswold escarpment enters the north-western part of the district, but the rest comprises a rolling upland plateau, dissected by attractive winding valleys which drain south-eastwards to the River Thames, just beyond the southern boundary of the district. The town of Cirencester, the 'Capital of the Cotswolds', lies in the south-west of the district, and the easternmost outskirts of the busy town of Cheltenham lie in the extreme north-west. Otherwise the area is rural and sparsely populated. There are many attractive villages, popular with tourists, of which the best known are Bibury and Fairford.

Cirencester town and the surrounding villages derive their character from the attractive buildings, built and roofed with local limestone quarried from the Middle Jurassic Great Oolite and Inferior Oolite groups. The use of local stone is also ubiquitous in the dry-stone field walls of the district, and walkers will soon become aware of the numerous ancient quarries which pockmark the landscape. As a result, the geology of the district, with its varied lithologies and abundant fossils, is hard to ignore and has been studied by geologists from the earliest days of the science. Nevertheless, the district had never been systematically surveyed in detail until the present survey was completed in 1994. This memoir integrates the information gathered during that survey with information from the literature. It provides a valuable synthesis of the geology of a classic area of Middle Jurassic stratigraphy, and gives an insight into the more ancient rocks at depth, as well as the more recent geological development of the area. It also deals with the more practical and commercial aspects of the geology, and includes data of value to those concerned with planning, civil engineering, and the water and mineral industries.

*Cover photograph*

Arlington Row, Bibury [SP 115 066]. This ancient row of weavers' cottages is an attractive example of Cotswold village architecture, of which many others may be found within the Cirencester district. The cottages are built of locally quarried freestone, and are roofed with 'Cotswold Slates' or tilestones, another type of limestone from within the district (A 15457). (Photographer: T P Cullen)

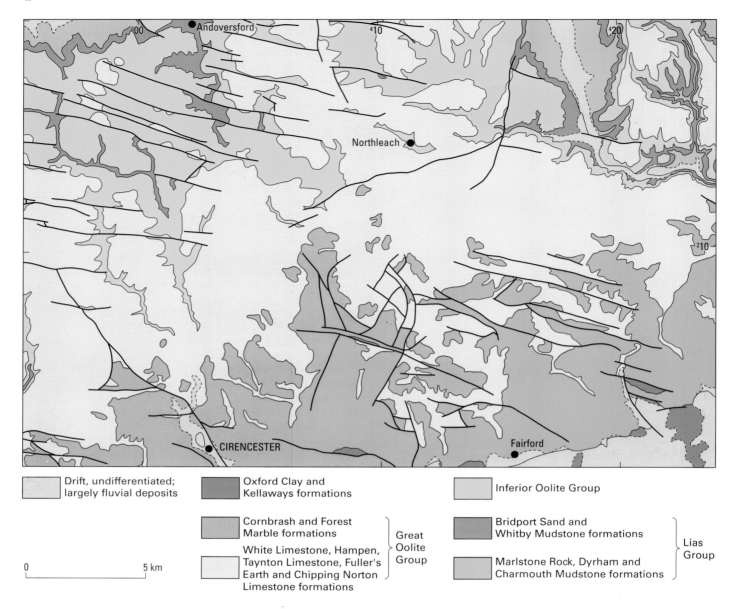

**Figure 1**   Simplified geological map of the Cirencester district.

BRITISH GEOLOGICAL SURVEY

M G SUMBLER
A J M BARRON
A N MORIGI

# Geology of the Cirencester district

Memoir for 1:50 000 Geological Sheet 235
(England and Wales)

CONTRIBUTORS

*Stratigraphy*
B M Cox
H C Ivimey-Cook
A Horton
G K Lott
G Warrington
I T Williamson

*Basement structure and geophysics*
T C Pharaoh

*Engineering geology*
A Forster

*Hydrogeology*
D K Buckley
V K Robinson

UNIVERSITY LIBRARY DATE DUE FOR RETURN

3 0 AUG 2002

GGL VAR 39

This book may be recalled before the above date

90014

London: The Stationery Office    2000

© NERC copyright 2000

*First published 2000*

The grid used in the figures is the National Grid taken from the Ordnance Survey map. Figure 2 is based on material from Ordnance Survey 1:50 000 scale maps, numbers 162 and 163.
© Crown copyright reserved
Ordnance Survey Licence No. GD272191/2000

ISBN 0 11 884555 1      1001979527

*Bibliographical reference*

SUMBLER, M G, BARRON, A J M, and MORIGI, A N. 2000. Geology of the Cirencester district.   *Memoir of the British Geological Survey*, Sheet 235 (England and Wales)

*Authors*

M G Sumbler, MA, CGeol, FGS
A J M Barron, BSc, CGeol, FGS
A N Morigi, BSc, FGS
*British Geological Survey, Keyworth*

*Contributors*

B M Cox, BSc, PhD, CGeol
A Forster BSc, CGeol
G K Lott BSc, PhD
T C Pharaoh BSc, PhD, CGeol
G Warrington DSc, CGeol
I T Williamson BSc, PhD
*British Geological Survey, Keyworth*

D K Buckley BSc
*British Geological Survey, Wallingford*

A Horton, BSc
H C Ivimey-Cook BSc, PhD
*formerly British Geological Survey*

V K Robinson MSc, CGeol
*The Environment Agency (Thames Region), Reading*

*Other publications of the Survey dealing with this and adjoining districts are listed in Information Sources on p.87*

## Acknowledgements

This memoir was written and compiled chiefly by Mr Sumbler with assistance from Mr Barron (who is largely responsible for chapters 1 and 5), and Mr Morigi (Chapter 2 and Information Sources). In Chapter 2, the account of engineering geology is by Mr A Forster, and that of hydrogeology by Mr D K Buckley, with a contribution from Mr V K Robinson (Environment Agency). Dr G K Lott drafted the account of building stones. Chapters 3 and 9 incorporate work by Dr T C Pharaoh on the basement geology and structure, and the account of the Permo-Triassic in Chapter 3 is based largely on a report by Dr G Warrington. The accounts of the Stowell Park and Upton boreholes in Chapter 4 are based on work by Dr H C Ivimey-Cook. Dr B M Cox is largely responsible for the account of the Cornbrash in Chapter 6, and for most of Chapter 7. All parts of the memoir borrow heavily from the numerous Technical Reports listed in Information Sources. The manuscript was edited by Dr S G Molyneux.

The geological survey of the district was in part supported by the Thames Water Authority.

## Notes

Throughout the memoir, the word 'district' refers to the area covered by the 1:50 000 Series Geological Sheet 235 Cirencester. National Grid references are given in square brackets. Grid references of boreholes cited in the text are given in Information Sources (p.87). The authors of fossil taxa are cited on p.99.

Enquiries concerning the availability of geological data for the district should be addressed to the Manager, National Geosciences Records Centre, Keyworth.

# CONTENTS

FIGURES

## PLATES

## TABLES

# PREFACE

The Cirencester district lies in the heart of the Cotswold Hills, a designated Area of Outstanding Natural Beauty. The charm of this area is related directly to the underlying geology, not only through the influence that it has on the natural landscape, but also because towns and villages throughout the district, including Cirencester itself, derive much of their character from the use of local limestone for building and roofing. In addition, local stone is used to construct the dry-stone wall field boundaries which are such a distinctive feature of the Cotswold countryside, the vast quantities of stone used for this and building purposes being extracted from numerous quarries, now mostly disused. Some knowledge of the geology thus helps the visitor to appreciate the development of the landscape of the area, and also helps the conservationist to preserve its beauty.

More than this, however, an understanding of geology is essential for the proper management of natural resources and the avoidance of ground hazards, so that geology has a fundamental contribution to make to the decision-making process in matters of land-use planning. Aspects of geology relating to ground conditions and the management of water resources are particularly important in the Cirencester district. The fact that relatively hard limestones often overlie comparatively soft, plastic mudstones can create problems of slope instability and can affect foundation conditions, so that civil engineering works depend on a proper understanding of the local geology. Backfilling of quarries throughout the district creates its own ground condition problems, not only in relation to the geotechnical properties of the backfill material, but also in relation to potential hazards that might arise from the latter's chemical composition. As regards water resources, Jurassic limestones, including those that underlie much of the Cirencester district, are an important source of groundwater supplies for the United Kingdom. A detailed knowledge of their distribution, at outcrop and at subcrop beneath overlying beds, is necessary for the proper management of groundwater resources, for their protection, for water extraction, and for the development of underground storage facilities. Limestone is still quarried at several sites, and sand and gravel deposits have been exploited in the recent past; where extractive industries are concerned, a systematic assessment of resources is essential to help planners balance the needs of development against the needs of conservation.

In recognition of the importance of geology to decisions regarding land use, the British Geological Survey is funded through central Government to undertake a programme of geological data collection, interpretation, publication and archiving. One aim is to ensure coverage of the UK land area by modern 1:50 000 geological maps, accompanied by explanatory memoirs. The 1:50 000 scale map and memoir for the Cirencester district constitute part of the output from that programme of work.

For geologists, the Cotswolds constitute a classic area of Jurassic stratigraphy. The Middle Jurassic limestones, with their abundant and attractive fossils, have been studied by geologists since the early nineteenth century, but the Cirencester district had never been surveyed systematically or in detail until the work reported in this memoir was completed. Comparison of the map and memoir with the previous editions that were based essentially on small-scale surveys of the nineteenth century, shows the considerable advances made in geological knowledge and interpretation since that time. The memoir provides a valuable insight into the geology of the Cirencester district, including the more ancient rocks underlying the district at depth, and gives an indication of the substantial body of data held by the British Geological Survey that relate to the district. It is intended to be of practical value to a wide range of users who require geological information, including those involved in land-use planning and development, and those working in resource management, but will also enhance the understanding of the many people who visit the area simply to enjoy its natural and man-made beauty or to learn about its geological history.

David A Falvey, PhD
*Director*

*British Geological Survey*
*Keyworth*
*Nottingham*
*NG12 5GG*

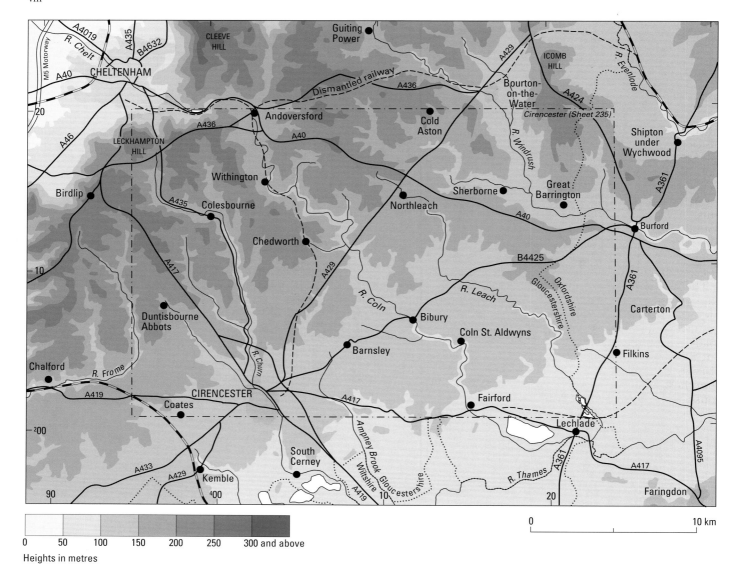

**Figure 2**  Physiography of the Cirencester district.

# ONE

# Introduction

This memoir describes the geology of the Cirencester district, covered by the 1:50 000 series Geological Sheet 235 (Figure 1). The district lies in the heart of the Cotswolds Hills, a designated Area of Outstanding Natural Beauty. In the extreme north-west, part of the Cotswold escarpment, here facing north, overlooks the southern outskirts of Cheltenham. The remainder of the district comprises a rolling upland plateau, dissected by winding valleys that are often dry or occupied by intermittent or transient streams. This plateau slopes gently to the valley of the upper Thames in the south-east (Figure 2).

The town of Cirencester lies in the south, with the large villages of Fairford to the east and Northleach to the north-east. Cirencester stands at a crossing point of the River Churn and the junction of three major Roman roads. The town boasts many important Roman remains, but like the many villages and hamlets throughout the district, it derives its present character from the later churches, houses and other buildings which have been constructed from the local Cotswold limestones. These have provided fine stone for building and roofing, which when weathered give the pleasing yellow and grey hues to the architecture of the region (see *Cover* photograph). The Cotswolds countryside is further renowned for the dry-stone walls that separate many of the fields; these are also built of local limestone.

Apart from the Roman roads, there are other ancient trackways notable for their straightness, including the White Way and Salt Way which cross the plateau seemingly regardless of the terrain. The modern A40 Oxford–Cheltenham road also traverses the high ground, and now bypasses Northleach. At the time of writing (1997), the Cirencester Bypass was under construction (opened 1998).

The district includes only a short section of operating railway track, part of the Swindon–Gloucester line in the extreme south-west, where there is also a stretch of the disused Thames–Severn Canal. However, disused railway lines run eastwards from Fairford, and between Cirencester and Andoversford, the latter including a number of cuttings which provide excellent exposures in the strata.

The River Chelt in the extreme north-west and the Frome in the extreme west both flow into the Severn, but otherwise all of the district's rivers drain south-eastwards into the Thames, which traverses the low ground beyond the southern margin. From the west, they are the Churn, Ampney Brook, Coln, Leach and Windrush (Figure 2). These are all more or less permanent watercourses, although parts of the course of the River Leach, and the upper reaches of the Ampney Brook (also known as the Winterwell), are intermittent or seasonal, appearing or disappearing with fluctuations in the groundwater table (See Chapter 2; Plate 12).

Concealed strata comprise a Precambrian to Lower Devonian basement of mudstone, sandstone and volcanic rocks, overlain in the east by an extension of the unexploited Oxfordshire Coalfield (Table 1). These are unconformably overlain by a Permo-Triassic sandstone and mudstone sequence, which has been investigated for hydrocarbon potential. The Permo-Triassic succession is covered by mudstones and limestones of the lowermost Jurassic. These Mesozoic strata were deposited in the 'Worcester Basin', the eastern boundary of which corresponds to the 'Vale of Moreton Axis'. The axis the district from north to south and accounts for a significant eastward thinning of the Mesozoic succession.

The strata that crop out in the district are all of Jurassic age. They range from the mudstones and siltstones of the Lias Group, through the predominantly limestone sequences of the Inferior Oolite and Great Oolite groups which crop out across most of the area, up to the mudstone and sandstone beds of the Kellaways and Oxford Clay formations (Figure 1). The beds are almost flat-lying, with a regional dip to the south-south-east of around 1°, but dips may attain 5° or more locally. The strata are cut by a number of faults with a predominant west-north-west to east-south-east trend, some of which exceed 10 km in length and have displacements of up to 60 m.

Outside the district, the mudstones of the Lias Group and the Oxford Clay Formation are important sources of brick clay, but within the district only the former has been exploited, near Cheltenham, Colesbourne and Sherborne. The outcrops of all the limestone formations are pockmarked by quarries, large and small, almost all now disused and degraded, but indicating the ubiquitous and abiding usage of the stone for local construction. Particularly valuable building stones were mined underground in several places. There are a number of larger quarries, the result of more recent industrial-scale extraction, but only a few are currently operational, notably at Daglingworth, 5 km north-west of Cirencester, and at Farmington, 2 km north-east of Northleach.

The highly permeable limestones of the Inferior Oolite and Great Oolite groups, underlain by the largely impermeable mudstones of the Lias Group and Fuller's Earth Formation respectively, form major aquifers in the region, from which numerous springs emerge, and from which water is abstracted both locally and in the district to the south.

Close to the surface, the various mudstone units weather to clay, and where they underlie steeper slopes, these are liable to fail. In consequence, there are extensive landslips along the escarpment in the north-west, and along the slopes of the Vale of Bourton and many other valleys, which may pose engineering hazards.

This juxtaposition of competent limestone strata with weak squeezable clays has also led to widespread cambering, which may include disrupted strata and concealed natural voids, a possible source of further engineering difficulties. An additional hazard may be posed by shallow stone-mines.

The upland of the district is largely drift free, but on the low ground in the extreme north-west and south-east, and around Cirencester town and in the Vale of Bourton, there are broad tracts of Quaternary superficial deposits. These are largely of fluvial origin and include substantial sand and gravel deposits. Some of these, particularly those bordering the lower reaches of the Coln and Leach, have extensive disused workings, mostly back-filled or flooded.

The broad, undulating upland plateau that dominates the district slopes from a high point of just under 300 m above sea level in the north-west to about 80 m in the south-east. It is underlain by the predominantly limestone sequence of the Inferior Oolite and Great Oolite groups. Prominent spurs, benches or slacks on the hillsides are mainly the result of the difference in resistance to erosion of the various limestone and mudstone strata, and the propensity to landslipping of the Fuller's Earth Formation and the Lias Group. Retreat of the escarpment in the north-west and in the Vale of Bourton continues by gradual landslipping, though less rapidly today than in the Pleistocene.

The plateau is dissected by a number of river valleys which cut across the geological grain in a south-eastwards direction. These are relics of an ancient drainage network, accentuated by seasonal meltwater torrents during the Pleistocene 'ice-ages'. As the flow diminished in intervening times, these evolved into meandering rivers, cutting down as the groundwater-table fell. In places they follow lines of weakness in the bedrock, for instance straight stretches of the Duntisbourne, Coltsmoor and Leach valleys lie along fault lines. The relief associated with the mudstone-dominated Kellaways and Oxford Clay formations is more subdued, and the rivers and streams crossing it occupy shallow valleys flanked by nearly flat terraces of sand and gravel.

## OUTLINE OF GEOLOGICAL HISTORY

The volcanic and volcaniclastic rocks inferred to be present at depth beneath the district are thought to have been deposited as part of a volcanic arc complex in the Late Precambrian, about 600 million years ago (Ma). They were folded and cleaved during the Cadomian orogeny (c.550 Ma) to form the floor of the Midland Platform, a stable crustal area throughout the early Palaeozoic. During Cambrian to earliest Ordovician times, these rocks were buried beneath a thick pile (up to 2.3 km) of marine shales and siltstones, deposited in a basin that extended from mid-Wales possibly as far as Belgium.

By about 480 Ma (early Ordovician), the Midland Platform (including the Cirencester district) was probably low-lying land, and remained emergent through much of the remainder of the Ordovician. Following a major transgression during the early Silurian (c.435 Ma), the entire platform was covered by a shallow sea. Volcanicity in the area of the Mendips, on the northern edge of a large landmass (Pretannia), generated basalt lava flows which, intercalated with mudstone, siltstone and sandstone beds, formed a thick sequence that may have extended across the entire region.

The extensive shallow sea endured into the late Silurian, and a considerable thickness of fossiliferous marine mudstone and limestone accumulated to the north of Pretannia. By then (c.415 Ma), however, the situation had reversed; gradual marine regression, resulting from silting up of the Welsh Basin and re-emergence of the Midlands Platform, heralded the onset of continental conditions in central England and Wales, while an ocean was created by the submergence of Pretannia to the south. In the latest Silurian, alluvial or littoral sedimentary regimes were established across much of England and Wales, with occasional marine incursions. Fluvial Old Red Sandstone facies spread progressively south-eastwards across England and Wales, depositing a thick sequence of red-brown mudstone and sandstone in early Devonian times.

The Acadian orogeny, the final phase of the Caledonian mountain-building episode, caused considerable deformation, uplift and erosion of the whole of southern Britain in mid-Devonian times (c.380 Ma). Predominantly fluvial deposition resumed in the late Devonian, on a wide coastal/littoral plain that extended through much of southern Britain, forming the red-brown sandstones and conglomerates of the Upper Old Red Sandstone that rest unconformably on the Lower Devonian sequence.

A major marine transgression in early Carboniferous times (355 Ma) established a broad tropical carbonate shelf across south Wales and southern England, on which a thick limestone sequence was deposited. However, from mid-Carboniferous times, a further orogenic episode (the Variscan) closed the ocean to the south, and caused uplift that extended the Wales–Brabant High southwards, such that no Namurian strata were deposited in southern England. In addition, the Lower Carboniferous limestones were exposed to severe erosion and were completely removed from the Cirencester district, although remnants are preserved in the areas to the east and west. By latest Carboniferous times (c.310 Ma), the Welsh, Malvern and London–Brabant highs had subdued relief, and were largely surrounded by broad floodplains on which red-brown and grey mudstone, siltstone and sandstone were accumulating, with, from time to time, coals and thin limestones (Upper Coal Measures).

The final phase of the Variscan orogeny uplifted most of southern England at the end of the Carboniferous (290 Ma). Through most of the Permian, the entire region was a desert in which the Palaeozoic strata at the surface suffered intense weathering and erosion. In the Cirencester district, erosion was most severe in the west, where Cambro-Ordovician strata are thought to have been exposed, with the Carboniferous succession being preserved only within the Oxfordshire Coalfield Syncline in the east. Hence, the earliest Permo-Triassic strata were deposited on a marked angular unconformity.

Crustal tension from early Permian to late Triassic times created the north–south-trending, fault-bounded Worcester Basin, in which a thick succession of continental sediments accumulated. The Permo-Triassic succession thins markedly eastwards from the basin onto the adjoining London Platform, as revealed by boreholes in the district. The earliest sediments to be deposited were Permian aeolian dune sands of the Bridgnorth Sandstone Formation. As the basin subsided, a substantial northward-flowing river became established in the Triassic, depositing conglomerates and sandstones of the Sherwood Sandstone Group.

As the Worcester Basin filled, a broad arid plain became established across the English Midlands and onto the London Platform. Red-brown windblown silt and mud (the Mercia Mudstone Group) accumulated to a considerable thickness, at least partly in brackish water from which evaporite layers and nodules were precipitated. The Mercia Mudstone displays greater marine influence in the last phase of its deposition (the Blue Anchor Formation), foreshadowing a transgression that established widespread shallow shelf seas across the region towards the end of the Triassic (c.210 Ma), represented by the grey, fossiliferous mudstones and limestones of the Penarth Group.

Continued sea-level rise from latest Triassic times caused the shallow sea to extend further, establishing marine deposition across much of England and Wales. The remaining land areas in southern Britain were low-lying, generating relatively little coarse clastic sediment, and so predominantly fine-grained sediments (Lias Group) were deposited throughout the Early Jurassic. At first, these were fossiliferous marine mudstones, with interbedded limestones at the base (Blue Lias and Charmouth Mudstone formations). As sedimentation transgressed eastward over the London Platform, the Mercia Mudstone and Penarth groups were overlapped to the east of the Cirencester district. A marked eastward thinning of the Lias succession is partly a result of progressive overlap of the lower beds, but may also be partly due to differential subsidence across the buried platform margin (the so-called Vale of Moreton Axis), such that the sequence to the east is condensed relative to that in the west. Later, increased terrigenous sediment supply, possibly accompanied by slight regression, added silt and fine sand to the mud being deposited (Dyrham Formation). Following this (c.190 Ma), rapid shallowing led to the formation of shoals across the region, with local erosion, in which iron-rich ooids were deposited with sand, silt and shell debris, to form the Marlstone Rock Formation.

With a deepening of the sea, mud deposition resumed to form the Whitby Mudstone Formation, which thins eastwards over the Vale of Moreton Axis because of both condensation of the sequence and subsequent erosion. Once again, regression or uplift of the land areas generated coarser sediment, and sandy beds began to appear within the mudstone succession forming the Bridport Sand Formation which is most fully developed to the south-west of the district. Open-marine conditions were abruptly terminated by a sea-level fall at the end of the Early Jurassic (c.180 Ma), which caused erosion of the highest part of the Lias Group.

By the earliest Mid Jurassic, a shallow shelf sea was established across the Cotswold region, and persisted through most of the Aalenian, Bajocian and Bathonian. It was bordered by landmasses to the north-west and south-east on which Lower Jurassic strata were probably exposed. A warm climate and a low input of terrigenous sediment were conducive to widespread carbonate formation and proliferation of marine life.

The widely deposited basal unit of the Inferior Oolite Group was deposited upon the exposed Lias Group strata. Following this, through much of the period of deposition of the Birdlip Limestone Formation, high-energy, open-water environments predominated, depositing ooid and bioclastic limestones from shoals or sheets of grains on a steadily subsiding shelf. The greatest thickness of sediment accumulated in the Cheltenham area, over the central part of the buried Worcester Basin. Periodically, more protected, lagoonal conditions were established locally, and marl, mud and algal pisoids accumulated. Early lithification at some horizons is indicated by the presence of hardgrounds, which in some cases may indicate local, temporary emergence. Later, regression resulted in deposition of terrigenous sand and mud, probably in an intertidal situation. Further sea-level fall led to these strata and older parts of the Birdlip Limestone Formation being eroded.

A subsequent rise of sea level led to the widespread deposition of the Aston Limestone Formation. This includes facies indicative of both a shallow shelf with a diverse bottom-dwelling fauna, moderate energy conditions and periodic terrigenous sediment input, and very shallow, high-energy shoal conditions.

A major hiatus in deposition followed. Uneven subsidence, coupled with a slight sea-level fall and consequent erosion, resulted in the Salperton Limestone Formation, at the top of the Inferior Oolite Group, overstepping strata ranging from the Aston Limestone to the Whitby Mudstone formations. Deposition was no longer constrained by the Vale of Moreton Axis, whose influence on sedimentation seems to have declined considerably, such that from about 170 Ma, the Salperton Limestone and younger Jurassic beds were deposited across a wider area, extending eastwards across much of the London Platform.

Deposition of the Salperton Limestone was succeeded in the east by deposition of the Chipping Norton Limestone Formation (Great Oolite Group) in very shallow water. In the deeper waters to the south-west, calcareous mudstones with thin limestones (the Fuller's Earth Formation) accumulated, eventually extending across the entire district. They thin eastwards, passing beyond the district into a predominantly limestone sequence that encroached onto the 'Oxford Shallows', at the margin of the remaining land area in the heart of the London Platform. Sandy beds near the top of the Fuller's Earth Formation reflect this terrigenous influence.

As sediment built up, marine carbonate deposition was re-established across the north Cotswolds. Ooids formed in the shallow, current-swept waters and were deposited with shell detritus from prograding shoals (Taynton Limestone Formation). In western parts, fine-grained ooids were deposited in thin, ripple-laminated beds, passing eastwards into very low-energy, interbedded marls and micritic limestones (Hampen Formation).

As an increasingly protected lagoonal environment developed, the passage from low to higher energy conditions shifted westwards, such that mainly low-energy micritic limestones (White Limestone Formation) were deposited in the Cirencester district, with oolite deposition continuing to the south-west. Periods of non-deposition in very shallow water resulted in extensive hardground formation, consistent with intermittent sea-level fluctuations. Younger parts of the formation display higher energy influences, and locally include coralline patch-reefs.

Following deposition of the White Limestone, a sea-level fall resulted in submarine erosion of its upper part, and the basal limestone beds of the Forest Marble Formation, representing high-energy conditions, accumulated in channels. In addition, thick beds of terrigenous silty clay with lignite fragments, derived from the landmass to the east, were deposited. Minor regression and erosion was followed by a major transgression (c.162 Ma) that deposited shallow marine limestones of the Cornbrash Formation across most of southern and eastern England.

As the water deepened, fine-grained marine sediments were deposited over an increasing area of the London Platform. Initially these were muds and sands of the Kellaways Formation, the latter perhaps representing reworked coastal or alluvial sands. The Kellaways Formation is succeeded by a thick sequence of mudstones of the Oxford Clay Formation, which accumulated in an open, fully marine environment. Widespread marine sedimentation continued through the Late Jurassic, depositing mudstones, sandstones and limestones of which no trace remains in the Cirencester district, but which are preserved to the south-east.

In latest Jurassic times, uplift of much of north-west Europe led to a fall in relative sea level, such that most of England and Wales, including the Cirencester district, formed an extensive landmass by the early Cretaceous (c.140 Ma). This tectonic activity may have produced most of the faulting seen at the surface in the district. The land area remained emergent until about 120 Ma, when a major transgression gradually submerged the Wessex Basin and East Midlands Shelf. The extent of the late Cretaceous sea which deposited the Chalk is unknown, as no deposits of that age occur in the district.

The commencement of the Alpine orogeny in earliest Palaeogene times (c.65 Ma) caused major compression of north-west Europe, resulting in uplift of many of the pre-existing lows, and formation of new basins such as the London and Hampshire basins. As a result of these movements, coupled with a global fall in sea level, the Cirencester district and the surrounding region became emergent, and has remained so ever since. Subaerial erosion through the Palaeogene and Neogene removed all the Upper Jurassic, Cretaceous and higher strata, originally perhaps several hundred metres thick, from the Cirencester district.

The predominant drainage pattern now seen in the district may have been instigated by this uplift, but the Thames–Evenlode system of the early to mid Pleistocene (c.1.5–0.5 Ma) is thought to have had a far larger catchment, including parts of the Midlands and Wales. Development of the Severn and the Cotswold escarpment truncated the upper part of the Thames–Evenlode during the mid Pleistocene. Later, the advance of the Anglian ice-sheet deposited till as far south as Moreton-in-Marsh, and material eroded as a result of the extreme arctic climate accumulated as 'head' and fluvial sediments along the rivers. These gravelly 'terraces' were later dissected, and lower terraces and modern alluvium were deposited by the river and its tributaries. This process continues to a minor degree to the present day.

## HISTORY OF RESEARCH

Study of the rocks of the Cotswolds dates back to the earliest days of English geology, when canal engineer William Smith deduced the constancy of the order of strata and their included fossils in the neighbourhood of Bath. In 1799, he compiled a geological map of the district and a *Table of the Order of Strata and their embedded Organic remains...* which extended from the Coal Measures up to the Chalk. This was published in 1813, and in the following years was revised and refined, the Jurassic portion notably by Buckland (1818).

Among the earliest geological studies which included the Cirencester district is Murchison's *Outline of the geology of the neighbourhood of Cheltenham* (1834; second edition, 1845), in which he gives an account of the strata from the 'New Red Sandstone' (Mercia Mudstone Group) to the Great Oolite, with sections on the structure (including landslip), drift and water supply. The variety, fossil content and accessibility of the rocks of the Cotswolds attracted many scholars, including Brodie (1850) and Wright (1856, 1860). In addition, a great spur to the study of the area was created by the founding of the Cotteswold Naturalists' Field Club in 1846.

The Geological Survey's maps at the scale of one inch to one mile of the north Cotswolds, Old Series sheets 34 and 44, were published in 1857 and 1856 respectively, and showed the disposition of the solid strata and alluvium. The maps covering the Cirencester district were surveyed by Edward Hull, who contributed to the accompanying explanatory memoirs (Ramsay, Aveline and Hull, 1858; Hull, 1857).

Following publication of these maps and memoirs, the district continued to attract the attention of many geologists, including W C Lucy (1872, 1890), and with the opening of railway lines, access was improved and new exposures became available. The cuttings on the newly constructed railways between Cirencester, Andoversford and Bourton-on-the-Water were first described by S S Buckman (1887, 1892) and A Harker (1890), and were figured in H B Woodward's (1894) account of the English Middle Jurassic. In a number of landmark papers, Buckman went on to elucidate the stratigraphy of the Inferior Oolite of the north Cotswolds, deducing a number of important stratigraphical breaks (Buckman, 1893, 1895, 1897, 1901).

In 1904, Linsdall Richardson published his 'Handbook to the geology of Cheltenham and neighbourhood'. Over the years, he described many exposures in the district (e.g. Richardson, 1906, 1907a, 1911) and wrote the memoirs for the Geological Survey New Series 1:63 360 scale sheets 217 (Moreton-in-Marsh) and 235 (Cirencester) (Richardson, 1929, 1933), the latter being the forerunner of the present account. The geology shown on these maps is taken from Hull's maps of the 1850s, with the addition of drift and the Chipping Norton Limestone by H G Dines. Around the same time, W J Arkell (1933a) compiled an overview of the Jurassic stratigraphy of Great Britain, providing a comprehensive framework for all future work. Later, the Geological Survey commissioned two major stratigraphical boreholes in the district, at Stowell Park and Upton, reported on by Green and Melville (1956) and Worssam (1963) respectively. During the drilling of the latter borehole, in 1952–1953, a detailed geological map of the immediate neighbourhood was made, as described by Worssam and Bisson (1961).

The first systematic, detailed survey of the Cirencester district began in 1984. The first phase of work, carried out by BGS in 1984 and 1985, involved the survey, at 1:10 000 scale, of the southern half of the district, together with parts of the district to the south. This survey was partly funded by the Thames Water Authority, whose responsibilities are now shared between Thames Water plc and the Environment Agency. The survey of the northern half of the district was carried out between 1992 and 1994; this included updating and amending Worssam and Bisson's earlier maps. Geological maps at 1:10 000 scale are available for the entire district, and corresponding descriptive reports are available for most of the maps. These items are listed in the Information Sources section of this memoir, together with other pertinent BGS maps, reports and publications, and an indication of other data held by BGS.

# TWO

# Applied geology

The key geological factors pertinent to planning and development in the Cirencester district are:

- Engineering geology: geotechnical properties, foundation conditions and slope stability
- Hydrogeology: water resource management and conservation
- Mineral and energy resources
- Soils and agriculture

## ENGINEERING GEOLOGY

### Geotechnical properties of formations

The solid (bedrock) geological formations that crop out in the Cirencester district are, in engineering terms, mainly weak to moderately strong limestones (with a few strong to very strong limestone units), overconsolidated, fissured, very stiff clays, and dense sands (Table 2). Natural superficial deposits overlie the bedrock as river alluvium, river terrace deposits, head, colluvium, hillwash and landslip deposits. They comprise combinations of normally consolidated clay, silt, sand and gravel. The varied nature of the geological materials present in the district, and the action of periglacial processes in the recent geological past, have exerted a considerable influence on ground conditions pertinent to end use and construction.

The intense freezing and thawing activity which took place during Pleistocene times has caused the bedrock to be disrupted, to a greater or lesser extent, to a depth of several metres. Limestone units are generally broken-up in the near-surface zone, and bedding and joint planes are dilated. Mudstone units have been similarly disrupted, with an attendant increase in their moisture content, and they may have been reduced in strength to a value approaching that for their remoulded condition (residual strength). In these circumstances, strength measurements may be more meaningful if obtained by in-situ methods, such as plate loading tests, rather than from laboratory determinations (Higginbottom and Fookes, 1971).

Although a particular geological formation may be dominated by limestone or mudstone, as generally indicated by the formation name, it may contain thin beds of material of contrasting properties which could have a significant influence on the engineering behaviour of the formation as a whole. Limestone blocks, for example, may slide on thin beds of clay where they dip outwards from a cut face, or thin limestone beds may

**Table 2** General classification of bedrock formations in terms of engineering behaviour.

| LIMESTONES — Generally weak to moderately strong, more rarely strong to very strong |
|---|
| Cornbrash Formation<br>White Limestone Formation<br>Hampen Formation<br>Taynton Limestone Formation<br>Chipping Norton Limestone Formation<br>Salperton Limestone Formation<br>Aston Limestone Formation<br>Birdlip Limestone Formation (Scottsquar, Cleeve Cloud, Crickley and Leckhampton members)<br>Marlstone Rock Formation |

| MUDSTONES — Overconsolidated, fissured, generally stiff (weathered clay) to weak (fresh mud rock) |
|---|
| Oxford Clay Formation<br>Kellaways Clay Member<br>Forest Marble Formation<br>Fuller's Earth Formation<br>Birdlip Limestone Formation (Harford Member (part))<br>Whitby Mudstone Formation<br>Dyrham Formation<br>Charmouth Mudstone Formation |

| SANDS — Generally dense to very dense |
|---|
| Kellaways Sand Member<br>Birdlip Limestone Formation (Harford Member (part))<br>Bridport Sand Formation |

impair the excavation of a predominately mudstone formation. Thus, after a desk study has ascertained the general geological environment, it is important to determine the precise nature of the materials present by an appropriate site investigation.

## Foundation conditions

In general, the **limestones** of the district offer good foundation conditions, but with some important exceptions. Limestone may contain cavities where water charged with carbon dioxide has dissolved the calcium carbonate of the rock fabric. This process is active at the present time, but would have been more vigorous under periglacial conditions because the solubility of carbon dioxide is higher at low temperatures. The magnitude of such voids is not likely to be very great, but they might be expected to occur as widened joints, perhaps of the order of tens of millimetres across.

More significant voids may be found in the form of linear, tensional features called gulls which occur in cambered strata (see Chapter 9). The ground conditions that result from cambering are very significant for land use and construction on upper valley slopes, and on the limestone plateau for some distance from the valley side. Gulls may either be open, or more or less infilled by material washed in from above; this may comprise a mixture of clay, sand and limestone debris with a bearing capacity and compressibility very different from that of the surrounding limestone. In some instances, open gulls may be bridged at rock head by naturally cemented limestone. Foundations which cross a gull, in whole or in part, might encounter problems due to lack of support and differential settlement and compaction. If a foundation cannot be relocated to better ground, it may be possible to design a reinforced raft or strip foundation capable of bridging areas of weak ground or voids (Hawkins and Privett, 1981). One way to investigate for the presence of gulls is by digging intersection trenches at right angles to the inferred gull direction.

In addition to the problem of natural rock cavities, the possibility of man-made voids should be considered. Many of the limestone formations of the area have been worked from quarries which, because of backfilling, may no longer be apparent at the surface. In addition, both the Taynton Limestone and White Limestone formations are known to have been worked by means of shafts and galleries between Farmington [SP 135 154] and Burford [SP 251 121], and near Barnsley [SP 098 055], and it is possible that these and other formations have been mined elsewhere.

In areas where either natural or artificial cavities may be suspected, investigation of the ground for voids before construction would be prudent. Appropriate techniques include black and white, colour and infra red aerial photography, and engineering geophysical and engineering geomorphological surveys. Care should be taken with the disposal of surface water, to avoid washing out material that infills voids, as this might induce surface collapse or initiate (or reactivate) landslipping.

Geotechnical data for similar geological formations in other districts (Forster et al., 1995) indicate that conditions for sulphate attack on concrete foundations excavated within limestone units below the water table are likely to fall into class 1, as defined in Building Research Establishment Digest 363 (Anon., 1991).

The **mudstones** in the district may offer reasonable foundation conditions if suitable designs are adopted. They are generally of high plasticity, but may range from intermediate to very high plasticity. In the weathered zone, strength is likely to be lower and plasticity higher because the original structure of the material is disrupted and moisture content increased. High plasticity clays are particularly prone to volume changes, with variation in moisture content resulting in clay shrinkage problems to foundations in times of drought (Anon., 1980a, 1980b, 1993) or when trees are planted too close to buildings (Anon., 1985). Conversely, when desiccated ground rehydrates following the removal of established trees, hedges or at the end of a drought period, the ground will swell. In order to avoid shrinking or swelling problems, deeper foundations may be needed to carry the load below the zone affected by moisture content changes. Provision of compressible material to accommodate lateral earth pressures may also be necessary. Soft material encountered below foundation level should be removed and replaced by suitable fill, and temporary excavations for foundations should be protected from the ingress of water.

Construction on mudstone or clay on valley sides, particularly on the Fuller's Earth Formation or Lias Group, may encounter landslip deposits with low (remoulded) strength values. A stability analysis may be necessary to ensure that the ground will support the structure, and that changes to the ground will not trigger instability up or down slope of the site. The disposal of surface water away from areas of actual or potential landslipping is particularly important.

Mudstone formations, where exposed in the bottom of valleys, may have suffered lateral squeezing and uplift that has left them in a contorted, partially remoulded condition with an increased moisture content. This phenomenon, known as valley bulging (see Chapter 9), is particularly common in the Whitby Mudstone Formation, for example near Turkdean [SP 106 173]. Foundations on such material should take account of the consequent loss of strength.

Geotechnical data for similar geological formations in other districts (Forster et al., 1995) indicate that conditions for sulphate attack on concrete foundations below the water table, for most mudstone units in the area, are likely to fall into class 1 or 2, except for the Oxford Clay which is likely to be class 3, as defined in Building Research Establishment Digest 363 (Anon., 1991). However, unless there is a high level of dissolved sulphate in groundwater which is flowing and in contact with the concrete structure, there is unlikely to be a significant problem of sulphate attack.

The **sandstone** units of the district should offer reasonable foundation conditions where they are sufficiently dense and are protected from erosion by surface water or groundwater flow. Foundations for most buildings are likely to be sufficiently deep to be unaffected by frost heave, but for very shallow foundations, such as those for roads and concrete hardstanding, the possibility of frost heave may need to be considered, particularly where the material is of a fine sand or silt grade and where the water table is sufficiently close to the surface for the upward migration of water by capillarity. Frost-susceptible siltstone and sandstone beds may also be present within predominantly mudstone units.

Of the **natural superficial deposits** present in the district, the most significant in the context of construction is alluvium. Many of the deposits of head which occur in valley bottoms may have similar properties. Alluvium is generally a normally consolidated, grey, brown, more or less calcareous silty clay or silt, often resting on a basal limestone gravel. It is generally a soft to firm, compressible material, and does not usually offer good foundation conditions. Where peaty or organic layers or lenses are present, it may suffer from differential consolidation. Alluvium may also have a desiccated crust with higher strength than the underlying material. Geotechnical data for alluvium in other areas (Forster et al., 1995) indicate that conditions for sulphate attack on concrete foundations below the water table are likely to fall into class 1, as defined in Building Research Establishment Digest 363 (Anon., 1991).

### Excavations

In the near-surface zone, where strata have been disrupted by weathering, frost action and solution, excavation of most of the limestones of the district should be possible using mechanical excavators, and by ripping as less-weathered material is encountered. However, more powerful machinery and the use of pneumatic tools may be necessary to deal with the more massive blocks, perhaps up to 2 m across, in some of the more thickly bedded units such as the White Limestone, Taynton Limestone and Birdlip Limestone formations. In general, the strength of most of the limestones is expected to fall in the moderately strong range, with an unconfined compressive strength of 12.5 to 50 MPa, but significantly stronger units are present locally. Some beds in the White Limestone Formation at Daglingworth Quarry [SP 001 061] (Plate 9) have been quoted as having an unconfined compressive strength of 136 MPa (Anon., 1972). Although such beds are usually less than 0.5 m thick, they are sufficiently strong to be a problem in small or narrow excavations, such as service trenches, where jointing and bedding are less easily exploited to remove material. Similarly, the more tabular limestones such as the Forest Marble might present problems in small excavations. Other significantly strong limestones include the Notgrove and Gryphite Grit members (Aston Limestone Formation), and the Upper Trigonia Grit Member (Salperton Limestone Formation).

The stability of cut faces in the limestone units may be expected to be good where they conform to the regional dip of about 1–2°, but where they have been affected by faulting, cambering or landslipping, they may have local dips of up to 15° or more. Cut faces in such areas may experience stability problems from rock fall and block slides where bedding planes dip out of the face, particularly where the rock is significantly fractured.

Excavations in the mudstone units should be possible using mechanical excavators, but may become progressively more difficult where limestone beds are encountered, as in the upper part of the Fuller's Earth Formation. In these situations ripping or pneumatic tools may be necessary. Mudstones exposed in the bottom of excavations may be prone to softening on the uptake of water, thus impairing the movement of wheeled vehicles on the site. Consequently, excavations for foundations may need to be protected from the inflow of surface water. The stand-up time of excavations in areas affected by valley bulging and landslipped material may be shorter than expected, and immediate support may be required.

Excavations in the sandstone units should be readily achieved with digging machinery, but support in excavations may be required, and groundwater inflow may need to be controlled. Similarly, it should be easy to make excavations in natural superficial deposits, but support may be required to maintain the stability of cut faces, and provision to control the flow of water into excavations below the water table may be necessary to avoid running sand conditions. If a desiccated crust is present, passage of wheeled vehicles on site may be impaired if it is removed or disrupted.

### Use as engineering fill

The limestones of the area should be well suited for use as engineering fill if crushed and graded; the mudstones should be suitable if the moisture content of the more plastic clays is controlled within suitable limits during placement. Bedrock sandstone formations and superficial gravels may also be suitable if the particle size grading is appropriate, but alluvium, head and landslip deposits are less appropriate due to their higher moisture contents and the likely presence of organic material.

### Slope stability

Ancient and/or modern slope movements are common on valley sides in the area. Landslips result when the strength of the material of the slope is too low to resist the downward shear stress due to the force of gravity. The slope changes shape until it reaches an equilibrium angle at which the material strength is in balance with the stress. Landslips may be triggered by an increase in the shear stress, or by a reduction of the shear strength of the slope-forming material. The former situation is encountered where the angle of slope is increased by undercutting, and the latter by changes in structure and composition due to weathering or an increase in pore water pressure.

All geological formations may exhibit some form of slope instability under some circumstances, but within the Cirencester district, the Fuller's Earth Formation and the mudstone formations in the Lias Group are most commonly affected (see Chapter 9). These formations include highly plastic clays and underlie limestones that act as aquifers. The clay at the interface reduces in strength as it takes in water, and is further reduced in strength as pore water pressures increase, ultimately reaching failure. Groundwater issuing at the base of the limestone, where it crops out on a slope, increases the moisture content of the weathered clay in the near-surface zone, and that of the landslipped material down-slope. If the water input is sufficient, the increasing satu-ration and disruption caused by landslipping leads even-tually to the development of mudflows. The progression from the terraced slopes of multiple rotational failure, downhill through hummocky ground of mud and debris-slides, to spreading, lobate mudflows, is commonly seen on slopes in the district (Plate 1). Water carried by thin limestone beds within the clay formations and from perched water tables within the landslips themselves may also adversely affect stability.

During the survey of the district, landslips were recog-nised and mapped by walk-over survey, aided by the use of aerial photographs. Some of these landslips are still inter-mittently active. For example, at Lineover Wood [SO 987 189], tilted trees provide evidence of very recent activity, and near Dowdeswell [SP 003 198], local residents have observed active landslipping within the last few years. On the north bank of Dowdeswell Reservoir, the stability of the ground is regularly monitored for possible slippage, and a few hundred metres to the east of the reservoir, just outside the northern boundary of the district, the A40 trunk road was recently disrupted because of landslipping.

The surface expression of landslips may be obscured by natural degradation or by agricultural practices within very few years, (Hutchinson, 1967). However, below the surface, material will remain in a weak, remoulded condition and contain shear surfaces which may be reac-tivated if the pore water pressure rises or the slope is undercut. Before any construction work on slopes in sus-ceptible clay formations, trial pits should be dug and

examined for evidence of past movement, such as relict shear surfaces.

## Made ground

Small areas of made ground occur at many localities in the district, not all of which are necessarily indicated on the map. They occur either as mounds on the existing ground surface, or as an infill within pre-existing excava-tions. The first category includes mainly engineered fill, such as road and rail embankments. There are many examples of the second category throughout the district ; these are mainly backfilled quarries or gravel pits. The most extensive are at the former Foss Cross Quarry [SP 055 093] (Plate 10), which has been largely back-filled with domestic refuse, and the abandoned, partly backfilled sand and gravel workings between Fairford and Lechlade in the south-east of the district. Construc-tion on artificial fill should only be carried out after a detailed site investigation has determined the geotechni-cal properties of the site, particularly those affecting bearing capacity and settlement. Other hazards may include gases such as methane derived from the breakdown of organic materials, and chemical wastes from industry and agriculture.

## HYDROGEOLOGY AND WATER RESOURCES

In terms of yield, Jurassic limestones are the third most important source of groundwater in the United Kingdom. In the Cirencester district, two separate and relatively thick aquifers occur, namely the Inferior Oolite aquifer and the Great Oolite aquifer (Figure 3). Although they are exposed and thus unconfined over much of the district, both dip south-eastwards beneath a cover of younger rocks which eventually confine them.

**Plate 1** Landslipped Fuller's Earth Formation, Pen Hill, Colesbourne [SO 995 124].

The terracing in the upper part of the slip results from rotational or translational movements on discrete shear surfaces, but the lower part is composed of mounded, lobate mudflows, some of which are still sporadically active (A 15452).

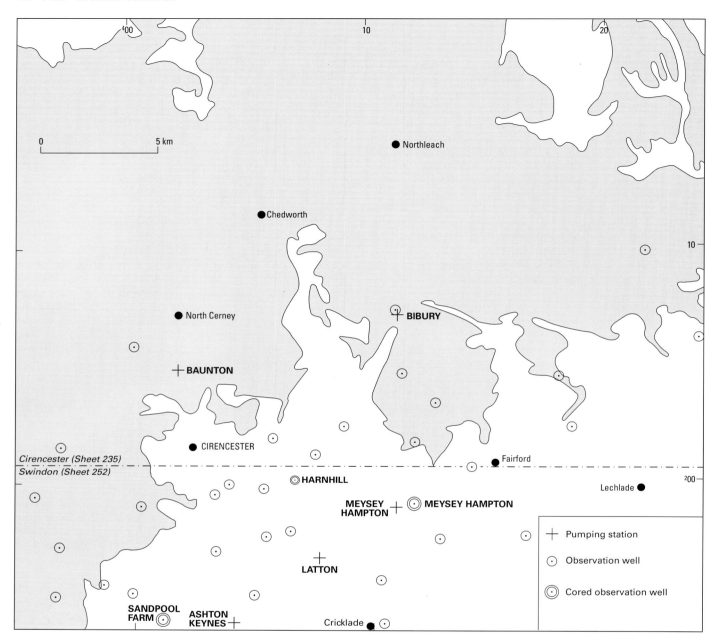

**Figure 3** Map showing combined outcrop of Inferior Oolite and Great Oolite aquifers (shaded), and location of main pumping stations and observation boreholes in the Cirencester district and the adjoining area to the south. The two aquifers are separated by the 'aquiclude' of the Fuller's Earth Formation (see 1:50 000 Geological Sheet 235).

The mean annual rainfall over the outcrop area is 760 mm, increasing to 890 mm in the south-west, and recharge of the limestone aquifer has been estimated at 370 mm/y (Morgan-Jones and Eggboro, 1981). The water resources in the district are administered by the Environment Agency (Thames Region).

The **Inferior Oolite aquifer** comprises the limestones which form the greater part of the Inferior Oolite Group (Chapter 5), together with any Bridport Sand Formation (Lias Group) which may be present below in the west,

and Chipping Norton Limestone (Great Oolite Group) which occurs above in the east. The aquifer crops out in the north and north-western parts of the district, forming the main part of the Cotswolds escarpment overlooking Cheltenham. It varies in thickness from over 80 m in the north-west, but thins slightly to the south, and also thins markedly across the Vale of Moreton Axis to little more than 15 m in the east. The Inferior Oolite aquifer is not as fissured as the Great Oolite; transmissivities (T) are typically 400–600 m²/d. Where the aquifer is confined in the southern part of the district, the aquifer porosity and permeability is reduced, and water quality is poor.

The Inferior Oolite aquifer becomes confined by the mudstones of the Fuller's Earth Formation some 6–7 km down dip. This unit, actually a part of the Great Oolite Group (Chapter 6), forms an aquiclude of variable efficiency that separates water in the Inferior Oolite aquifer from that in the overlying Great Oolite aquifer. The seal is most effective in the west, where the mudstones are thickest (locally up to 30 m). In places in the north-east, the Fuller's Earth is absent, and the Inferior Oolite and Great Oolite aquifers are in continuity.

The **Great Oolite aquifer** comprises the limestone formations in the middle part of the Great Oolite Group, above the Fuller's Earth mudstones. The aquifer is 40 to 45 m thick throughout the district, without the marked thickness variation of the Inferior Oolite. It offers a large area for recharge, being exposed over approximately 50% of the district and having an outcrop width of approximately 10 km, before becoming confined by overlying mudstone units that comprise the upper part of the Forest Marble Formation and the succeeding Kellaways and Oxford Clay formations. Three main limestone units, the Taynton Limestone Formation, the White Limestone Formation, and the beds that dominate the lower part of the Forest Marble Formation, are the main producing units. More clayey and less permeable units are present, notably in the Hampen Formation and sporadically in the White Limestone Formation, especially in the eastern part of the district. These locally restrict and divert recharge to contact springs, and are responsible for slight chemical differences between groundwaters of the limestone units. The Cornbrash Formation (topmost Great Oolite Group) forms a separate, relatively insignificant aquifer between the mudstones of the Forest Marble and Kellaways formations.

The Great Oolite limestones are brittle and fractured, and contain numerous fissured horizons. A small number of main fissures concentrate groundwater movement and contribute high transmissivity, and are responsible for high borehole yields. Transmissivity (T) of unconfined Great Oolite is high, typically up to 4500 m$^2$/d. Where confined at shallow depth, as in the southern part of the district, transmissivity decreases to 1200–1500 m$^2$/d, reducing further to about 400 m$^2$/d down dip. The aquifer storage (S) is small, so that aquifer diffusivity (T/S) is high. This imparts a rapid response to recharge and drainage events. In upland areas, it is not unusual for the recharge in the Great Oolite aquifer to be rapidly dissipated via the fissure system, and for groundwater levels to fall several tens of metres and drain down close to the base of the aquifer during the summer months. This is shown by characteristic 'flat-bottomed' well hydrographs (Figure 4a), and by the seasonal or intermittent flow of streams such as the Ampney Brook and River Leach (Plate 12).

A feature of the Cotswold escarpment in the north-west of the district is the general paucity of escarpment springs. Instead, several streams are developed on the dip slope of the limestones; these flow generally towards the south-east, up-sequence across progressively younger rocks. They include, from west to east, the Duntisbourne Brook, the River Churn, the Ampney Brook, and the rivers Coln, Leach and Windrush (Figure 2). On the valley slopes, contact springs are thrown out from the Inferior Oolite aquifer at the junction with the underlying Whitby Mudstone Formation, and at the base of the Great Oolite aquifer at the junction with the Fuller's Earth mudstones. Other springs may be associated with clay or marl horizons within the aquifers, or more rarely, where the aquifer is faulted. A good example of the latter is the Swan Spring [SP 1144 0698] at Bibury, which was a source of water for many years. A well constructed nearby in the 1950s proved dry, however, and mapping suggests that, although the spring is sited on the Great Oolite outcrop, the waters derive from the Inferior Oolite via a fault.

Dip slope springs may rise in the valley floor where the Inferior Oolite becomes confined beneath the Fuller's Earth, but this water may be lost where the streams cross onto the Great Oolite outcrop. Thus some of the Inferior Oolite groundwater discharged to the streams in the north recharges the Great Oolite aquifer farther south. Several streams therefore have an intermittent character, as typified by the accretion hydrograph for the River Churn which shows a loss of flow where it crosses the aquifers (Figure 5). The Great Oolite aquifer eventually discharges in a series of dip slope springs in the south and south-east, for example at Ampney Park [SP 062 023], near Quenington [SP 147 030], and at Boxwell Springs [SU 059 977] just south of the district. A small proportion of groundwater continues to flow south in the aquifer under increasing confinement, but the water quality soon deteriorates.

Maximum groundwater levels in both aquifers may be limited by the elevation of springs in valleys, so that some boreholes close to the spring line display flat-topped hydrographs (Figure 4b). Consistent breaks in the rate of water level rise and fall are also an indication of the position of important fissured horizons. A natural consequence of the well-developed fissure system and high diffusivity is that head changes caused by borehole abstractions are transmitted rapidly over long distances, affecting borehole water levels and spring flows several kilometres distant from abstraction sources. This, together with the large seasonal change in water levels, affects the yields of boreholes tapping the unconfined Great Oolite aquifer. The depth to water in the Great Oolite aquifer varies, depending upon location, and ranges from zero (i.e. overflowing) to 48 m depth, but is generally of the order 20 m below surface.

## Groundwater abstraction

Licenced groundwater abstractions within the district total some 11.2 × 10$^6$ m$^3$/y. The great majority (c.95 per cent) is taken from the Inferior Oolite aquifer, and most of this (94 per cent of the total) is used for the public supply, the remainder serving agricultural and private needs (Table 3). Groundwater abstraction for public supply takes place at pumping stations operated by

**Figure 4a**
Typical 'flat-bottomed' well hydrograph, caused by the aquifer draining to its base during the summer months. Unconfined Great Oolite aquifer, Coln St Aldwyns observation borehole.

**b** 'Flat-topped' well hydrograph, confined Great Oolite aquifer, Ampney St Peter observation borehole.

The maximum groundwater level is controlled by the level of springs which drain to the nearby Ampney Brook. The lowest water levels are seen in the 1976 and 1991 droughts; the lower elevation recorded in 1991 reflects groundwater abstraction caused by nearby pumping at that time.

a.

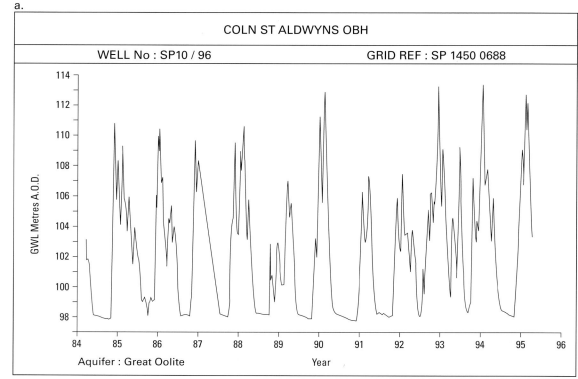

b.

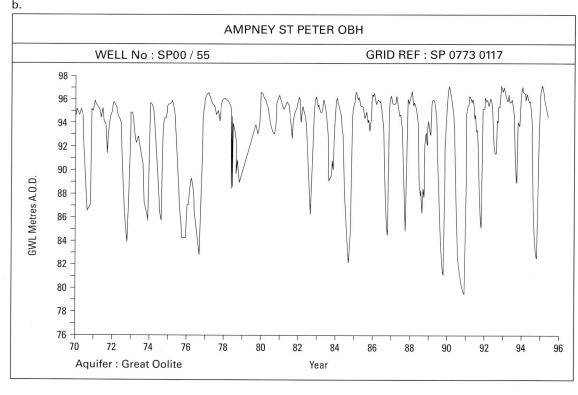

**Figure 5** Flow accretion diagram for the River Churn (September, 1975).

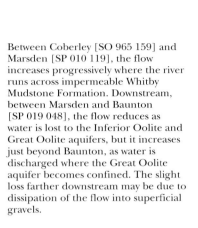

Between Coberley [SO 965 159] and Marsden [SP 010 119], the flow increases progressively where the river runs across impermeable Whitby Mudstone Formation. Downstream, between Marsden and Baunton [SP 019 048], the flow reduces as water is lost to the Inferior Oolite and Great Oolite aquifers, but it increases just beyond Baunton, as water is discharged where the Great Oolite aquifer becomes confined. The slight loss farther downstream may be due to dissipation of the flow into superficial gravels.

Thames Water plc, at Baunton [SP 0195 0484] and Bibury [SP 1123 0712] (Figure 3), where water is pumped from the confined Inferior Oolite aquifer. However, three other major pumping stations that lie just beyond the southern margin of the district, should be considered, as their recharge area lies within the sheet boundaries. The pumping stations at Ashton Keynes [SU 042 941] and Latton [SU 081 968] exploit the confined Great Oolite, whilst that at Meysey Hampton [SU 113 989], extracts water from both aquifers. Taking these into account, the total quantity of licensed abstractions from the Inferior Oolite is about $13.5 \times 10^6$ m³/y, and that from the Great Oolite is about $35 \times 10^6$ m³/y, giving a better indication of the relative importance of the aquifers in the Cirencester district.

Boreholes which penetrate both the Great Oolite and the Inferior Oolite are not permitted by the Environment Agency to connect the two aquifers hydraulically. Thus a borehole drilled to abstract water from the Inferior Oolite aquifer must be sealed with blank casing where it penetrates the Great Oolite, to avoid any mixing. At Baunton Pumping Station, for example, the boreholes are cased within the Great Oolite aquifer, and instead pump from the underlying Inferior Oolite aquifer. At Meysey Hampton Pumping Station there are four boreholes, two of which abstract from the confined Great Oolite aquifer, and two of which abstract from the confined Inferior Oolite. As abstraction from the Inferior Oolite affects the flow of the Swan Spring at Bibury on the River Coln, some 8 km to the north, pumping from the Inferior Oolite at Meysey Hampton is permitted only when the Coln at Bibury weir exceeds a certain threshold level. In practice, this is only during the winter months; in summer, pumping is switched to the Great Oolite aquifer.

**Table 3** Summary of licensed abstraction of groundwater in the Cirencester district (from Environment Agency, Thames Region data).

The figures for abstraction for public supply do not include the pumping stations at Latton, Ashton Keynes and Meysey Hampton, which lie just to the south of the district; together, these are licensed to abstract a further $34.7 \times 10^6$ m³/y from the Great Inferior Oolite aquifer, and $2.91 \times 10^6$ m³/y from the Inferior Oolite (see text). Groundwater abstracted from gravels (mainly in the valleys of the rivers Churn, Coln and Leach) is derived ultimately from the limestone aquifers.

| AQUIFER | USE | | | |
|---|---|---|---|---|
| | **Public supply** | **Agriculture** | **Private Domestic** | **Other** |
| Alluvium, gravels | — | 19 931 | 850 | 250 |
| Great Oolite (GO) | 277 306 | 63 877 | 36 266 | 2130 |
| Inferior Oolite (InO) | 10 564 948 | 37 603 | 23 191 | 4923 |
| GO and InO (undifferentiated) | — | 187 130 | 9318 | — |
| | 10 842 254 (96.5%) | 308 541 (2.7%) | 69 625 (> 1%) | 7303 — |

## Groundwater chemistry

The regional groundwater flow in both aquifers is from north-west to south-east, in the down-dip direction. As a general rule, groundwaters show increased mineralisation in this direction, typically with increased calcium carbonate hardness, increased alkalinity, and increased fluid electrical conductivity (EC). These changes in groundwater chemistry reflect progressive reaction with the aquifer rock, and the change from oxidising to reducing conditions under the confined areas. In more detail, the changes are complicated by local recharge of the upper part of the aquifer by streams, and by slight changes in chemistry during water level decline during the summer, when the water is pumped from deeper horizons with increased mineralisation.

Calcium and bicarbonate are the dominant major ions in the unconfined sections of both aquifers, but the waters become soda (sodium bicarbonate; $NaHCO_3$) rich with increasing confinement and, under deep confinement, become saline (sodium chloride; NaCl-type). The change in groundwater chemistry as the water moves down dip has been described in detail by Morgan-Jones and Eggboro (1981). They observed that the onset of reducing conditions in the Inferior Oolite aquifer takes place some 4 km down-dip from confinement, but for the Great Oolite aquifer it takes place within 1 to 2 km of confinement. The difference reflects the incomplete confinement of the Inferior Oolite by the Fuller's Earth, which results in part from faults that allow hydraulic connection between the aquifers.

Analyses of groundwater sampled by the Environment Agency are given in Tables 4 and 5. Whilst Table 4 shows the general increase in mineralisation where the aquifer is confined, the range of analyses in Table 5 also show the importance of local conditions on groundwater chemistry. Water from several of the springs and a few borehole sources exceeds the World Health Organization recommended nitrate limit of 11.3 mg/l $NO_3$-N, due to agricultural inputs of fertiliser and contamination from septic tank discharges.

## Water resources conservation

As a result of the highly fissured nature of both the Great Oolite and Inferior Oolite limestones, the two aquifers are very permeable. Recharge from rainfall reaches the water table quickly, and conduit flow ensures that groundwater flow down-gradient is rapid. As a result, the rivers flowing off the unconfined aquifers have very high peak flows in winter but flows fall rapidly in summer, as groundwater levels decline.

It is during the summer periods of low flow that groundwater abstraction is seen as being detrimental to the river corridor environment, by reducing flows still further. Water resources are brought into the area from farther downstream in the Thames catchment, but these are limited and are more expensive.

A new option is the approach known as ASR (Aquifer Storage and Recharge). In winter, treated water from surplus river flow is injected via boreholes into the confined aquifer. This forms a 'bubble' of high-quality water that displaces the natural groundwater which may be of inferior quality, or even quite saline. After a few recharge–abstraction cycles, using the same boreholes, the recovered water is good-quality potable water, needing relatively little further treatment. Both the confined Inferior Oolite and Great Oolite aquifers are likely to be suitable for this type of operation, even where they contain brackish groundwater, although the practicalities have yet to be assessed. By using ASR to take water, from deeply confined sources situated too far down dip to affect the flows of rivers, it may be possible to avoid the problems hitherto associated with summertime groundwater abstraction, thus combining good groundwater resource management with conservation of the riverine environment.

**Table 4**  Chemical analyses, Great Oolite aquifer groundwaters.

| Sample location<br><br>Grid reference | Trowel Covert Spring, Easington<br>SP 1332 1158 | Fossebridge Spring<br><br>SP 0771 1121 | Hampnett Village Spring<br>SP 0985 1590 | South Farm Spring, Shipton Oliffe<br>SP 0409 1868 | Dean Farm Borehole, Coln St Aldwyns<br>SP 1656 0796 | Homeleaze Farm Borehole, Hatherop<br>SP 1740 0415 |
|---|---|---|---|---|---|---|
| EC (µs/cm) | 382 | 521 | 540 | 546 | 619 | 676 |
| $CaCO_3$ Hardness (mg/l) | 212 | 284 | 302 | 307 | 365 | 330 |
| Alkalinity ($CaCO_3$) (mg/l) | 132 | 169 | 196 | 196 | 266 | 250 |
| Ca (mg/l) | 75.7 | 110 | 111 | 110 | 125.2 | 123.2 |
| Mg (mg/l) | 2.02 | 2.27 | 2.0 | 2.4 | 6.98 | 12.49 |
| Na (mg/l) | 4.05 | 4.57 | 7.51 | 7.81 | 8.04 | 8.1 |
| K (mg/l) | 0.55 | 0.47 | 0.35 | 0.49 | 2.15 | 1.29 |
| Cl (mg/l) | 13.1 | 20.1 | 25.8 | 28.7 | 16.6 | 26.0 |
| $SO_4$ (mg/l) | 23.3 | 24.3 | 34.3 | 30.3 | 39.6 | 49.6 |
| $NO_3$-N (mg/l) | 10.63 | 12.9 | 12.03 | 12.3 | 9.77 | 16.5 |

Note the greater mineralisation of the water from the two boreholes (shallowly confined aquifer) when compared with that from the springs (unconfined aquifer).

**Table 5**   Chemical analyses of Inferior Oolite groundwaters.

| Sample location | Woodbridge Spring, Withington | Upcote Farm Spring, Withington | Northfield Barn, Spring, Sherborne | Clear Cupboard, Spring, Farmington | Baunton Pumping Station Borehole | Bibury Pumping Station Borehole |
|---|---|---|---|---|---|---|
| Grid reference | SP 0360 1445 | SP 0226 1601 | SP 1764 1535 | SP 1330 1577 | SP 0195 0484 | SP 1123 0712 |
| EC ($\mu$s/cm) | 317 | 382 | 607 | 687 | 472 | 494 |
| $CaCO_3$ Hardness (mg/l) | 176 | 212 | 324 | 378 | 253 | 266 |
| Alkalinity ($CaCO_3$) (mg/l) | 129 | 132 | 184 | 240 | | 218 |
| Ca (mg/l) | 64.2 | 75.7 | 118.8 | 140.5 | 89 | 101 |
| Mg (mg/l) | 2.48 | 2.02 | 2.6 | 4.0 | 5.1 | 6.4 |
| Na (mg/l) | 4.12 | 4.05 | 7.7 | 10.4 | 6.7 | 8.1 |
| K (mg/l) | 0.2 | 0.55 | 2.25 | 3.5 | 1.2 | 1.6 |
| Cl (mg/l) | 12.6 | 13.1 | 23.7 | 27.6 | 17 | 17 |
| $SO_4$ (mg/l) | 20.6 | 23.3 | 41.2 | 39.0 | 38.5 | 44 |
| $NO_3$-N (mg/l) | 4.0 | 10.6 | 20.6 | 21.47 | 5.3 | 4.5 |

The degree of mineralisation of the waters is essentially dependent on the length of time it has spent in the rock, which in turn is partly controlled by local hydrogeological conditions. Thus, the waters from the two boreholes, which pump from the confined Inferior Oolite aquifer, are actually less mineralised than that from some of the springs (unconfined aquifer). Compare Table 4.

## Groundwater protection

Groundwater in the district, although usually of high quality, is highly vulnerable to contamination from both diffuse and point source pollutants, either from direct discharges into the ground or indirect discharges into or onto land. Successful aquifer remediation is difficult, prolonged and expensive, and therefore the prevention of pollution is important.

The Environment Agency has responsibility for, amongst other matters, the protection of groundwater. The Soil Survey and Land Research Centre and the BGS have produced a series of 1:100 000 scale Groundwater Vulnerability maps, which form a component of the Agency's Policy and Practise for the Protection of Groundwater. The Cirencester district is covered by sheets 37 and 38 of the series (HMSO, 1995). This account is largely a summary of the relevant parts of these maps.

The limestones of the Inferior Oolite and Great Oolite groups at outcrop over much of the area are, for the most part, highly permeable formations that constitute major aquifers. Minor aquifers, or variably permeable units, include the Dyrham, Marlstone Rock, Forest Marble and Cornbrash formations, the Kellaways Sand Member, river terrace deposits, alluvium, calcareous tufa and landslip deposits. The remaining, mainly mudstone formations are classified as non-aquifers or are negligibly permeable.

The soils that have developed on the majority of the major and minor aquifers, including those of the Elmton, Sherborne, Badsey, Kelmscott and Thames associations (see Soils and Agriculture), have little ability to attenuate diffuse source pollutants, and non-adsorbed diffuse source pollutants and liquid discharges have the potential to move rapidly through them to underlying strata or shallow groundwater.

## MINERAL AND ENERGY RESOURCES

### Building stone

The ready availability of a wide variety of local limestones for building purposes has given the villages of the district their typical Cotswold character (see *Cover* photograph). Pale grey to pale yellow-brown, ooidal, sandy and shelly limestones from the Great Oolite and Inferior Oolite groups have been quarried for building purposes since Roman times. The Roman walls of Cirencester and the large villa complex at Chedworth [SP 053 135] both contain locally quarried, dressed limestone blocks in their wall fabric. In the 11th century, the quarries at Taynton (Plate 2) were significant enough to gain a mention in the Domesday Book. From the village churches and manor houses, built for the prosperous wool merchants between the 15th and 18th centuries, to the railway bridges of Victorian times and the local housing projects of today, the limestones have been in continuous demand for building purposes (Arkell, 1947a; Clifton-Taylor 1972).

The dry-stone field walls that are so characteristic of the Cotswolds were generally constructed from the most convenient material that came to hand; almost every field had its quarry. However, for constructing dwellings and other buildings, the masons were more particular, and various beds of stone gained high reputations. The limestones from the lower part of the Inferior Oolite Group (Birdlip Limestone Formation) were quarried for building stone at many localities, most notably to the north of Colesbourne [SP 000 132] and Withington [SP 031 057], near Turkdean [SP 108 175], and at Leckhampton Hill [SO 949 174], immediately west of the district (Plate 4). They are still quarried on a large scale in the Moreton-in-Marsh district to the north. Quarries at Bourton Hill [SP 157 196] yielded a distinctive yellowish brown oolite (Plate 5) that is much in evidence in the

**Plate 2**   Lee's Quarry, Taynton, the type locality of the Taynton Limestone Formation (Great Oolite Group) [SP 236 152].

The photograph, taken in 1975, shows the method of working this fine freestone, which was split into blocks using 'plug and feathers'. The steep dip of the bedding surface in the foreground is the result of cambering. On the right-hand side of the photograph, pale marls of the Hampen Formation are faulted against the Taynton Limestone. They occur within a small graben structure which may also be associated with superficial movements (Chapter 9) (A12424).

village of Bourton-on-the-Water [SP 167 207]. A contrast is provided by many of the buildings in the nearby villages of Great Rissington [SP 199 172] and Little Rissington [SP 192 197], which are built largely of reddish brown ironstone from the Marlstone Rock Formation (Lias Group). There are signs of ancient quarries from which the material may have been obtained at several places nearby [SP 197 178; SP 195 185].

Many of the limestone beds of the Great Oolite Group have been worked in the past, as is evident from the numerous abandoned quarries in the district, but only two sites are currently active. The best-quality building stone came from the Taynton Limestone Formation of the Windrush valley. This was formerly quarried near Taynton [SP 232 137], Great Barrington [SP 209 137], Windrush [SP 193 131] and Sherborne [SP 156 144], and was used extensively in local buildings such as Sherborne Hall (c. 1651), Windrush Manor (c. 1700), Barnsley Park (c. 1713) and Barrington Park (1736). It was also used farther afield, for example in various Oxford colleges, Blenheim Palace (1705–1723), and parts of St Paul's Cathedral, Windsor Castle and Eton College (Hull, 1857; Arkell, 1947a). Much of the best stone was obtained from underground galleries, the entrances of which can still be seen at Windrush and Sherborne. The one remaining quarry at Taynton (Plate 2) has been largely disused since the 1970s, but the Taynton Limestone Formation is still worked at the thriving Farmington Quarry [SP 131 169] (Plate 7), near Northleach, which produces sawn blocks and a variety of mouldings and decorative carved work.

Oolites in the middle part of the White Limestone Formation (Ardley Member) were also worked on a moderate scale for building. The most extensive workings were at Quarry Hill [SP 101 057] between Barnsley and Bibury, where the beds ('Bibury Stone')

were worked from both open quarries and underground galleries. It was used for the house at Barnsley Park (Verey, 1979) and elsewhere, and for some Oxford buildings (Arkell, 1947a). Oolites from the same part of the succession are still worked at Daglingworth for rough walling. There, the White Limestone Formation once supported a small industry producing the much sought-after Dagham Stone, a distinctive hard, white, vuggy limestone once favoured for rustic work (see Richardson, 1933, plate 4). In the Northleach area, a hard, grey, sandy limestone at the base of the Ardley Member has been quarried at numerous localities, probably mainly for the construction of field walls.

### Roofing tilestone

The almost ubiquitous use of natural stone 'slates' or tilestones for roofing, contributes as much to the character of local buildings as does the stone of their walls. The traditional 'Cotswold Slate' roof exhibits an attractive gradation of size of individual 'slates' (large at the eaves, and small at the ridge; see cover photograph) which is very hard to emulate with artificial materials. The fissile, sandy limestones of the Eyford Member in the upper part of the Fuller's Earth Formation were the premier source of 'Cotswold Slates', and were quarried for the purpose near Cold Aston [SP 129 198], Hazleton [SP 080 180], Turkdean [SP 108 175], Compton Abdale [SP 061 166], Rendcomb [SP 021 098] and Elkstone [SO 968 122]. Production involved exposing the quarried blocks of stone ('pendle') to frosts over the winter period. By the spring, the stone split readily along the bedding planes into thin sheets suitable for dressing. The 'Cotswold Slates' from the Eyford Member are essentially similar to the 'Stonesfield Slates' of Oxfordshire, although the former were obtained from open quarries whilst the latter, which occur at a slightly higher horizon, were obtained exclusively from mines.

The Througham Tilestones, a unit of fissile, sandy, silty limestones, were worked in drifts and pits for roofing 'slates' around the village of Througham [SO 920 080], just to the west of the district (Arkell and Donovan, 1952). 'Slates' may also have been obtained from equivalent beds in the Hampen Formation in the western part of the Cirencester district (see Figure 16).

The thinly bedded shelly limestones of the Forest Marble Formation were once extensively worked for flooring slabs and decorative mantelpieces (Woodward, 1894). The formation also yielded tilestones, though they are generally thicker, heavier and of poorer quality than those of the Eyford Member. Many of the houses in Cirencester and the surrounding villages are roofed with tilestones from this formation, which is still worked intermittently for the purpose at Ampney Down [SP 048 070] and to the north of Filkins [SP 232 062].

**Crushed limestone aggregate**

Most of the limestones have the potential for use as crushed aggregate in construction, and nearly all have been used at some time for this purpose, albeit in a piecemeal fashion. The Cornbrash and Clypeus Grit, in particular, were once favoured for road building, but in more recent times, the White Limestone Formation has been the principal source of aggregate. Currently, it is worked for this purpose at Daglingworth Quarry [SP 001 061], where some finely crushed limestone for agricultural liming is also produced. The quarry, operated by ARC-Southern, extends over an area of approximately 18 hectares and is up to about 30 m deep, so that formations underlying the White Limestone are also worked (Table 6; Plate 9). Until relatively recently, Foss Cross Quarry [SP 055 093] (Plate 10) also produced aggregate from the White Limestone Formation, but the quarry is now disused and largely back filled with domestic waste. Similarly, Forest Marble limestones were worked in conjunction with underlying White Limestone at several quarries around Sunhill [SP 117 027]; all the workings there are now defunct and the quarries partially backfilled and restored.

**Sand and gravel**

The principal sand and gravel resources of the district are located in the south-east, where they comprise the river deposits of the River Thames and its tributaries, chiefly the Coln and the Leach (see Chapter 8). They were the subject of an assessment by Robson (1975, 1976). Sand and gravel deposits of potential economic interest are present in the Windrush valley between Bourton-on-the-Water and the confluence of the River Windrush and Sherborne Brook. These deposits, and others in the district that are less promising as a potential resource, were reviewed by Barron (1995). This account is intended as a brief summary of the earlier reports, insofar as they relate to the Cirencester district, updated as necessary.

SAND AND GRAVEL RESOURCES OF THE THAMES VALLEY

Sand and gravel-bearing deposits crop out over some 9 km$^2$ (excluding areas sterilised by development, but without consideration of other possible constraints) between Meysey Hampton and Little Faringdon along the valley of the River Thames. They are disposed in four terraces above the level of the present floodplain, and also occur beneath its alluvium. The suballuvial deposits are thought to be contiguous with the those of the First (Northmoor) and, locally, the Second (Summertown–Radley) terraces. An area of about 1.4 km$^2$ has been worked out, mainly between Little Faringdon and Lechlade and east of Fairford, but there are currently no active workings within the district. Immediately south of the district, at Thornhill Farm [SP 181 005] however, the sand and gravel deposits continue to be exploited commercially (Plate 11).

The resources of this area were considered as part of a wider assessment of the Upper Thames valley as a whole (Robson, 1975, 1976). The results were expressed in terms of resource blocks that not only straddled the boundary of the Cirencester district, but were based on geological maps that have since been superseded. Consequently, the statistics presented by Robson (1975, 1976) cannot be specifically or accurately applied to the district. Nevertheless, the information given remains relevant in general terms.

Fifteen of the boreholes drilled for the assessment were located within or very close to the district. They proved thicknesses of mineral ranging from 1.3 to 6.9 m, with the Second Terrace deposits showing the greatest variation. Overburden, consisting of clay and silt, was generally less than 1 m thick, and did not exceed 1.2 m. Pit sections show that the sand and gravel deposits contain thin layers of clay and silt, but none were encountered in the boreholes. There is little variation

**Table 6**  Technical data for Great Oolite Group limestones at Daglingworth Quarry.

Tests carried out to BS 812 Pt3 1990, BS 812 Pt2 1975, BS 6463 Pt2 (1984). Information supplied by ARC. The stratigraphical classification used in this table may differ from that used in this memoir (see Chapter 6).

| Stratigraphical unit | 10% fines value | | Relative density (SSD) | Water absorption | Neutralising value |
|---|---|---|---|---|---|
| | dry | wet | | | |
| White Limestone (top) | 95 | 75 | 2.50 | 4.4 | 53 |
| White Limestone (base) | 55 | 25 | 2.48 | 5.9 | 53 |
| Hampen Marly Formation | 75 | 65 | 2.53 | 5.3 | 49 |
| Taynton Limestone Formation | 80 | 70 | 2.45 | 5.6 | 55 |
| Througham Tilestone Formation | 95 | 85 | 2.51 | 4.5 | 51 |

between the terraces in the composition of the sand and gravel. Typically, the gravel fraction comprises sub-rounded, platy and tabular, sandy, shelly, ooidal limestone with subordinate ironstone, a little subangular flint and well-rounded quartzite and quartz, and a trace of igneous and metamorphic lithologies. The sand consists of sub-rounded oolitic limestone grains and discrete ooids, with some subangular quartz and ironstone; minor components include glaucony and shell grains. The upper parts of the older Third (Wolvercote) and Fourth (Hanborough) river terrace deposits contain a higher proportion of siliceous lithologies, as a result of leaching-out of the calcareous components.

Most of the assessment boreholes proved mineral that was classified as either sandy gravel or gravel, falling within the range 37 to 59 per cent gravel. Clay and silt ('fines') usually make up less than 10 per cent of the deposit; exceptionally, two boreholes (SP 20 SW 5; SP 20 SW 9) encountered clayey sand and gravel containing up to 14 per cent fines. The gravel is mainly fine grained (i.e. < 16 mm) but contains a proportion of coarser clasts, up to cobble size, which tend to be concentrated near the base of the terrace deposits. The sand fraction is mostly medium and coarse grained.

## SAND AND GRAVEL RESOURCES OF THE WINDRUSH VALLEY

Unlike the sand and gravel deposits of the Thames valley, those of the Windrush valley can only be regarded as an inferred resource because of the lack of samples and measurements. The following information is derived from Sumbler (1995a).

Remnants of the First (Rissington) Terrace have been mapped in several places along the Windrush valley, between Bourton-on-the-Water and Sherborne Brook. The largest spread, to the west of Great Rissington, has an area of about 50 hectares. An outcrop at the confluence of the rivers Dikler and Windrush has been sterilised by urban development south of Bourton. There are other, smaller outcrops near Marsh Farm [SP 176 193; SP 177 187] and on the south side of Sherborne Brook near its confluence with the Windrush.

Deposits of the First Terrace are thought to extend beneath the alluvium of the present-day floodplain. Indeed, until the 1970s, suballuvial gravels of the First Terrace were worked by the Hoveringham Gravel Company from pits on the floodplain [SP 179 192]. These workings, now flooded and abandoned, covered an area of about 10 hectares. It can be reasonably assumed that the suballuvial gravels are co-extensive with the alluvium at least as far south as Sherborne Brook, giving a total area of about 3.5 km² of potentially workable sand and gravel deposits in the Windrush valley.

The First Terrace deposits are up to about 5 m thick, and comprise medium to coarse, subrounded, limestone gravel in a loamy clay matrix. For the suballuvial gravels, the alluvium constitutes a clay and silt overburden that is typically about 1 m thick.

Small, isolated outcrops of Second (Sherborne) Terrace deposits occur near Sherborne Common [SP 18 15]. These have been worked on a small scale in the past but are not considered to represent a significant resource.

## OTHER SAND AND GRAVEL DEPOSITS OF THE DISTRICT

River terrace deposits in the lower Churn valley, covering about 1 km² and up to 7 m thick, have been effectively sterilised by the urban area of Cirencester. Between Cirencester and Stratton, a small area of dissected terrace deposits consists of sandy, medium to coarse gravel up to 5 m thick. Several small, isolated outcrops of river terrace deposits occur adjacent to the streams and rivers of the district. Most have been worked piecemeal for gravel in the past, but are not now considered to have any significant economic value.

The Cheltenham Sand and Gravel occupies an area of about 1 km² in the extreme north-west of the district. It is a heterogeneous deposit, up to 3.5 m thick, consisting of medium-grained sand with limestone and ironstone gravel. It has been worked at several localities, notably at Little Herbert's [SO 965 197], Pilley [SO 954 199] and Coxhorne [SO 981 199], but is now entirely sterilised by the urban area of Cheltenham.

## Clay

Because of the ready availability of stone for both walling and roofing, there has been little demand for clay bricks or tiles in the district. Even today, natural or reconstituted stone and concrete products are favoured for most building work, in order to blend in with existing buildings. Nevertheless, there are several sites in the area where mudstone formations were worked to produce bricks, tiles and pipes (Hull, 1857; Woodward, 1893; Richardson, 1933). The largest was the Pilley or Pilford Brickworks [SO 952 194], in the north-west corner of the district, which is still marked by a degraded and partially flooded pit. This, and several smaller pits nearby, exploited the silty mudstones in the upper part of the Charmouth Mudstone Formation (Lias Group). Brick and tile works at Sherborne and Colesbourne worked the Whitby Mudstone Formation, but no trace of this activity remains.

Contrary to a prevalent local belief, the hummocky terrain typical of the outcrop of the Fuller's Earth Formation (Great Oolite Group) is not the result of quarrying activities, but of landslipping (see above; Chapter 9; Plate 1). There is no evidence that the formation has ever been worked in the district, either for brick-making or to provide fuller's earth which was once an important commodity for the local wool industry. Commercial fuller's earth, a clay rich in the mineral smectite or calcium montmorillonite, is still a valuable product, with many uses in modern industry. The formation takes its name from the presence of this material in the Bath area where it was worked until 1979 (Moorlock and Highley, 1991). There, it occurs as single bed in the upper part of the formation (Upper Fuller's Earth). However, the Fuller's Earth Formation of the Cirencester district corresponds only to the Lower Fuller's Earth of the type area, and does not contain smectite in commercial quantities. X-ray diffraction analysis of a number of samples from a borehole at Daglingworth shows that, whilst smectite commonly forms a high proportion (up to 90 per cent) of the clay

**Table 7** The relationship between geology and soil, showing the soil types developed on various stratigraphical units (based on Soil Survey of England and Wales, 1983, 1984).

| Stratigraphical unit | Soil subgroup | Soil association |
|---|---|---|
| alluvium (Coln, Leach, Churn) | calcaro-cambic gley soils | Kelmscott |
| alluvium (Windrush) | pelo-calcareous alluvial gley soils | Thames |
| river terrace deposits | brown calcareous earths | Badsey 1 |
| limestones | brown rendzinas | Elmton 1 and 2 Sherborne |
| Great Oolite clays (Fuller's Earth, Forest Marble clays) | calcareous pelosols | Evesham 1 |
| Lias Group clays | stagnogley soils | Martock Wickham 2 |
| Lias Group clays, Oxford Clay | pelo-stagnogley soils | Denchworth |

fraction, it is a poorly crystalline, detrital form of the mineral, and in any case only forms a relatively modest proportion of the whole rock.

## Coal

The eastern part of the district includes the westernmost part of the Oxfordshire Coalfield (Chapter 3; Dunham and Poole, 1974). The Geological Survey Upton Borehole, drilled near Burford in 1952–1953, proved 15 coal seams in the Upper Coal Measures between depths of 402.8 m and 1032.6 m (Worssam, 1963), with a maximum thickness of 0.61 m. A possible 16th seam was indicated by the gamma-ray log (Bullerwell, in Worssam, 1963). Analysis of the coals (Adams, 1963) indicated that, although two of the coal seams were around the minimum seam thickness then worked in Great Britain, none of the seams were of workable quality. Given the contraction of the coal industry during the 1990s, there is little likelihood of these coals being worked in the forseeable future.

## Hydrocarbons

Commercial exploration surveys, including seismic profiling and the drilling of the Sherborne No. 1 borehole, were carried out during the 1970s and 1980s in this and adjoining districts. Despite minor gas shows at

some levels, the lack of suitable source rocks for much of the region indicates low prospectivity.

## SOILS AND AGRICULTURE

The close relationship between geology, topography, soils and agriculture is particularly marked in the Cirencester district (Table 7; Soil Survey of England and Wales, 1983, 1984). The soils of the Sherborne association, which have developed on the limestones of the Great Oolite and Inferior Oolite groups, are the most widespread, and cover much of the Cotswold dip slope. Arable and mixed farming predominate here, with cereals forming the most extensive crop. In undisturbed ground, the soil may be up to 0.5 m thick, but ploughing disrupts the soil profile, bringing debris of the limestone subsoil to the surface and producing the characteristically brashy soils seen in every arable field. Where thick clay units are interbedded with limestones, the patchwork of Sherborne association soils and the deeper, more clayey soils of the Evesham 1 association tend to be used for mixed dairy and cereal farming. Steep limestone slopes and rough landslipped clay slopes are generally given over to dairying or sheep grazing. Woodland is particularly extensive on steep ground, and small-scale commercial forestry is becoming increasingly common.

# THREE

# Basement geology: concealed Palaeozoic and Triassic rocks

The regional context of the Cirencester district, and the locations of principal boreholes mentioned in this chapter, are shown in Figure 6. Boreholes in the eastern part of the district have proved Devonian and Carboniferous strata at depth. The nature of the pre-Devonian rocks is known from boreholes in adjacent districts, and from interpretation of seismic reflection data acquired during hydrocarbon exploration. The probable subcrop distribution of the pre-Permian basement rocks in the district, based on that information, is shown in Figure 7.

## PRECAMBRIAN AND LOWER PALAEOZOIC BASEMENT

Precambrian rocks are inferred at depth beneath the district. They are probably similar to those encountered in the Kempsey Borehole near Worcester, which proved heterogeneous lithic sandstones and tuffs, the latter having a broadly calc-alkaline, andesitic composition and a probable Charnian affinity (Barclay et al., 1997).

Seismic reflection data indicate the presence of 1.5 to 2 km of Cambrian and Tremadoc strata beneath the Permo-Triassic cover in the western part of the district (Figure 7). Cooles Farm 1 Borehole, 20 km south-south-west of Stowell Park, proved 2282 m of Upper Cambrian to Ordovician (Tremadoc) shale and siltstone, overlying 27 m of Lower Cambrian quartzite (base not proved). A highly reflective seismostratigraphic unit that overlies the Cambro–Tremadoc strata is interpreted as a succession of lower Silurian rocks (Smith, 1987). This sequence, about 500 m thick, may comprise basaltic volcanic rocks ('traps') and intercalated sedimentary rocks, including limestones, comparable to those seen at outcrop to the west of the Worcester Basin at Tortworth (Cave, 1977) and in the Mendips (Kellaway and Welch, 1993). Volcanic rocks of probable early Silurian age were encountered by boreholes at Netherton near Evesham, and at Bicester, showing their extensive development along the southern margin of the Midland Platform (Pharaoh et al., 1991). Seismic reflection data indicate that they are overlain by about 2000 m of ?middle Silurian to Lower Devonian strata. The Batsford Borehole, near Moreton-in-Marsh, encountered about 52 m of shallow marine, lower Silurian (upper Llandovery or Wenlock) strata, and Highworth Borehole, to the south of the district, about 100 m of upper Silurian strata. The Cambrian to Silurian rocks are only slightly metamorphosed because of their position within the Midlands Microcraton which, in contrast to the surrounding Caledonides, was only mildly affected by Acadian (late Caledonian) deformation and metamorphism (Merriman et al., 1993).

## DEVONIAN

The oldest strata proved in the district are known from the Sherborne No. 1 Borehole, drilled for hydrocarbon exploration by Shell UK Exploration in 1975. Beneath the base of the Carboniferous, at a depth of 1146.0 m, the borehole penetrated some 800 m (not bottomed) of Devonian strata. Cuttings samples indicate that the strata are mainly reddish brown sandstones. The terminal core (1937.2 to 1945.5 m), held by BGS, comprises purplish grey to purplish brown sandstone, with beds of purplish brown silty mudstone and siltstone. The lithologies and sedimentary structures present suggest that the strata are fluvial channel sandstones and overbank mudstones (Sumbler, 1994a), probably belonging to the Lower Old Red Sandstone (Early Devonian). The Guiting Power Borehole, to the north of the district, proved similar strata beneath the Permo-Triassic, and it is probable that sandstones encountered by Staverton Borehole, to the west of Cheltenham, are also Lower Old Red Sandstone. They had been regarded as Precambrian (British Geological Survey, 1985), but their sonic velocity is lower than that of typical Precambrian volcaniclastic strata (see Barclay et al., 1997).

The upper 264 m or so of the Devonian succession at Sherborne may represent the Upper Old Red Sandstone (mainly Late Devonian). Geophysical logs show that these beds have a lower sonic velocity than the underlying strata, indicating a lesser degree of cementation and compaction. This is comparable with the situation in the Apley Barn and Faringdon boreholes to the east and south-east of the district, where continental Lower Old Red Sandstone is overlain unconformably by Upper Old Red Sandstone with marine intercalations. The unconformity, spanning Mid Devonian time, corresponds to the Acadian orogenic phase, the climax of the Caledonian orogeny in southern Britain (Soper et al., 1987). There is no evidence for a strong angular discordance at this unconformity, which emphasises the importance of Variscan rather than Caledonian deformation in the pre-Permian structural evolution of the district.

## CARBONIFEROUS

The presence of Carboniferous rocks in the district was first proved by the Signet (or Burford) Borehole, drilled for coal exploration in 1875, about 1 km beyond the eastern margin of the district. According to Woodward (1894, p.303), Coal Measures were penetrated from a depth of 360.88 m to the bottom of the borehole at 429.77 m. De Rance's (1878, p.437, 1879, p.384) descriptions of the succession include red and green mottled

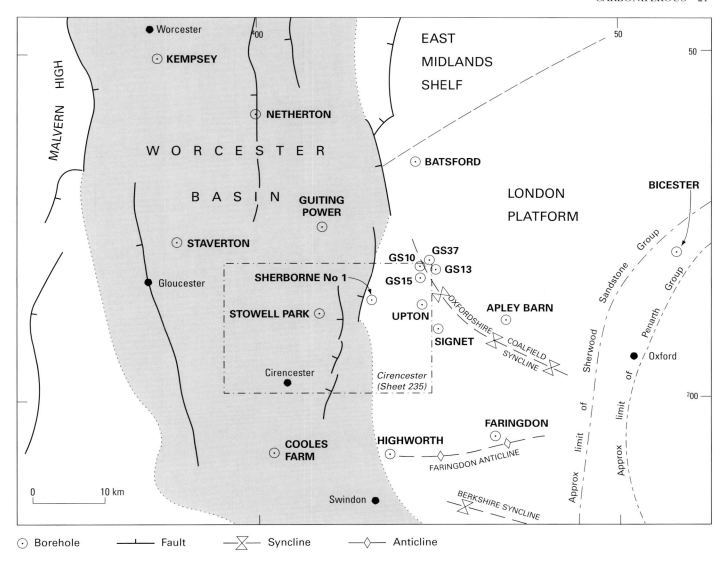

| ⊙ Borehole | ── Fault | ⊠ Syncline | ◇ Anticline |

**Figure 6**   Sketch-map showing fault and fold structures in the sub-Permian basement, the main structural elements affecting Mesozoic sedimentation, and the location of boreholes mentioned in the text.

Brown shaded area indicates top of pre-Permian basement more than 1000 m below Ordnance datum; this approximates to the Worcester Basin, which was controlled by faults in the basement. The so-called Vale of Moreton Axis is the manifestation of the eastern margin of the Worcester Basin with the London Platform within the Mesozoic cover rocks. The boundary of the London Platform and East Midlands Shelf is gradational and arbitrary. Limit of Sherwood Sandstone and Penarth groups from Whittaker (1985) and Horton et al. (1995).

sandstones, red marl and 'coal measures', with a coal seam (no thickness given) at 411.48 m.

The Stowell Park Borehole was drilled by the Geological Survey in 1949–1951, principally to prove the presence or otherwise of Coal Measures to the west of Signet (Green and Melville, 1956). As is now known, the borehole was sited close to the north–south-trending axis of the Worcester Basin, in which a thick Mesozoic sedimentary succession is preserved. The borehole terminated whilst still within Triassic beds, but subsequent boreholes and seismic data show that, although Coal Measures are present on the London Platform to the

east, none are preserved in the Worcester Basin (see below).

The Carboniferous strata in the eastern part of the district are preserved in a large synclinal fold, the Oxfordshire Coalfield Syncline (Figures 6, 7; Dunham and Poole, 1974; Foster et al., 1989). The axial trace of this structure runs north-north-west to south-south-east along the eastern edge of the district, to the east of the Upton Borehole, the second of the Geological Survey deep boreholes in the region, which proved the fullest Coal Measures succession in the district (Table 8). South of the Upton Borehole, the axial trace turns in a south-

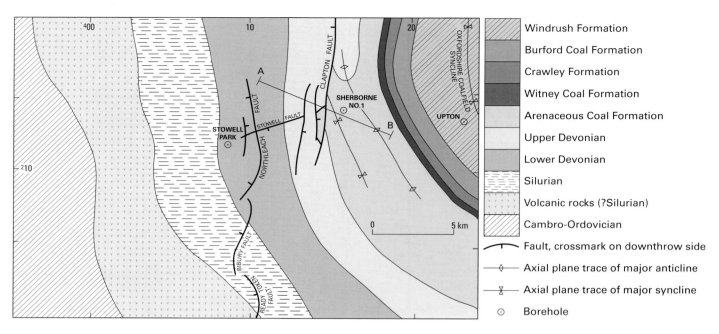

**Figure 7** Subcrop map showing inferred distribution of sub-Permian basement strata at the Variscan unconformity (modified after Smith, 1985). Line A–B indicates location of seismic section CT 28 (see Figure 8).

easterly direction, parallel to the Berkshire Syncline (Figure 6). The two synclines are separated by the westerly trending Faringdon Anticline, whose northern limb affects strata in the south-eastern part of the district. A further anticline, of lower amplitude, affects the subcrop pattern north of Sherborne No. 1 Borehole, 7.5 km west of Upton (Figures 7, 8). These fold structures were generated during the climactic phase of the Variscan orogeny, probably in latest Carboniferous times. The Upper Coal Measures (late Westphalian C to early Westphalian D) unconformably overlie older Westphalian strata, and earlier Variscan deformation cannot be excluded. The Variscan orogenic movements caused uplift of the area which later became the Worcester Basin, and perhaps 4 km of strata were eroded in the western part of the district in latest Carboniferous and early Permian times, resulting in the subcrop distribution shown in Figure 7.

The core of the Upton Borehole provided details of the Carboniferous succession on the London Platform (Worssam, 1963). Below the base of the Trias at a depth of 337.49 m, some 810.74 m of Carboniferous strata were proved. The entire succession belongs to the Upper Coal Measures, of Westphalian D age (Worssam, 1963), and includes 15 coal seams, up to 0.6 m thick. Comparison with the Apley Barn Borehole, 11.5 km to the east-south-east, and with other boreholes in Oxfordshire (Poole, 1969, 1977, 1978), shows that the succession at Upton corresponds to the upper part of that proved at Apley Barn. The lithostratigraphical classification of the strata (Table 8), based on core lithology, is supported by borehole geophysics and a certain amount of palaeontological data.

Poole (1969) described the Crawley Formation (of Apley Barn) as comprising primary and penecontemporaneously brecciated and reddened mudstones, alternating with espley-type breccias and grey seatearths, sandstones and mudstones. In the Upton Borehole, the formation, penetrated between depths of 1049.88 and the bottom of the borehole at 1148.23 m, is dominated by grey to reddish brown, mottled and variegated mudstones and siltstones, with a number of beds of sandstone. The strata are predominantly grey between about 1095 and 1109 m, and from 1119 m to the bottom of the borehole. These lowest beds contain plant-rich levels. Beneath the Crawley Formation, underlying units that were proved in the Apley Barn Borehole, namely the Witney Coal Formation and Arenaceous Coal Formation (Poole, 1969), are probably present at depth (see 1:50 000 Sheet 235, cross-section).

The Burford Coal Formation in the Upton Borehole (928.29 to 1049.88 m) comprises normal grey 'coal measures', made up of rhythmically bedded mudstones, siltstones and sandstones, with seatearths and coals. In the Upton Borehole, at least six coal seams (Upton Nos. 10 to 15) are present, of which the thickest (Upton No. 12, at 974.32 m) is at least 0.61 m thick. In the upper part of the succession, four beds of grey to brown limestone, typically about 0.6 m thick and containing *Spirorbis* and ostracods, occur above seatearths or listric mudstones, i.e. in a position in the sedimentary cycles analogous to the coals. One of the limestones, at 955.79 m, overlies the Upton No. 11 coal.

The Windrush Formation was proved between 337.49 and 928.29 m in the Upton Borehole. A greater thickness is preserved beneath the Trias at Upton (590.80 m) than

**Table 8** Lithostratigraphical succession proved by the Geological Survey Stowell Park and Upton boreholes.

**STOWELL PARK BOREHOLE** (1951) [SP 0835 1176] SL +170.7 m

| | | | |
|---|---|---|---|
| JURASSIC | GREAT OOLITE GROUP | | |
| | White Limestone Formation | 20.93 m | |
| | Hampen Formation | 30.50 m | |
| | Taynton Limestone Formation | 32.79 m | |
| | Fuller's Earth Formation (Eyford Member) | 34.62 m | |
| | Fuller's Earth Formation (undifferentiated) | 49.02m | |
| | INFERIOR OOLITE GROUP | | |
| | Salperton Limestone Formation | | |
| | Clypeus Grit Member | 60.55 m | |
| | Upper Trigonia Grit Member | 62.13 m | |
| | Aston Limestone Formation | | |
| | Gryphite Grit Member | 65.30 m | |
| | Lower Trigonia Grit Member | 66.45 m | |
| | Birdlip Limestone Formation | | |
| | Scottsquar Member | 74.68 m | |
| | Cleeve Cloud Member | 105.51 m | |
| | Crickley Member | 112.45 m | |
| | Leckhampton Member | 122.28 m | |
| | LIAS GROUP | | |
| | Whitby Mudstone Formation | 220.50 m | |
| | Marlstone Rock Formation | 222.28 m | |
| | Dyrham Formation | 276.51 m | |
| | Charmouth Mudstone Formation | 560.48 m | |
| | Blue Lias Formation | 618.29 m | |
| TRIASSIC | PENARTH GROUP | | |
| | Lilstock Formation | | |
| | Langport Member | 623.75 m | |
| | Cotham Member | 629.56 m | |
| | Westbury Formation | 635.08 m | |
| | MERCIA MUDSTONE GROUP | | |
| | Blue Anchor Formation | 643.97 m | |
| | Twyning Mudstone Formation | 765.68 m | |
| | Arden Sandstone Formation | 785.65 m | |
| | Eldersfield Mudstone Formation | 1075.26 m | |
| | SHERWOOD SANDSTONE GROUP | | |
| | Bromsgrove Sandstone Formation | | |
| | Sugarbrook Member | 1083.06 m | |
| | Finstall Member | 1168.86 m | |
| | Burcot Member | 1372.49 m (TD) | |

**UPTON BOREHOLE** (1952) [SP 2315 1313] SL +114.00 m

| | | | |
|---|---|---|---|
| JURASSIC | INFERIOR OOLITE GROUP | | |
| | Salperton Limestone Formation | | |
| | Clypeus Grit Member (ex situ) | 0.30 m | |
| | LIAS GROUP | | |
| | Whitby Mudstone Formation | 10.90 m | |
| | Marlstone Rock Formation | 16.18 m | |
| | Dyrham Formation | 36.04 m | |
| | Charmouth Mudstone Formation | 156.62 m | |
| | Blue Lias Formation | 165.23 m | |
| TRIASSIC | PENARTH GROUP | | |
| | Lilstock Formation: | | |
| | Langport Member | 166.62 m | |
| | Cotham Member | 172.57 m | |
| | Westbury Formation | 177.47 m | |
| | MERCIA MUDSTONE GROUP | | |
| | Blue Anchor Formation | 184.48 m | |
| | Twyning Mudstone Formation | 232.13 m | |
| | Arden Sandstone Formation | 240.41 m | |
| | Eldersfield Mudstone Formation | 305.41 m | |
| | SHERWOOD SANDSTONE GROUP | | |
| | Bromsgrove Sandstone Formation | | |
| | Sugarbrook Member | 313.48 m | |
| | Finstall Member | 337.49 m | |
| CARBONIFEROUS | UPPER COAL MEASURES | | |
| | Windrush Formation | 928.29 m | |
| | Burford Coal Formation | 1049.88 m | |
| | Crawley Formation | 1148.23 m (TD) | |

The classifications given differ somewhat from those in the original accounts by Green and Melville (1956) and Worssam (1963). The changes result from both updating of nomenclature and revisions of certain boundaries. For the most part, boundary revisions are based on re-examination of core specimens by the authors of this memoir.

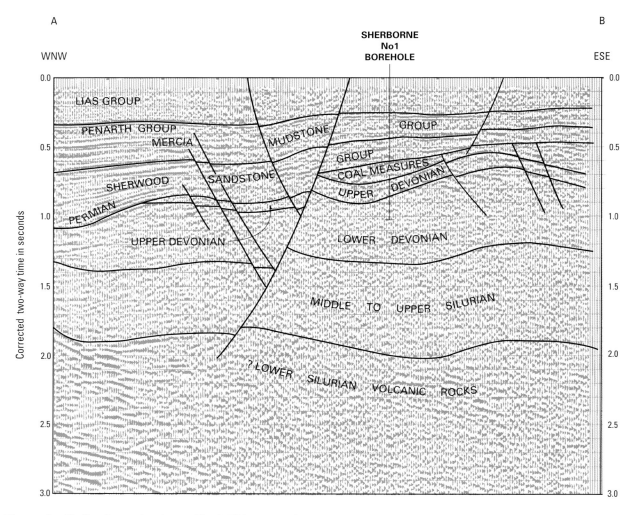

**Figure 8** Reflection seismic profile CT28 across the eastern margin of the Worcester Basin. For location, see Figure 7. Reproduced by permission of Shell U.K. Limited.

at Apley Barn (199.39 m), despite the more axial position of the Apley Barn Borehole within the Oxfordshire Coalfield Syncline. According to Poole's (1969; fig. 6) correlation, the Windrush Formation at Upton is thickened compared with that at Apley Barn. An alternative interpretation, based on borehole geophysics, is that the upper part of the succession at Upton is repeated by thrusting (Peace and Besly, 1997, fig. 10). The Windrush Formation is dominated by reddened and variegated mudstones, siltstones and sandstones. Worssam (1963) commented on the similarity of the upper 50 m or so to the Keele Formation of the Midlands coalfields; it includes lithologies with chocolate-brown and lilac tints, and contains several beds of small pebble conglomerate (between 372.45 and 387.17 m) with clasts of possibly pedogenic limestone. Between 388.24 and 431.72 m, and between 601.22 and 668.27 m, the strata are predominantly grey mudstones, siltstones and sandstones, with eight coal seams (Upton Nos. 2 to 9), the Upton

No. 2 coal (at 608.84 m) being 0.56 m thick. The strata originally proved in the Signet Borehole also belong to the Windrush Formation.

The Sherborne No. 1 Borehole penetrated 167.9 m of Carboniferous strata, between the base of the Triassic at 978.1 m and the unconformable contact with the underlying Devonian strata at 1146 m. Cuttings samples and records of sidewall cores indicate a succession of purplish brown to brownish grey mudstones and sandstones; traces of coal were seen at some levels, and coal seams are also suggested by geophysical logs. The gamma log characteristics of the succession are reminiscent of the Windrush Formation at Upton, but it is likely that the strata are older than any proved in the Upton Borehole as they lie at the base of the local Carboniferous succession, resting unconformably on Devonian rocks. They may correspond to the Arenaceous Coal Formation at the base of the Oxfordshire Coal Measures (Poole, 1969; see 1:50 000 Sheet 235, cross-section).

## PERMIAN AND MESOZOIC STRUCTURAL SETTING

After the uplift and erosion associated with the late Carboniferous Variscan orogeny, subsidence, beginning in Permian times, formed the fault-bounded Worcester Basin (Chadwick, 1985; Whittaker, 1985; Chadwick and Smith, 1988; Chadwick and Evans, 1995). The western margin of this major north–south-trending graben is marked by the Malvern Hills, while the eastern margin traverses the Cirencester district at depth as a series of *en échelon* faults, approximately midway between the Stowell Park and Upton boreholes (Figures 6 and 8). The main subsidence of the Worcester Basin occurred during Late Permian, Triassic and Early Jurassic times, when more than 3 km of strata accumulated in the deepest part of the basin, near Worcester, with some 2 km in the Cirencester district. Intermittent subsidence on a smaller scale continued into Mid, and possibly Late Jurassic times (see Chapter 9). The axis of maximum subsidence, to the west of the district, is virtually coincident with the axis of maximum Variscan uplift.

The area to the east of the bounding faults of the Worcester Basin remained a relatively stable basement high during the Mesozoic. Known as the London Platform (Figure 6), it is characterised by relatively thin Triassic and Jurassic sedimentary successions; a marked thinning takes place across the narrow boundary zone between the Worcester Basin and the London Platform. Thinning of the Lias succession was proved by the Stowell Park and Upton boreholes (Green and Melville, 1956; Worssam, 1963), but had previously been suggested by Hull (1857, plate 2). Buckman (1901, pp.143–146) was the first to recognise the importance of structural control on sedimentation of the Inferior Oolite, even though he did not acknowledge it in the Lias. He ascribed the eastward attenuation of the Inferior Oolite to the progressive erosion of beds uplifted along a north–south syndepositional anticlinal axis, following the vales of Moreton and Bourton. This concept is still widespread in the literature; following Arkell's (1933a, p.64) use of the term, it is generally known as the Vale of Moreton Axis (or Vale of Moreton Swell). However, the idea of an axis of relative uplift, with the implication of a thicker sedimentary succession on either side, is misleading; in fact, the Vale of Moreton Axis acted as a 'hinge' so that, in general, the succession thins eastwards across it onto the London Platform (see also Structure; Chapter 9). A slight thickening as the outcrops are traced to the north-east, across Oxfordshire, is related to the gradational boundary of the London Platform with the East Midlands Shelf to its north (Figure 6).

## PERMO-TRIASSIC

Triassic rocks were proved in 1875 by the Signet Borehole, about 1 km beyond the eastern margin of the district (De Rance, 1878, p.437, 1879, p.384; Woodward,1894, p.303). More details were subsequently provided by the Geological Survey Stowell Park and Upton cored boreholes (Green and Melville, 1956; Worssam, 1963; Sumbler, 1994b; see Table 8 and Figure 9). The Sherborne No. 1 Borehole, sited midway between the two, penetrated the entire succession (Sumbler, 1994a), and the uppermost beds were proved in several Gas Council Boreholes, drilled in the 1970s, in the north-eastern part of the district (Horton et al., 1987). The information from these latter boreholes comprises mainly geophysical logs and sporadic cuttings samples.

Regional considerations indicate that Permo-Triassic rocks are present at depth throughout the district, with a succession that is probably up to 1.5 km thick in the Worcester Basin, but much more attenuated over the London Platform in the east, in places perhaps less than 150 m thick.

## PERMIAN

Seismic data show that the Stowell Park Borehole is sited close to the axis of the Worcester Basin, where the thickest Permo-Triassic succession is preserved. Due to drilling difficulties, the borehole terminated without reaching the base of the Triassic beds, but it is likely that the full succession at the site would be much like that proved in the Guiting Power Borehole, some 12.5 km farther north (Figure 9). There, the basal part of the succession, resting upon Devonian rocks, comprises 155.45 m of orange to red-brown, fine- to medium-grained, argillaceous sandstone. This succession probably represents the **Bridgnorth Sandstone Formation**, of Permian age, which crops out in the west Midlands. It is largely of aeolian origin. These strata appear to be confined to the deepest, central part of the Worcester Basin, and are absent from the London Platform to the east. An overlying unit of mudstone and siltstone, 30.78 m thick in the Guiting Power Borehole (Figure 9), is unknown elsewhere in the region, but is perhaps analogous to upper Permian or lower Triassic mudstones that occur in the north Midlands and south-west England.

## TRIASSIC

### Sherwood Sandstone Group

The oldest beds proved in the Stowell Park Borehole are assigned to the Sherwood Sandstone Group of Early to Mid Triassic age. Whilst only 297.23 m of Sherwood Sandstone were proved (between 1075.26 m and terminal depth at 1372.49 m), seismic data show that the total thickness of the group is much greater. Some 814 m were proved in the Guiting Power Borehole, and the succession at Stowell Park is probably similar, both in thickness and in its component units. This thickness contrasts with the 213.7 m of Sherwood Sandstone in the Sherborne No. 1 Borehole, sited on the margin of the Worcester Basin, and only 32.08 m in the Upton Borehole, on the London Platform. These attenuated successions result mainly from the loss, due to overlap, of older parts of the succession (Figure 9).

In both the Guiting Power and Cooles Farm boreholes (Figure 6), the basal part of the Triassic succession is

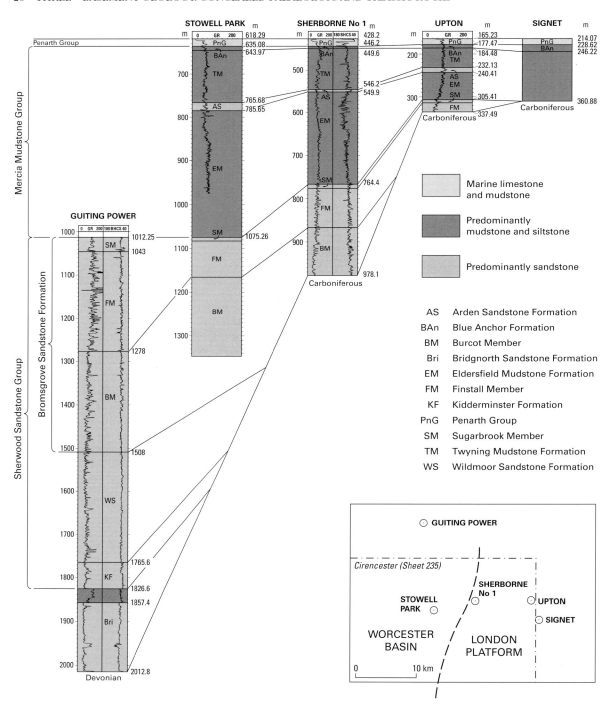

**Figure 9** Permian and Triassic succession proved in the Guiting Power, Stowell Park, Sherborne No. 1, Upton and Signet boreholes, illustrating the marked eastward attenuation of the succession.

assigned to the **Kidderminster Formation** (formerly the 'Bunter Pebble Beds'), a succession of conglomerates and sandstones, probably about 60 to 70 m thick. It is succeeded by the **Wildmoor Sandstone Formation** (formerly the 'Upper Mottled Sandstone'), comprising reddish brown sandstones, mainly of fluvial origin which,

from borehole geophysical logs, are of the order of 250 m thick at Guiting Power (Figure 9). Both units are probably present only within the deeper parts of the Worcester Basin, having been overstepped by younger beds elsewhere. Based on geophysical log characteristics and the presence of 'pebbles' in sidewall cores, however, it is possible that the basal 72.9 m of the Sherwood Sandstone in the Sherborne Borehole (905.2 to 978.1 m) represents the Kidderminster Formation, although they have been included here in the Bromsgrove Sandstone Formation (see below). The Wildmoor Sandstone is definitely absent at Sherborne, and neither unit is present at Upton (Figure 9).

The highest unit of the Sherwood Sandstone Group is the **Bromsgrove Sandstone Formation** (formerly the 'Lower Keuper Sandstone'). It comprises the whole 297.23 m of Sherwood Sandstone proved at Stowell Park, but the total thickness at that site is probably much greater; some 495 m are present at Guiting Power. In its type area to the south of Birmingham, the formation is divisible into three members (Old et al., 1991). These can be tentatively identified in the Stowell Park succession as recorded by Green and Melville (1956; Table 8, Figure 9).

The basal 203.63 m of the Bromsgrove Sandstone Formation at Stowell Park (between 1168.86 and 1372.49 m) resembles the Burcot Member of the type area. It is dominated by reddish brown sandstones that are conglomeratic at many levels, with quartz and quartzite pebbles, and intraformational mud-flakes. Overlying strata, 85.8 m thick (from 1083.06 to 1168.86 m), have many of the features of the Finstall Member. They consist of whitish to yellowish brown sandstones with some thin, reddish brown siltstones and mudstones, organised in fining-upwards, fluvial-type sedimentary rhythms, which typically comprise a coarse-grained or conglomeratic channel sandstone with an erosional base, passing upwards into finer-grained sandstone and overbank mudstones. Within the conglomerates, mudstone intraclasts are common, and extraformational pebbles include sandstones, quartz and perthitic feldspar. Coaly streaks and possible plant debris occur at several levels, and spores and pollen recovered from 1108.71 m (Warrington, 1970) are indicative of an Anisian (early Mid Triassic) age. The uppermost 7.8 m of the Bromsgrove Sandstone Formation (between 1075.26 and 1083.06 m) is similar to the Sugarbrook Member (formerly the 'Keuper Waterstones'), comprising relatively thinly interbedded sandstones, argillaceous sandstones and red, green and grey mudstones, with small patches of anhydrite. These beds were placed in the 'Keuper Marl' (now the Mercia Mudstone Group) by Green and Melville (1956).

The Bromsgrove Sandstone Formation is probably 213.7 m thick at Sherborne (764.4 to 978.1 m), although it remains possible that the basal 72.9 m of beds belong to the Kidderminster Formation (see above). No cores are available, but from the downhole geophysical logs it seems that all three members are present (Figure 9). The Burcot Member appears to be about 114 m thick. The rhythmic succession within the Finstall Member, 92 m thick, is evident from the gamma-ray log. The Sugarbrook Member, about 8 m thick, also has a distinctive gamma-ray signature, almost identical with that from the Upton Borehole.

In the Upton Borehole, the Bromsgrove Sandstone Formation forms the basal 32.08 m of the Triassic succession (305.41 to 337.49 m), resting unconformably on Carboniferous strata. The lower part (below 313.48 m), probably corresponding to the Finstall Member of Stowell Park, is mainly dark reddish brown, coarse-grained sandstone; the basal 7 m, containing scattered quartz pebbles, conceivably represents an attenuated Burcot Member. The Sugarbrook Member, 8.07 m thick, comprises grey, yellowish or reddish brown, soft, 'loamy', fine-grained, micaceous sandstones, with some beds of reddish brown and greenish grey mottled sandy mudstone containing sporadic plant remains and conchostracan crustaceans (*Euestheria*).

There is no indication of the Bromsgrove Sandstone in the log of the Signet Borehole (Woodward, 1894); it may be overstepped by the Mercia Mudstone to the west of that site, although it is present farther east in the Apley Barn Borehole near Witney (Poole, 1969).

### Mercia Mudstone Group

The Mercia Mudstone Group (formerly the 'Keuper Marl') is dominated by reddish brown mudstone, silty mudstone and siltstone; these lithologies are traditionally and conveniently referred to collectively as 'marl', although they are essentially non-calcareous. Anhydrite is present throughout most of the succession, accompanied by some gypsum in the upper part.

The Stowell Park Borehole proved Mercia Mudstone between 635.08 m and the top of the Bromsgrove Sandstone at 1075.26 m. The thickness of the group, 440.18 m, is close to that proved at Guiting Power (446.23 m) and Cooles Farm (406 m), which also lie within the axial zone of the Worcester Basin (Figure 6). It is greater than that in the Sherborne No. 1 Borehole (c. 318.2 m), and considerably more than the thicknesses in the Upton Borehole (127.94 m) and Signet Borehole (132.25 m), although the thickness changes are less pronounced than in the Sherwood Sandstone Group (see above; Figure 9).

In the Worcester Basin, the group comprises four formations (Barclay et al., 1997), all of which apparently persist throughout the district, indicating that the thin successions at Sherborne and Upton are largely complete, i.e. that the thinning is due to overall condensation, and not loss of beds by overlap (Figure 9). The same conclusion was reached by Wills (1970, 1976) from the recognition of 'miocyclothems', based essentially on the proportion of evaporites to clastic sediment.

The **Eldersfield Mudstone Formation** (formerly 'Lower Keuper Marl') is 289.61 m thick at Stowell Park (785.65 to 1075.26 m). It consists largely of red marl with some thin beds of green and grey marl, particularly in the higher part. Green mottling is developed in the lower and upper parts, but seems to be absent from the middle. Anhydrite is present as small veins, speckles and patches throughout, with larger patches (up to 0.1 m) between 857.4 m and 901.3 m.

The **Arden Sandstone Formation** (formerly 'Upper Keuper Sandstone') is 19.97 m thick at Stowell Park (765.68 to 785.65 m). It comprises lower (3.81 m) and upper (7.78 m) units of thinly bedded, fine-grained, green-grey and white sandstone with minor marl beds, separated by 8.38 m of red, purple and green marls. The sandstones in the upper unit are cross-bedded, with common desiccation cracks in mudstone intercalations. Veins and small patches of anhydrite occur sporadically.

The **Twyning Mudstone Formation** (formerly 'Upper Keuper Marl') is 121.71 m thick at Stowell Park (643.97 to 765.68 m). It consists largely of red-brown marl. Thin beds of green marl occur in the lower and upper parts, and green mottling is also present near the top. Anhydrite is present throughout the lower 93 m of the formation, but is absent from the higher beds. It occurs largely as specks and larger patches, up to 0.1 m in size, with six irregular bands up to 0.1 m thick between 682.75 and 701.04 m; veins are rare.

The **Blue Anchor Formation** (formerly 'Tea Green Marl') is 8.89 m thick in the Stowell Park Borehole (635.08 to 643.97 m). It consists largely of pale green and greenish white, slightly sandy mudstones with some pyrite; a few fish scales were found at about 638.9 m. The basal 4 m or so are sandier, with rare grains and granules of quartz (0.5 to 1.5 mm in diameter). Interbedded dark green mudstones impart a banded appearance to the middle part of the sequence; small-scale brecciation and injection structures occur in these banded units. The base of the formation is marked by a change to red marls below, but there is no other lithological difference, nor any sign of a break in sedimentation.

In the Sherborne Borehole, the Mercia Mudstone Group is about 318.2 m thick (from about 446.2 m to 764.4 m). The Arden Sandstone is probably represented by low gamma-ray values, and a sonic velocity peak between 546.2 and 549.9 m (Figure 9). The Blue Anchor Formation is difficult to recognise from geophysical logs alone, but may be present between depths at 446.2 and about 449.6 m.

In the Upton Borehole, the Mercia Mudstone Group is 127.94 m thick (177.47 to 305.41 m). A unit of sandy mudstones between 232.13 and 240.41 m, with a 0.91 m-thick bed of greyish green, fine-grained sandstone at the top, probably represents the Arden Sandstone Formation. The strata below, i.e. the Eldersfield Mudstone Formation, are paler in colour and more silty than those above, and below a depth of about 295 m are generally sandy. They contain occasional gypsum nodules and veins. The strata above, i.e. the Twyning Mudstone Formation, contain irregular greenish grey patches and gypsum veins. The highest 7.01 m of the Mercia Mudstone (177.47 to 184.48 m), assigned to the Blue Anchor Formation, comprise greenish grey, often dolomitic mudstones, with scattered fish scales and slump structures.

The only other borehole in the district to prove the Mercia Mudstone is the Gas Council GS13 Borehole near Fifield, which penetrated the topmost 5.49 m before terminating at a depth of 128.02 m. The strata, comprising greenish grey, finely silty and micaceous mudstones, with some sandstone and brick red 'marl', probably belong to the Blue Anchor Formation. The record of 'Top of Keuper Sandstone' (i.e. Bromsgrove Sandstone Formation) at +0.9 m OD in this borehole (Horton et al., 1987, p.148) is erroneous, and should read 'Top of Keuper Marl' (i.e. Mercia Mudstone Group).

Just outside the district, the Mercia Mudstone was penetrated by the Signet Borehole (Figure 9). Comparison with the succession in the Upton Borehole suggests that the classifications given by De Rance (1878, 1879) and Woodward (1894) are incorrect. The Mercia Mudstone is probably represented by the 132.25 m of beds between 228.62 m and the top of the Carboniferous at 360.88 m (Sumbler, 1994b). The strata are dominated by 'variegated marls with gypsum'; the upper 17.6 m (above 246.22 m) are described as green, and presumably include the Blue Anchor Formation.

No biostratigraphical evidence of age has been obtained from the Mercia Mudstone Group in the district, but by analogy with correlative successions farther north (Barclay et al., 1997), the Eldersfield Formation ranges from Anisian (early Mid Triassic) to Carnian (early Late Triassic), the Arden Sandstone Formation is late Carnian, and the Twyning Mudstone Formation and Blue Anchor Formation are of Norian and Rhaetian age.

## Penarth Group

The Penarth Group (formerly the 'Rhaetic') comprises the Westbury Formation and the succeeding Lilstock Formation, the latter divided into lower (Cotham) and upper (Langport) members (Warrington et al. 1980). In earlier accounts (e.g. Green and Melville, 1956; Worssam, 1963), the Langport Member, as the 'White Lias', was treated as the lowest unit in the Lias succession, and considered to be of Jurassic age. The Penarth Group is now known to be latest Triassic (Rhaetian) in its entirety (Cope, 1980a; Warrington et al., 1980).

The group is 16.79 m thick in the Stowell Park Borehole (from 618.29 to 635.08 m) and 12.24 m thick (165.23 to 177.47 m) at Upton. Similar thicknesses (in the range 12 to 20 m) were proved elsewhere in the region, and the formation seems little affected by the Vale of Moreton Axis (i.e. the boundary between the Worcester Basin and London Platform) (Figure 9), although farther east it pinches out towards an inferred shoreline on the London Platform in the Oxford–Bicester area (Horton et al., 1987, 1995; Figure 6).

The **Westbury Formation** is 5.52 m thick at Stowell Park, and 4.90 m at Upton. In both boreholes, a thin (25–50 mm) 'Bone Bed' with phosphatic debris, including fish debris (*Gyrolepis* and *Saurichthys*), rests disconformably on an uneven and probably eroded surface of the Blue Anchor Formation. The overlying beds comprise dark grey to black shaly mudstone with silty and sandy laminae. Some greyish green calcareous mudstone interbeds in the upper part herald a transition to the succeeding Lilstock Formation. The mudstones contain pyritised bivalves, notably *Eotrapezium* (*E. germari* and *E. concentricum*), *Protocardia rhaetica* and *Rhaetavicula contorta*; gastropods, ophiuroid fragments and fish also occur. Palynomorph assemblages from the Upton Borehole (Orbell, 1973) are dominated by spores and pollen, but include a large number of marine dinoflagellate cysts.

The **Cotham Member** of the Lilstock Formation, 5.81 m thick at Stowell Park and 5.95 m at Upton, comprises pale bluish to greenish grey calcareous mudstone, with streaks and laminae of white to pale grey, ripple-bedded sandstone and siltstone. At the top, a thin (0.15 to 0.18 m) bed of dark grey silty mudstone occurs; this was included in the 'White Lias' (Langport Member) by Green and Melville (1956) and Worssam (1963). Although the successions in the two boreholes are superficially similar in terms of lithology and thickness, the faunas contrast markedly. At Stowell Park, bivalves, notably *Chlamys*, *Eotrapezium*, *Gervillia* and *Protocardia* are dominant. At Upton, bivalves are rare, but ostracods and conchostracan crustaceans (*Euestheria*) are relatively common, as is plant material (including *Botryococcus*, *Naiadita lanceolata* and *Stenixys*). The first report of dinoflagellate cysts of Triassic age (Sarjeant, 1963) was from this member in the Stowell Park Borehole; in the Upton Borehole (Orbell, 1973), dinoflagellate cysts are much less common than in the underlying Westbury Formation. These features suggest lower salinity at Upton during deposition of the Cotham Member because of the influence of the land that lay to the east (Figure 9).

The **Langport Member** of the Lilstock Formation comprises pale grey, hard, splintery micritic limestone with some thin, undulating or stylolitic seams of dark grey mudstone. Although 5.46 m thick at Stowell Park, the member is only 1.39 m thick at Upton, possibly as a result of erosion in latest Rhaetian or early Hettangian times. The member yielded a few macrofossils, mostly bivalves including *Atreta (Dimyopsis) intusstriata*, *Meleagrinella fallax*, *Modiolus hillanoides* and *Modiolus langportensis*.

The member can be readily recognised on downhole geophysical logs by its marked low gamma-ray peak and high sonic velocity. In the Sherborne No. 1 Borehole, it is 5.5 m thick, close to that in the Stowell Park Borehole. It is considerably thinner in Gas Council boreholes GS15, GCN10 and GCN37 in the north-eastern corner of the district, from which Horton et al. (1987) quoted thicknesses of 2.50 m, 2.40 m and 1.90 m respectively.

In the Signet Borehole, Woodward (1894, p.303) placed the top of the Trias at depth of 218.56 m. However, 'jointed limestone', 1.83 m thick between 214.07 and 215.90 m, is probably the Langport Member, and underlying 'shales', 'limestone' and 'clay', with a basal 'black shale' at 228.62 m, represent the Cotham Member and Westbury Formation, giving a total thickness of 14.55 m for the Penarth Group.

Above the Langport Member in the Worcester Basin, the basal beds of the Lias Group are of Triassic age; these strata, 0.78 m thick in the Stowell Park Borehole, are dealt with in Chapter 4.

# FOUR

# Lower Jurassic: Lias Group

Rocks of the Lias Group are the oldest to crop out within the district. Only the upper part of the group is seen at the surface, most extensively in the north-west around Cheltenham and farther east in the Vale of Bourton, with narrow outcrops present in valley bottoms farther to the south and east. Underlying beds are known from boreholes, most notably the cored BGS Stowell Park and Upton boreholes, first described by Green and Melville (1956), Spath (1956), Melville (1956, 1963) and Worssam (1963). These demonstrate a dramatic thinning of the succession, from some 496 m at Stowell Park in the deepest part of the Worcester Basin, to about 165 m at Upton, 15 km to the east on the London Platform (Figure 10). These thicknesses differ slightly from those quoted by Green and Melville (1956) and Worssam (1963), due to revisions of both the upper and lower boundaries of the group. The thickness at Stowell Park is fairly typical for the Worcester Basin, although the basal part of the succession is slightly attenuated compared to successions in the Tewkesbury and Worcester districts (Worssam et al., 1989; Barclay et al., 1997), perhaps indicating some thinning towards the eastern margin of the basin during the early stages of its infill.

The Lias Group is almost entirely of Early Jurassic age, and the standard zonation (Table 9) is based on ammonite faunas which are generally abundant in the predominantly mudstone succession. The zonal nomenclature and boundary depths for the Stowell Park and Upton boreholes (Figure 10) have been updated from the original accounts by Spath (1956) and Worssam (1963) in reports by Ivimey-Cook (summarised by Sumbler 1994b, and Sumbler and Barron, 1995). In most cases, the zone and subzone boundaries are positioned at the lowest occurrence of particular ammonite taxa, and the depths quoted refer to individual specimens in the BGS collections. As the recovery of an ammonite specimen from a borehole core is partly a matter of chance, most of the zonal boundaries of Figure 10 are necessarily approximate, and are not precisely correlative between the boreholes. A more detailed, bed-by-bed correlation can be achieved using downhole gamma-ray and other geophysical logs; these enable a fairly detailed lithological correlation of the cored Stowell Park and Upton boreholes with others, such as the Sherborne No. 1 Borehole, sited midway between them on the edge of the Worcester Basin (Figure 10), and with various Gas Council boreholes in the north-east and beyond (Horton et al., 1987) for which no cores are available. Together, the ammonite zonation and lithological correlation indicate that the eastward thinning of the succession across the district results from loss by overlap of the basal beds, and condensation of the remainder (Figure 10; Table 9).

The Lias Group has traditionally been subdivided into Lower, Middle and Upper Lias. As originally used, these were lithostratigraphical terms but, commencing with Woodward (1893), they acquired a chronostratigraphical connotation which has led to some confusion over the definition of boundaries. To avoid such confusion in the present account, the succession is described in terms of six lithostratigraphical formations Cox et al. (1999).

## BLUE LIAS FORMATION

The Blue Lias, like most of the Lias Group, is dominated by grey, more or less calcareous marine mudstones, but is characterised by the presence of thin beds of grey argillaceous limestone ('cementstone'). This facies of interbedded mudstone and limestone is widespread in the lower part of the Lias Group throughout England and Wales. Although some of the limestones are nodular and of secondary diagenetic origin, the majority are probably primary (Hallam, 1964), and demonstrate repetitive cycles of sedimentation that were probably related to climate and sea-depth variations. The facies is diachronous, being preferentially developed in shallower depositional environments. The diachronous relationship is particularly marked between the Worcester Basin and adjoining shelf area of the London Platform (Figure 10).

In the Stowell Park Borehole, the Blue Lias Formation was proved between 560.48 m and the base of the Lias Group at 618.29 m. Its thickness, 57.81 m, is less than that at outcrop in the Vale of Severn, west of the district, where the formation is divisible, in ascending order, into the Wilmcote Limestone Member, Saltford Shale Member and Rugby Limestone Member (e.g. Worssam et al., 1989; Barclay et al., 1997). At Stowell Park, only the latter two are present; the Wilmcote Limestone Member, characterised by limestones, is absent, and beds of equivalent age are represented within an expanded Saltford Shale Member. At Upton, only the Rugby Limestone Member is present.

The **Saltford Shale Member**, comprising the basal 21.01 m of the Lias in the Stowell Park Borehole (from 597.28 to 618.29 m) consists of very dark grey to black, finely laminated, pyritous mudstone ('paper shales'), yielding scattered bivalves such as *Astarte*, *Cardinia*, *Lucina*, *Modiolus*, *Plagiostoma*, *Parallelodon* and *Pteromya*. Following Torrens and Getty (in Cope, 1980a), the base of the Jurassic System (corresponding to the base of the Planorbis Zone and Hettangian Stage) is taken at the first record of the ammonite *Psiloceras*, at 617.51 m. The underlying 0.78 m of Lias mudstone, down to the top of the Langport Member, thus belongs to the uppermost Triassic (Rhaetian Stage). These 'Pre-Planorbis Beds' are

**Figure 10**   Lithostratigraphical correlation of the Lias Group in the Stowell Park, Sherborne No. 1 and Upton boreholes, and relationship to the ammonite-based zonation.

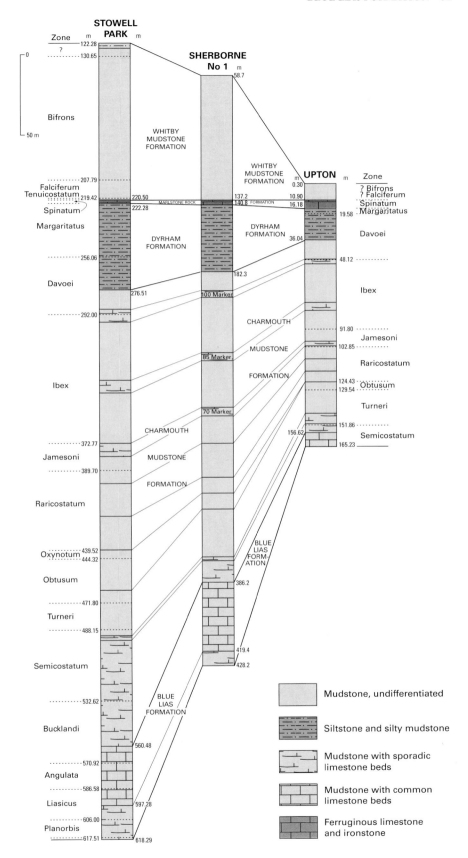

Classification of Sherborne No. 1 Borehole based entirely on downhole gamma-ray logs. The tie-lines between the boreholes indicate inferred correlation of lithostratigraphical units based on gamma-ray logs. Ammonite zonal nomenclature and boundaries for Stowell Park and Upton boreholes updated from the original accounts by Spath (1956) and Worssam (1963). The zones (and subzones) are, in most cases, defined by first appearances of ammonite taxa, and the boundaries shown in the boreholes (by pecked lines) may not be precisely correlative between them.

**Table 9** Lithostratigraphical classification of the Lias Group, and relationship to the standard chronostratigraphical framework. Not to scale.

| CHRONOSTRATIGRAPHY | | LITHOSTRATIGRAPHY |
| --- | --- | --- |
| SUBSTAGE | ZONE | FORMATION |
| UPPER TOARCIAN | Levesquei | WHITBY MUDSTONE / BRIDPORT SAND |
| | Thouarsense | |
| | Variabilis | |
| LOWER TOARCIAN | Bifrons | |
| | Falciferum | |
| | Tenuicostatum | |
| UPPER PLIENS–BACHIAN | Spinatum | MARLSTONE ROCK |
| | Margaritatus | DYRHAM |
| LOWER PLIENS–BACHIAN | Davoei | CHARMOUTH MUDSTONE (pars) |
| | Ibex | 100 marker / 85 marker |
| | Jamesoni | 70 marker |
| UPPER SINEMURIAN | Raricostatum | |
| | Oxynotum | CHARMOUTH MUDSTONE (pars) |
| | Obtusum | |
| LOWER SINEMURIAN | Turneri | |
| | Semicostatum | |
| | Bucklandi | BLUE LIAS |
| HETTANGIAN | Angulata | Rugby Limestone Member |
| | Liasicus | Saltford Shale Member |
| | Planorbis | |
| (RHAETIAN) | | |

Vertical ruling indicates non-sequence. The ammonite-based zonation follows Dean, Donovan & Howarth (1961), incorporating revisions of Cope (1980a), Ivimey-Cook and Donovan (1983), Phelps (1985) and Howarth (1992).

somewhat thinner than in adjoining areas to the west, where they are typically about 3 m thick. Above, the greater part of the member is assigned to the Planorbis Zone, but the lowest occurrence of the ammonite *Waehneroceras* at depth of 606.00 m indicates the succeeding Liasicus Zone (Figure 10).

The **Rugby Limestone Member** comprises grey calcareous mudstones and black shaly mudstones, with interbeds of grey, fine-grained, argillaceous limestone. As well as ammonites, the fauna includes brachiopods (*Lingula*, *Calcirhynchia*) and bivalves such as *Gresslya*, *Gryphaea*, *Liostrea*, *Lucina*, *Modiolus*, *Oxytoma*, *Placunopsis*, *Plagiostoma* and *Pseudolimea*. The member is 36.80 m thick in the Stowell Park Borehole (560.48 to 597.28 m), and corresponds to the 'Blue Lias' noted by Green and Melville (1956). The limestones, about 31 in number, range from 0.05 to 0.53 m in thickness, are typically about 0.18 m thick, and make up some 14 per cent of the thickness of the member. The strata span the upper part of the Liasicus Zone, the Angulata Zone (recognised by the presence of *Schlotheimia*), and the lower part of the Bucklandi Zone, the base of which is taken at the lowest occurrence of arietitid ammonites (Figure 10).

In the Upton Borehole, the basal 8.61 m of the Lias (156.62 to 165.23 m) contain 15 beds of limestone, typically 0.1 m thick. The ammonite fauna indicates the upper part (Resupinatum Subzone) of the Semicostatum Zone, and so is significantly (perhaps of the order of 1 million years) younger than the youngest Blue Lias at Stowell Park. Blue Lias beds of similar age and character occur in the Apley Barn Borehole, some 11.5 km to the east of Upton (Poole, 1969), and seem to be fairly typical for this part of the London Platform.

## CHARMOUTH MUDSTONE FORMATION

Overlying the Blue Lias Formation, the Charmouth Mudstone Formation corresponds to the Lower Lias Clay [Formation] of other accounts (e.g. Worssam et al., 1989; Barclay et al., 1997). The succession is 283.97 m thick in the Stowell Park Borehole (276.51 to 560.48 m), but only 120.58 m in the Upton Borehole (36.04 to 156.62 m). It ranges from the Bucklandi Zone to the Davoei Zone (Figure 10).

The formation is dominated by mudstone, with certain units recognisable from both the lithological and gamma-ray logs. These include the 70, 85 and 100 geophysical marker 'members', first described by Horton and Poole (1977) in the Chipping Norton district on the basis of resistivity logs, on which they form notable rightward (high) peaks. They form corresponding leftward (low count) peaks on the gamma-ray logs, and can be related to more calcareous units in the cores of the Stowell Park and Upton boreholes, despite minor depth discrepancies which probably result from inaccuracies in the depth marking of the cores. The vertical separation of these and other unnamed geophysical markers indicates a significant condensation of the succession between Stowell Park and Upton (Figure 10). Addition-

ally, some strata may be missing at Upton; for example, neither the Oxynotum Zone nor the upper part of the underlying Obtusum Zone was proved, probably being cut out by an erosional non-sequence at the base of the Raricostatum Zone, as is typical elsewhere over the London Platform (Donovan et al., 1979). The non-sequence may be present at Stowell Park too, as the Oxynotum Zone, though present, is rather thin.

As well as an extensive and varied ammonite fauna, the Charmouth Mudstone contains a variety of bivalves (e.g. *Astarte*, *Bakevellia*, *Camptonectes*, *Chlamys*, *Gervillia*, *Grammatodon*, *Gryphaea*, *Hippopodium*, *Lucina*, *Mactromya*, *Meleagrinella*, *Modiolus*, *Oxytoma*, *Palaeoneilo*, *Palaeonucula*, *Parallelodon*, *Pholadomya*, *Pleuromya*, *Plagiostoma*, *Protocardia*, *Pseudolimea*, *Pseudopecten*), with gastropods and rarer brachiopods, echinoids and crinoids. Sporadic belemnites also occur, mainly in higher parts of the succession.

In the Stowell Park Borehole, the basal part of the succession, belonging to the Bucklandi Zone, the Semicostatum Zone and lowest part of the Turneri Zone, comprises dark grey and black calcareous mudstone, commonly indurated, with occasional limestone nodules and beds. At Upton, a similar facies extends up to approximately the same horizon (Figure 10), although limestones are better developed.

Overlying beds, up to the base of the 85 Marker (in the Ibex Zone), comprise grey mudstones, more shaly in the lower part, with rare limestone nodules and beds. Within this succession, the prominent leftward gamma-ray signature of the 70 Marker apparently corresponds to an interval of indurated calcareous mudstone and soft argillaceous limestone in the Jamesoni Zone. In the Stowell Park Borehole and elsewhere, the 70 Marker is known to occur in the upper part of the zone (Brevispina Subzone), and its apparent position lower in the zone in the Upton Borehole (Figure 10) reflects the relatively poor ammonite control on the zonal boundaries there.

Within the Ibex Zone, the 85 Marker is notable on gamma-ray logs, occurring in the uppermost part of the middle (Valdani) of its three subzones. In borehole cores, it corresponds to calcareous, often highly fossiliferous mudstones, with some limestone bands and nodules. In the logs (based on cuttings) of the Gas Council boreholes in the north-east of the district, it is typically recorded as 'mudstone with cementstone fragments'. It crops out immediately beyond the northern boundary of the district, near Rissington Mill [SP 1815 2028]. Northwards, in the Vale of Bourton, it forms a marked scarp feature associated with slabs of bluish grey to yellow, slightly ferruginous, shelly, argillaceous limestone, and yellowish, ferruginous limestone nodules. The 85 Marker probably corresponds, at least in part, to the so-called 'Yellow Lias' (Buckman, 1843), formerly exposed in the Battledown Brickworks [SO 962 217] in Cheltenham, just to the north of the district (Richardson, 1929). Ammonite faunas from approximately this level, in the Ibex Zone, are known from sections near Leckhampton Station [SO 949 203] (Richardson, 1904; Spath, 1938) and the 'Cotswold Potteries' [SO 950 202] (Richardson, 1913).

The topmost part of the Charmouth Mudstone Formation, above the 85 Marker, consists of grey calcareous mudstones, with scattered sideritic ('clay ironstone') nodules. These are the oldest Lias strata to crop out in the district, producing a brownish grey clay soil in the northwest and Vale of Bourton. Most of this interval belongs to the uppermost (Luridum Subzone) part of the Ibex Zone, but the top (marked by the presence of *Androgynoceras*) belongs to the Davoei Zone. Although now very poorly exposed, a brickpit at Pilley (or Pilford) [SO 952 194] formerly exposed mudstones with ironstone and limestone nodules that yielded ammonites and bivalves of the Davoei Zone. Richardson (1913), noted other claypits, such as those by Lilley Brook [SO 9650 1925] and off Little Herbert's Road [SO 9965 1940], where the strata were assigned to the '*Capricornus*-Beds', i.e. middle Davoei Zone. Beds of the Davoei Zone are also known from a pit near the northern end of the dam [SO 9880 1982] at Dowdeswell Reservoir (BGS collections).

The 100 Marker on the geophysical logs corresponds to a unit of silty or sandy mudstones with some thin limestones in cored boreholes. It lies about 10 to 12 m below the top of the Charmouth Mudstone Formation, and approximately at the boundary between the Ibex and Davoei zones. It has not been detected at outcrop, perhaps because of obscuring landslip and downwashed material from the succeeding Dyrham Formation.

## DYRHAM FORMATION

The Dyrham Formation comprises grey mudstones and silty mudstones, with interbeds of highly micaceous, weakly cemented siltstone or very fine sandstone. It incorporates the lower and greater part of the 'Middle Lias' of many previous accounts, i.e. the 'Sandy Beds' of Richardson (1933). In the Cirencester district, the Dyrham Formation extends from the upper part of the Lower Pliensbachian Davoei Zone to the upper part of the Margaritatus Zone. It thins significantly across the district, reflecting the general eastward attenuation of the Lias succession when traced from the Worcester Basin onto the London Platform (Figure 10). Although ammonite control is poor compared with some parts of the Lias succession, it appears that the thinning is a result of both overall condensation, and a loss of the youngest beds beneath an erosive non-sequence at the base of the Marlstone Rock Formation, which cuts down to lower stratigraphical levels in the east.

The Dyrham Formation crops out in the valley of the River Chelt, in the north-western part of the area. Exposure is extremely limited due to extensive landslipping, although a section showing 2.3 m of silty mudstone and limestone near the top of the formation is visible in a sunken trackway [SO 9711 1939]. The thickness of the formation is estimated to be approximately 35 m, much the same as at Robins Wood Hill [SO 836 149] and Stonehouse [SO 816 050], just to the west of the district, where the base of the formation is marked by a bed of calcareous sandstone, named the 'Capricornus Sandstone' by Palmer (1971).

Exposure is slightly better in the Vale of Bourton, where the formation is 20 to 25 m thick, and in the Evenlode valley in the north-eastern corner of the district, where it is only about 15 m thick. The outcrop is characterised by a silt or silty clay soil, of a pale bluish grey colour, weathering to pale yellowish or reddish brown. Small chips of limonite are common in places; these result mainly from the weathering and disintegration of sideritic nodules within the mudstones, but probably also include downwashed material from the Marlstone Rock and Whitby Mudstone. Small exposures in stream gulleys and ditches typically show bluish grey, very silty and micaceous mudstone with ferruginous bands and, particularly in the upper part of the succession, limonitic concretions or lenticles of grey calcareous siltstone. Locally, minor groundwater seepage indicates a particularly sandy unit at the base of the formation, probably the 'Capricornus Sandstone'. The Dyrham Formation is slightly more resistant to erosion than the underlying Charmouth Mudstone, and so gives rise to steeper slopes. This facilitates mapping the base of the formation where exposure is poor, for example near Great Rissington.

The Dyrham Formation was penetrated in both the Stowell Park and Upton boreholes (Green and Melville, 1956; Worssam, 1963; Sumbler, 1994b; Sumbler and Barron, 1995; see Figure 10). In the Stowell Park Borehole, the formation is 54.23 m thick (222.28 to 276.51 m), the maximum known in the region. The base corresponds to a fairly sharp increase in the arenaceous content of the sediment, which is obvious from the core specimens and probably corresponds to the 'Capricornus Sandstone' seen at outcrop. On the gamma-ray log, it is indicated by a significant leftward swing in the trace, a feature that can be recognised in other (uncored) boreholes in the region. The lowest 24 m or so of the formation in the Stowell Park Borehole are dark grey, very finely sandy or silty mudstones, with wisps and laminae of pale grey, fine-grained sandstone, and rare sideritic nodules. Succeeding strata are dominated by grey and greenish grey, very fine- to fine-grained, commonly cross-laminated sandstones. Conglomeratic horizons at depths of about 247 m, 241.30 m and 225.17 m, give an indication of cyclicity. At 227.00 m, in the upper part of the formation, 1.83 m of dark green muddy sandstone with abundant fine-grained berthierine ooids (the 'oolitic ironstone' of Green and Melville, 1956) is overlain (at 225.17 m) by finely sandy mudstone with scattered berthierine ooids, conglomeratic at the base. According to Simms (1990, fig. 6), this 'oolitic ironstone' bed represents the 'Subnodosus Sandstone', a supposed marker bed high in the subzone, although there is insufficient evidence to confirm this and other correlations are possible (e.g. Palmer, 1971).

The fauna of the Dyrham Formation in the Stowell Park Borehole is dominated by bivalves such as *Goniomya*, *Grammatodon*, *Mactromya*, *Modiolus*, *Parallelodon*, *Pinna*, *Pleuromya*, *Protocardia* and *Pseudolimea*, commonly preserved uncrushed in the more sandy beds. Ammonites also occur. *Aegoceras capricornus*, from about 275 m in the basal sandstone bed of the formation, indicates the middle (Capricornus) of the three subzones of the Davoei Zone, and *Oistoceras* at 267.37 m and above indicates the succeeding Figulinum Subzone. The occurrence of *Amaltheus* at and above 256.06 m indicates the Upper Pliensbachian Margaritatus Zone. The Margaritatus Zone is divided into three subzones. The lowest, the Stokesi Subzone, has been proved below 242.95 m, and higher beds yield a small number of poorly preserved *Amaltheus* cf. *subnodosus,* suggesting the succeeding Subnodosus Subzone. No ammonites were recovered from the topmost 3.88 m of the Dyrham Formation (222.28 to 226.16 m), and so there is no evidence of the Gibbosus Subzone, which may be absent below the erosive base of the Marlstone Rock Formation. The Gibbosus Subzone is not well substantiated anywhere in the region (Palmer, 1971, 1973; Simms, 1990).

In the Upton Borehole, the Dyrham Formation is only 19.86 m thick (16.18 to 36.04 m). It comprises grey mudstones and silty mudstones, with interbeds of highly micaceous siltstone or very fine sandstone at some levels, although there is no evidence for the Capricornus Sandstone at the base. It includes a 0.05 m bed of pale fawn, kaolinised, argillaceous sideritic limestone with ferruginous staining immediately beneath the Marlstone Rock Formation; this limestone bed was included in the Marlstone Rock by Worssam (1963). The lower part of the succession belongs to the Davoei Zone; *Oistoceras* cf. *curvicorne* at 26.68 m provides the highest evidence of this zone. *Amaltheus,* at 19.58 m and above, indicates the Margaritatus Zone. Faunal evidence is inconclusive, but it seems unlikely that any Dyrham Formation younger than the Stokesi Subzone is present.

## MARLSTONE ROCK FORMATION

The Marlstone Rock Formation constitutes the upper part of the 'Middle Lias' of previous accounts, such as that of Richardson (1933). Within the Cirencester district, it is typically 2 to 3 m thick, but is absent in some places. At outcrop, it is best developed in the eastern part of the district, notably on the eastern side of the Vale of Bourton where it forms a prominent feature surmounted by a dip slope, in places more than 150 m wide. At the southern end of the vale [SP 193 150], the Marlstone Rock dips beneath the floodplain of the River Windrush, but it reappears farther downstream [SP 220 134] near Taynton. It forms marked features along the narrow valley of the Coombe Brook to the north of Taynton, and on the slopes of the Evenlode valley in the extreme north-east. It is also present in the Chelt valley, in the north-western part of the district. There, however, it is very poorly exposed because of landslip and may be locally absent.

In the Stowell Park Borehole, the Marlstone Rock (220.50 to 222.28 m) comprises 1.78 m of pale grey and slightly brownish grey, hard, medium-grained, shell fragmental and ooidal wackestone to packstone, with some darker, rather argillaceous layers. The ooids are composed of soft, whitish kaolinite, probably a diagenetic replacement of berthierine; the brownish tinge of the rock suggests that a certain proportion of iron is present. At outcrop, however, the formation is invariably oxidised to an orange, red or rust-brown, ferruginous, massive or poorly bedded limestone or ironstone, commonly with thin veins or coatings of brown, secondary limonite. Texturally, the weathered rock is a fine- to very fine-grained ooidal grainstone, containing abundant yellowish brown limonite ooids (probably altered berthierine), generally 0.125 to 0.25 mm in diameter, in a clear grey crystalline calcite and/or siderite cement. It contains a proportion of quartz sand, and exposed surfaces (as in brash) have a sandy texture, although the crystalline cement probably contributes to this. The dip slopes developed on the Marlstone Rock may carry brash of this material, although in many places the soil is a loam containing only small chips of limonite. The Marlstone Rock is commonly unfossiliferous, but brachiopods occur both sporadically and concentrated in small 'nests'. A characteristic species found in the area is *Tetrarhynchia tetrahedra*; species of *Lobothyris, Gibbirhynchia* and *Rudirhynchia* also occur. Various bivalves may be found, most conspicuously the large *Pseudopecten equivalvis*. Robust belemnites may be common locally, particularly near the top of the formation, where they occur in current-winnowed concentrations, commonly in association with crinoid debris. Ammonites are generally rare, but those known from the Cotswolds indicate the Upper Pliensbachian Spinatum Zone (Howarth, 1958; 1980). Within the district, a specimen of *Pleuroceras solare* found [SP 2250 1409] near Great Barrington indicates the Apyrenum Subzone, the lower of the two subzones of the Spinatum Zone, and a *Pleuroceras hawskerense?*, found in brash near the top of the Marlstone Rock north of Great Rissington [SP 1996 1880], suggests the succeeding Hawskerense Subzone.

Several exposures of the Marlstone Rock occur in the eastern part of the district. An overgrown quarry [SP 2001 1921], 1.3 km south-east of Little Rissington, shows, 1.35 m of rust-brown, sandy textured, shell-fragmental, limonite-ooid grainstone, with rare nests of *T. tetrahedra* and sporadic belemnites and crinoid fragments, beneath Whitby Mudstone. Other sections occur in the valley of the Coombe Brook, where old quarry workings [e.g. SP 2332 1710; SP 2327 1793; SP 2327 1756] reveal up to 2.5 m of massive, poorly bedded, coarse-grained, sandy, ochreous limonitic and siderite-veined ironstone, with sporadic belemnites and shell fragments. The Marlstone Rock was also exposed near the now-ruined Dodd's Mill [SP 1900 1525], Great Barrington, where Woodward (1893, p.219) saw 'traces of the Rock-bed with *Rhynchonella* [=*Tetrarhynchia*] *tetrahedra*'. In the river bank, just north of the mill, Richardson (1933, p.9) recorded 'hard, brown slightly ferruginous and somewhat sandy limestone with 'nests' of *Lobothyris punctata* and occasional specimens of *L. edwardsi*', and Worssam and Bisson (1961, p.78) noted up to 1.2 m of 'massive ironstone' to the south-east [SP 1913 1500].

The Marlstone Rock is apparently 5.28 m thick in the Upton Borehole (10.90 to 16.18 m depth), although only 3.76 m of core were recovered (Worssam, 1963; Figure 10). This is the maximum confirmed thickness for the district; the log of a borehole [SP 1873 1107] on Windrush Airfield that records 8.4 m of limestone at this level may be unreliable. Most of the core samples from the Upton Borehole are brown, oxidised, sandy ironstone, containing pale, limonitised and kaolinitised ooids, and sporadic brachiopods including *Lobothyris* and *Gibbirhynchia micra*. A conglomeratic layer at the base contains small pebbles of 'buff marl', evidently reworked from an underlying bed of sideritic limestone (upper-most Dyrham Formation; see above), together with a few quartz granules. This basal, conglomeratic bed has also been noted in field brash [SP 197 150] near Dodd's Mill.

To the west of the Dodd's Mill, ditch dredgings [SP 1873 1550] indicate the presence of typical Marlstone Rock beneath the Windrush alluvium at the southern end of the Vale of Bourton, and the typical ironstone with abundant belemnites was seen in a ditch about 0.8 km to the north-west [SP 1843 1584]. However, northwards from this point, the Marlstone Rock appears to be absent, probably having been removed by erosion prior to deposition of the succeeding Whitby Mudstone Formation. The local disappearance of the Marlstone Rock is approximately coincident with the Vale of Moreton Axis, and may be related to this structure in some way, although it is present farther west in the Worcester Basin, as in the Stowell Park Borehole and in the Chelt valley (see above). The Marlstone Rock of the Cotswold scarp edge in adjoining districts has been documented by Palmer (1971, 1973) and Simms (1990). They showed that it rests erosively on underlying beds including, at some localities (e.g. Robins Wood Hill [SO 836 150]), sandstones of the Subnodosus Subzone; this may also be the case in parts of the Cirencester district. Such sandstones, hitherto included in the Marlstone Rock, are herein regarded as part of the Dyrham Formation.

## WHITBY MUDSTONE FORMATION

The Whitby Mudstone Formation corresponds to the Upper Lias of previous accounts. Dominated by bluish grey mudstones, the formation crops out on the slopes of the Chelt valley in the north-west of the district, in the Vale of Bourton, and in the Coombe Brook and Evenlode valleys in the north-east. The uppermost beds also crop out sporadically in the floors of other valleys in the northern part of the area as a result of localised valley bulging (Chapter 2). These topmost beds have been penetrated by a number of water wells in the district, but only a few boreholes proved the whole formation. Of these, the most important are the Stowell Park and Upton cored boreholes. The principal outcrops of the Whitby Mudstone are on the steep slopes capped by the limestones of the Inferior Oolite Group. These outcrops are characterised by bluish grey to fawn-weathering clays that are very finely silty and micaceous in places, although markedly less so than those of the Dyrham Formation. The Whitby Mudstone also lacks the yellowish and reddish weathering colours of the latter. The silty beds occur particularly in the upper part of the

formation in the west of the area, but are absent in the east because of overstep (see below).

Large areas of outcrop are obscured by wash and debris from the overlying beds, and the formation is affected by major landslips, particularly in the north-western part of the district. This makes estimates of its thickness uncertain, but the formation appears to be about 70 to 80 m thick in the north-west, and nearly 100 m were proved in the Stowell Park Borehole. It thins dramatically eastwards, however, being only about 25 to 35 m in the Vale of Bourton, and even less in the Windrush valley, on the eastern margin of the district. There, Worssam (1963) recorded a thickness of only 10.6 m in the Upton Borehole (0.30 to 10.90 m, Figure 10) but the overlying Inferior Oolite (0 to 0.30 m depth) is cambered. Nevertheless, the full thickness of the formation in this area is probably no more than 12 or 14 m. This thinning, even more pronounced than in underlying units of the Lias Group, is due to condensation of the succession over the London Platform, combined with the absence of the youngest beds as a result of eastward overstep by the Middle Jurassic Inferior Oolite Group across the Vale of Moreton Axis.

The Stowell Park Borehole (Figure 10) provides the best information on the Whitby Mudstone succession within the Worcester Basin. The 98.22 m thickness of the formation from 122.28 to 220.50 m, is slightly less than that quoted by Green and Melville (1956), as they included sandstones at the top that are now regarded as part of the Inferior Oolite Group (see Chapter 5). The greater part of the succession comprises dark grey mudstones with fossils typically preserved in pinkish aragonite. Ammonites are generally the most abundant macrofossils, although gastropods and bivalves (such as *Grammatodon*, *Lucina* and *Pseudomytiloides*) also occur. The upper 33 m (above 155.42 m, within the Bifrons Zone) comprise very poorly fossiliferous, pale grey, fine-grained argillaceous sandstones and siltstones with laminae and lenticles of smoother, darker grey mudstone. They contain a number of minor conglomeratic beds, giving an indication of cyclicity. These rather sandy strata, transitional to the Bridport Sand Formation, were also proved in the BGS Northfield Farm Borehole, about 7 km north-west of Stowell Park, and are probably widespread at the top of the formation in the western part of the district.

In the following account of the Stowell Park Borehole, the ammonite zonation, which supersedes that of Spath (1956), is based on a re-examination of the specimens by Dr M K Howarth (summarised by Ivimey-Cook in Cope, 1980a), with nomenclature updated after Howarth (1992).

The basal beds of the formation are dark grey shaly mudstones which rest sharply on the Marlstone Rock. The lowest 1 m (below 219.42 m) is attributed to the basal Toarcian Tenuicostatum Zone (Figure 10). *Tilton-iceras antiquum* and *Dactylioceras* cf. *semicelatum* at 219.84 m indicate the Semicelatum Subzone in the upper part of the zone; lower subzones of the Tenuicostatum Zone are thus likely to be absent, implying a non-sequence at the base of the formation. As well as ammonites, these beds have yielded small brachiopods such as *Nannirhynchia* cf. *pygmaea* and *Gibbirhynchia* cf. *tiltonensis*. The overlying 11.62 m of strata (below 207.79 m) belong to the Falciferum Zone. The lower part includes dark grey and brown 'paper shales' with fish debris and abundant ammonites. This facies is typical of the 'Fish Beds' which are widely developed near the base of the Whitby Mudstone in the Midlands. The lowest ammonite from the Falciferum Zone is a *Cleviceras exaratum* (from 219.42 m depth), a species that characterizes the middle part of the lower (Exaratum Subzone) of its two subzones; older beds, normally characterised by *Eleganticeras elegantulum* were not proved. The succeeding Falciferum Subzone, with abundant *H. falciferum* was proved above 214.42 m.

The base of the succeeding Bifrons Zone, taken at 207.79 m, at the lowest occurrence of *Pseudolioceras*, coincides with a conglomeratic bed that presumably marks a minor non-sequence. Of its three subzones, the Commune Subzone at the base has not been confirmed, but the succeeding Fibulatum Subzone has been recognised above 180.42 m. In contrast to the underlying beds, the Crassum Subzone, proved between 173.73 and 130.65 m, contains a diverse fauna with bivalves and gastropods as well as ammonites. Above a nodular bed with berthierine ooids at 157.28 m, the mudstones become silty and very finely sandy. A sandy limestone bed with bored pebbles, at 137.49 m in the Stowell Park Borehole, can also be recognised at a depth of 11.66 m in the Northfield Farm Borehole. The highest occurrence of *Hildoceras* in the Stowell Park Borehole, at 130.65 m, is the last confirmation of the Bifrons Zone. It occurs within a condensed bed with a conglomeratic base; a similar bed, also with *Hildoceras*, occurs at 10.05 m in the Northfield Farm Borehole. In both boreholes, interbeds of pale, fine-grained, soft sandstone become progressively more common in the overlying succession. At Stowell Park, the highest 2.76 m of the formation, above 125.03 m, are dominated by grey, fine-grained sandstones which could be regarded as the feather edge of the Bridport Sand Formation, but are herein classified with the Whitby Mudstone for convenience (Figure 10). These strata yielded a *Hammatoceras?* from 122.37 m, immediately below the top of the formation, suggesting a late Toarcian, post-Variabilis Zone age. Spath (1956) considered the specimen to be from the latest Toarcian Levesquei Zone, and this would seem to be confirmed by the presence of *?Dumortieria levesquei* from approximately the same level in the Northfield Farm Borehole (see below). *Hammatoceras* is particularly common in the Dispansum Subzone at the base of the Levesquei Zone.

In the north-eastern part of the district, the basal part of the formation appears to be further condensed relative to that in the Stowell Park Borehole, and it includes fossiliferous limestones and ironstones not developed in the borehole. These beds rest with marked non-sequence on the underlying Marlstone Rock, or on the Dyrham Formation where the former is absent on the western side of the Vale of Bourton. In the Upton Borehole, 0.1 m of ferruginous, argillaceous limestone, with scattered peloids, small dactylioceratid ammonites and a few pebbles of Marlstone, rests on an unevenly eroded and oxidised surface of the Marlstone Rock. In an old quarry [SP 2001 1921], 1.3 km south-east of Little Rissington, above a markedly uneven, eroded surface of the Marlstone Rock, the lowest bed of the Whitby Mudstone is a clay, 0.3 m thick, containing large pebbles of Marlstone and smaller phosphatic clasts. Above, a thin bed of greyish cream, sideritic limestone or ironstone is much like that in the Upton Borehole. Together with an overlying clay, it contains abundant ammonites, mainly dactylioceratids (*?Dactylioceras* (*Orthodactylites*)) but also rarer small hildoceratids including *Hildaites?* and *Harpoceras serpentinum?*. Above, lying about 0.4 to 0.5 m above the base of the Whitby Mudstone Formation, a yellowish cream to rust brown, ferruginous, shell fragmental wackestone to packstone is largely made up of crinoid debris, with some pale grey ?phosphatic peloids. It contains subangular pebbles of limestone (like the bed below), and abundant fragments of ammonites, mainly *Dactylioceras* (*Orthodactylites*), as well as belemnites and small rhynchonellids (*Gibbirhynchia?*).

These distinctive limestone/ironstone beds have been noted at several other localities in the eastern part of the district. The pebbly, crinoidal bed seems to be particularly widespread, and at one locality [SP 1834 1612], it yielded a worn, ferruginous fragment of *Pleuroceras?*, presumably reworked from the Marlstone Rock. Even where the limestones are not evident, loose dactylioceratid fragments, preserved in pale grey ?phosphatic limestone, are commonly found close to the base of the Whitby Mudstone Formation; this ammonite-rich horizon has been used to map the base of the formation on the western side of the Vale of Bourton where the Marlstone Rock is absent. From their ammonite fauna, these basal strata must belong largely to the Falciferum Zone, but may also include a thin representative of the preceding Tenuicostatum Zone, although that zone, being only about 1 m thick at Stowell Park, is likely to be absent due to overlap in the north-eastern part of the district. The limestone/ironstone strata correspond to the 'Transition Bed' sensu Horton et al. (1987), developed at the base of the 'Upper Lias' of Oxfordshire and Northamptonshire; the same term has been applied more generally to the upper (Toarcian) part of the Marlstone Rock as developed in the east Midlands (Howarth, 1980).

The immediately succeeding beds are poorly exposed but, in a few places, signs of fissile mudstone indicate the 'Fish Beds' of the Exaratum Subzone, as in the Stowell Park Borehole. At a number of localities in the north-eastern part of the district [e.g. SP 1691 1802; SP 1866 1493; SP 1869 1518; SP 1873 1495; SP 2000 1887], large fragments of hildoceratid ammonites, including *Harpoceras falciferum*, preserved in pale grey to cream argillaceous limestone, occur in the soil. They apparently originated from a level perhaps 1 to 2 m above the base of the formation, and represent the Cephalopod Limestone of the uppermost Falciferum Zone (Falciferum Subzone) and/or basal Bifrons Zone (Commune Subzone) (Horton et al., 1987).

Little is known of the overlying part of the Whitby Mudstone Formation in the north-eastern part of the district, but the strata appear to comprise fairly smooth, bluish grey mudstones, and the sandy and silty strata developed in the west (see above) seem to be absent. An exposure at a spring [SP 1658 1534] near Sherborne, for example, exposed 2 m of bluish grey, plastic, sparsely and very finely micaceous mudstone, with limonitic nodules and sparse limestone nodules, immediately beneath the Inferior Oolite. Comparison with the succession at Stowell Park suggests that the beds belong to the Bifrons Zone, and it is unlikely that any younger beds are present.

## BRIDPORT SAND FORMATION

The Bridport Sand Formation corresponds to the Cotteswold Sand of previous accounts of the region. Within the Cotswolds, the formation is best developed to the south-west of the district, e.g. in the Dursley area of Gloucestershire, where it is some 60 to 75 m thick (Cave, 1977). Traced northwards and eastwards, the formation passes into the mudstones of the Whitby Mudstone by a process of lateral passage and interdigitation from the base upwards, so that it is thin and only readily recognised in the western part of the Cirencester district. Farther east, the sandy strata pass into sandy mudstones better classified with the Whitby Mudstone Formation (see above), and even these beds are overstepped in the easternmost part of the district. Thus, although 'Cotteswold Sand' is shown as widespread between the 'Upper Lias' and Inferior Oolite on the first (1933) edition of Sheet 235, the sandy strata indicated (i.e. the 'Ammonite Beds' of Hull, 1857) belong, for the most part, to the Inferior Oolite Group, as Richardson (1933, p.10) recognised. The presence of these sandy Inferior Oolite beds (Leckhampton Member; see Chapter 5) inevitably complicates mapping of the Bridport Sand. Nevertheless, during this survey, Bridport Sand was recognised at outcrop in the north-westernmost parts of the district, where it may be up to 10 m thick. Whilst for the most part the outcrop is concealed by scree and landslip deposits, the formation locally gives rise to light, sandy soils ranging from orange-brown to grey-brown in colour, and sporadic exposures indicate finely sandy mudstone, siltstone and soft, clayey, fine-grained sandstone. Farther east, the outcrop is almost entirely obscured by cambered Inferior Oolite. Records of old sections (see below) show that the Bridport Sand is present at least as far east as Withington [SP 032 158], but it is absent at outcrop in the Vale of Bourton in the north-eastern part of the district. The transitional and interfingering relationship with the Whitby Mudstone make the precise eastern limit of the Bridport Sand difficult to define and somewhat arbitrary. However, at depth, it is deemed to be absent in the Stowell Park Borehole (see above), although it is present in boreholes at Harnhill and Meysey Hampton, a little farther east.

The best information on the Bridport Sand comes from Richardson's (1910a, 1933) details of a borehole on Hartley Hill [SO 952 179], on the western margin of the district. Beneath the Inferior Oolite, the borehole proved some 7.8 m of sandy, micaceous clay with a band of fossiliferous sandstone, 3.7 m below the top. The recent survey suggests that Richardson's record of a further 7.1 m of 'very fine blue sand' below the clay is unreliable. The ammonites from the sandstone include *Haugia grandis*, *Haugia* sp., *Dactylioceras* cf. *holandrei*, *D.* cf. *mucronatum* and '*Thysanoceras*' [=*Lytoceras*] *sublineatum*. The *Haugia* spp. clearly indicate the Variabilis Zone, whilst the *Dactylioceras* spp. suggest that the underlying Bifrons Zone may also be present. Richardson (1913, 1933) recorded similar sandy clays in a pit near Daisybank Road [SO 9531 1890], and also (1904, 1933) recorded '*Lillia* [=*Phymatoceras*] *lilli*' from a limestone nodule found [c. SO 975 187] on Wistley Hill, again suggesting the Variabilis Zone. There is no evidence for the condensed 'Cephalopod Bed' at the top of the Bridport Sand in this area, presumably because of overstep; it is well developed in districts to the south (Cave, 1977).

In a railway cutting at Sandywell Park [SP 013 204], immediately north of the district, Woodward (1893) recorded 'micaceous blue and brown sandy loam' overlying 'blue micaceous clay with cement nodules, septaria and pyrites' which yielded ammonites of the Bifrons Zone. According to records by Woodward (1894, pp.126–127) and others, the now-disused railway cutting [SP 032 173] near Northfield Farm exposed some 4.8 m of yellow, brown and blue ferruginous sands and bluish grey clays beneath the Inferior Oolite, and the cutting at Withington Station [SP 032 158] showed 9 m of 'micaceous clays alternating with greenish-grey sands'. The BGS Northfield Farm Borehole, sited in the railway cutting, just below the base of the Inferior Oolite Group, proved 23.6 m of silty to sandy mudstones with fine-grained sandstone interbeds, mostly assigned to the Whitby Mudstone, but the topmost 4.5 m, dominated by fine-grained, generally poorly bedded and uncemented sands, are herein assigned to the Bridport Sand Formation. The strata are generally medium grey in colour, but the highest core (1.50 to 1.90 m) was oxidised to a golden brown, with darker ferruginous banding. At a depth of 4.10 m, a small, poorly preserved ?*Dumortieria levesquei* is indicative of the youngest Toarcian Levesquei Zone (?and Subzone). In the southern part of the district, 6.12 m of Bridport Sand (128.40 to 134.52 m, not bottomed) were proved in the Harnhill cored borehole. The succession comprises grey to greenish grey, fine-grained, commonly micaceous, argillaceous sand and weakly calcareous sandstone with muddy wisps, interbedded with grey, finely sandy or silty mudstone. The cores contain sporadic bivalves such as *Gresslya*, *Meleagrinella* and *Hippopodium*. At a depth of 129.54 m (i.e. 1.14 m below the top), a poorly preserved *Hammatoceras* sp. suggests the Levesquei Zone.

FIVE

# Middle Jurassic: Inferior Oolite Group

The Inferior Oolite Group is made up predominantly of shallow marine, ooidal and shell-detrital limestones, with thin mudstone, marl and sandstone beds. It crops out in the north-west of the district, forming a broad plateau that ends at the main Cotswold escarpment, overlooking Cheltenham. From there, the outcrop extends southwards down the Churn valley to Perrott's Brook [SP 018 060], and the Coln valley to Fossebridge [SP 080 112]. In the north-eastern part of the district, the group crops out on broad spurs and the sides of the valleys of the River Windrush and its tributaries. Additionally, it has been proved by many water wells and boreholes down-dip of the outcrop, including the BGS Stowell Park Borehole (Table 8).

The Inferior Oolite of the Cotswolds has been studied from the earliest days of the science of geology, resulting in a plethora of stratal names. However, as a result of the survey of the Cirencester district, the lithostratigraphical terminology has been revised and rationalised by Barron, Sumbler and Morigi (1997; see Tables 10, 11). According to their scheme, which is followed in the present account, the group is divided into the Birdlip Limestone, Aston Limestone and Salperton Limestone formations (in ascending order). These lithostratigraphical units correspond to the Lower, Middle and Upper Inferior Oolite of Buckman (1905a), which are essentially chronostratigraphical terms, pertaining respectively to the Aalenian Stage, and the Lower and Upper Bajocian substages. Each of the three formations is divided into a number of members which, for the most part, correspond to one or more of the units traditionally recognised, e.g. by Buckman (1887, 1895, 1897, 1901), Richardson (1933) and Arkell

**Table 10** Lithostratigraphical classification of the Inferior Oolite Group of the district (Barron et al., 1997) and its relationship to previous schemes.

| Buckman, 1887, 1895, 1897, 1901, 1905, Richardson, 1929, 1933 Arkell, 1933 | | Mudge, 1978 (Cleeve Hill to Leckhampton Hill area) | This account (Barron et al., 1997) | |
|---|---|---|---|---|
| Upper Inferior Oolite | Clypeus Grit | | Clypeus Grit Member | Salperton Limestone Formation |
| | Upper Trigonia Grit | | Upper Trigonia Grit Member | |
| Middle Inferior Oolite | Phillipsiana Beds Bourguetia Beds Witchellia Grit | | Rolling Bank Member | Aston Limestone Formation |
| | Notgrove Freestone | | Notgrove Member | |
| | Gryphite Grit Buckmani Grit | | Gryphite Grit Member | |
| | Lower Trigonia Grit | | Lower Trigonia Grit Member | |
| Lower Inferior Oolite | Tilestone Snowshill Clay Harford Sands Naunton Clay | Harford Sands Member | Harford Member | Birdlip Limestone Formation |
| | Upper Freestone Oolite Marl | Scottsquar Hill Limestone Member | Scottsquar Member | |
| | Lower Freestone | Devil's Chimney Oolite Member Cleeve Hill Oolite Member | Cleeve Cloud Member | |
| | Pea Grit | Crickley Oncolite Member | Crickley Member | |
| | Lower Limestone | Crickley Limestone Member | | |
| | Scissum Beds | Leckhampton Limestone Member | Leckhampton Member | |

**Table 11**   Lithostratigraphical classification of the Inferior Oolite Group of the Cotswolds, and relationship to the standard chronostratigraphical framework, based on Barron et al. (1997, fig. 2). Not to scale.

Vertical ruling indicates nonsequence. Ammonite symbol indicates that member yields zonally indicative ammonite fauna (see text). The ammonite-based zonation used here (Callomon and Chandler, 1990; Callomon, 1995; Callomon in Callomon and Cope, 1995) is a modification of that used by Parsons (in Cope, 1980b): those Aalenian and Lower Bajocian zones marked with an asterisk were previously regarded as subzones.

| CHRONOSTRATIGRAPHY | | LITHOSTRATIGRAPHY | |
| --- | --- | --- | --- |
| SUBSTAGE | ZONE | MEMBER | FORMATION |
| LOWER BATHONIAN | Zigzag | | |
| UPPER BAJOCIAN | Parkinsoni | CLYPEUS GRIT 🐚 | SALPERTON LIMESTONE |
| | Garantiana | UPPER TRIGONIA GRIT 🐚 | |
| | Subfurcatum | | |
| LOWER BAJOCIAN | Humphriesianum | | ASTON LIMESTONE |
| | Sauzei | ROLLING BANK 🐚 | |
| | Laeviuscula * | NOTGROVE | |
| | Ovalis * | GRYPHITE GRIT 🐚 | |
| | Discites | LOWER TRIGONIA GRIT 🐚 | |
| AALENIAN | Concavum | HARFORD | BIRDLIP LIMESTONE |
| | Bradfordensis* | SCOTTSQUAR 🐚 | |
| | Murchisonae* | CLEEVE CLOUD 🐚 | |
| | | CRICKLEY 🐚 | |
| | Scissum | LECKHAMPTON 🐚 | |
| | Opalinum | | |

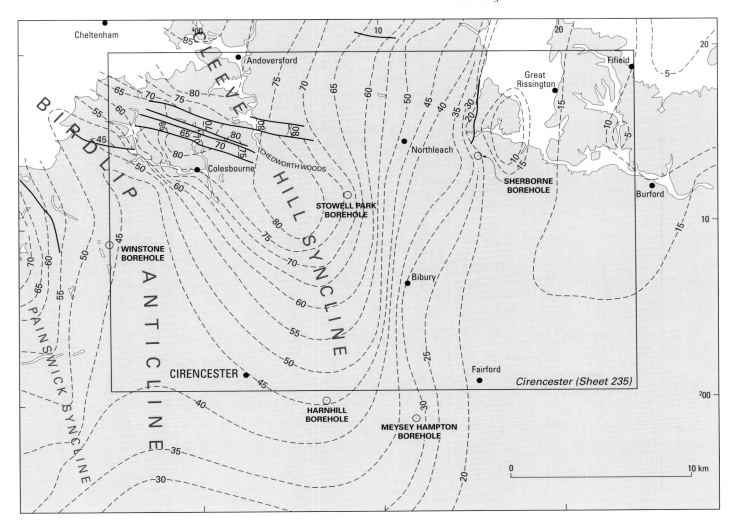

**Figure 11** Thickness of Inferior Oolite Group in the district and adjoining areas.

Outcrop and subcrop shown shaded. Contours in metres. Possible penecontemporaneous faults, across which thickness apparently changes, are shown by heavy lines. The 'Painswick Syncline', 'Cleeve Hill Syncline' and 'Birdlip Anticline' (Buckman, 1901) are better regarded as sedimentary troughs and highs rather than fold structures (see text).

(1933a) (Table 10). The outcrops of the three formations are depicted on the 1:50 000 geological map of the district and, where possible, individual members are shown separately.

As with the rest of the Jurassic, the standard zonation of the Inferior Oolite is based on ammonites, although these are rare throughout much of the succession in the Cotswolds. Nevertheless, sufficient specimens have been obtained to substantiate the zonation shown in Table 11, which is based essentially on the work of Parsons (1980, in Cope, 1980b).

Within the district, the Inferior Oolite Group is up to about 85 m thick, the thickest successions being present in the north-west near Colesbourne [SO 99 15] and in the Chedworth Woods area [SP 050 130] (Figure 11). At Cleeve Hill, just to the north of the district, the group is over 100 m thick, the maximum in Great Britain. Traced eastwards, the group thins dramatically, to 10 m or less in the Great Rissington–Fifield area (Figure 11). This

thinning indicates continued differential subsidence between the Worcester Basin and the London Platform, albeit on a smaller scale than in the Early Jurassic; it may have resulted largely from dewatering and compaction of the underlying argillaceous Lias Group, as there is no definite evidence for continued tectonic movement along the Vale of Moreton Axis. Sedimentation appears to have kept pace with subsidence; there is no indication of deeper water facies within the Worcester Basin area.

There were, however, interruptions to sedimentation, some of which are marked by bored and oyster-encrusted hardground surfaces. The most important of these non-sequences occur at the two levels which separate the three formations of the Inferior Oolite Group. Buckman (1887, 1901) demonstrated that the strata above these non-sequences variously overlap or overstep the strata beneath; the Aston Limestone Formation, for example, is overstepped by the Salperton Limestone Formation across the Vale of Moreton Axis (Figure 12). From the

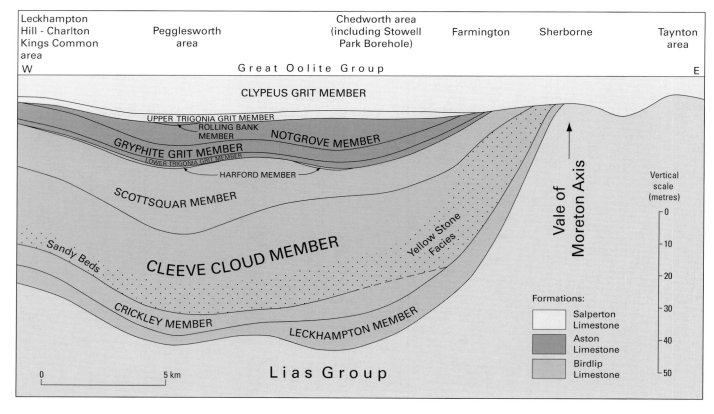

**Figure 12**  Schematic cross-section of the Inferior Oolite Group of the district. Vertical exaggeration ×150.

geographical distribution of the units below these non-sequences, Buckman built up a model in which episodes of 'earth movement' created gentle folds (the 'Painswick Syncline', 'Cleeve Hill Syncline' and intervening 'Birdlip Anticline', Figure 11), which were then subjected to differential erosion (the Aalenian and Bajocian denudations) followed by marine transgression (the Bajocian and Vesulian transgressions of Arkell, 1933a). This model is broadly consistent with the evidence, but considering the modest scale of the structures (with relative dips of a small fraction of a degree on the 'limbs'), and details of the thickness variation of individual units of the Inferior Oolite Group succession, these relationships are more compatible with a model of gentle, more or less continuous but slightly non-uniform subsidence, producing sedimentary troughs separated by highs with thinner sequences, with erosional truncation occurring during sea-level lowstands (Barron et al., 1997).

## BIRDLIP LIMESTONE FORMATION

The Birdlip Limestone Formation, corresponding to the Lower Inferior Oolite [Formation] of previous accounts (e.g. Arkell, 1933a; Mudge, 1978), comprises mainly ooidal, shell-fragmental, sandy and marly limestone, with subordinate sandstone, marl and mudstone beds. It is the thickest formation of the Inferior Oolite Group, reaching

a maximum of over 60 m in the north-west of the district, within the trough of the 'Cleeve Hill Syncline'. It is relatively thin in the area of the 'Birdlip Anticline', and thins even more dramatically towards the Vale of Moreton Axis, being absent to the east but for remnants of the lowest part. In each case, the thinning results from overstep by the Salperton Limestone Formation (Figures 12, 13). Locally, the pattern of thickness variation and overstep may have been affected by penecontemporaneous faulting, but the evidence for this remains inconclusive.

Where complete, the formation is divisible into five members (Table 10). These can be readily distinguished in sections and boreholes, and can also be recognised from field brash at outcrop. Where possible, the outcrops of the individual members are indicated on the map.

## Leckhampton Member

The Leckhampton Member (Barron et al., 1997) corresponds to the Scissum Beds of Richardson (1933) and others (Table 10). It is the basal unit of the Inferior Oolite throughout the Cotswolds, resting non-sequentially on the Bridport Sand Formation in the west of the district, and overstepping onto the lower beds of the Whitby Mudstone Formation in the east. It comprises grey, rubbly, ferruginous, sandy, argillaceous, shelly and shell-fragmental, peloidal and ooidal limestone with thin

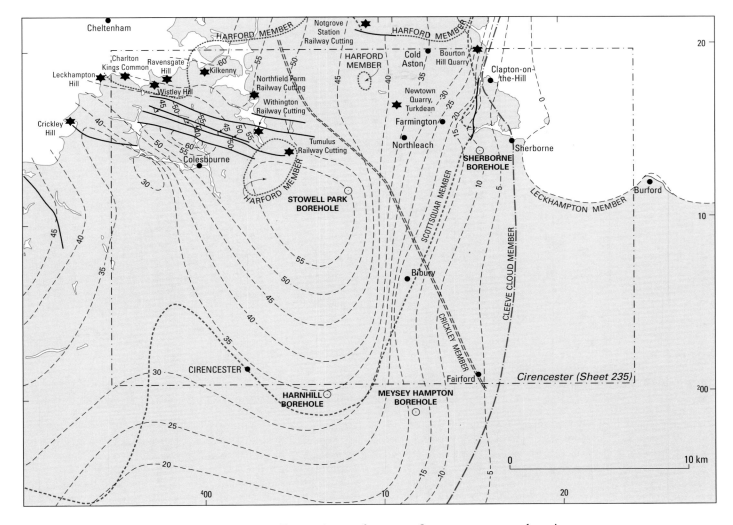

**Figure 13**   Thickness of Birdlip Limestone Formation and extent of component members in
the district and adjoining areas.

Outcrop and subcrop shown shaded. Contours in metres. Possible penecontemporaneous faults, across which thickness
apparently changes, are shown by heavy lines. Sections mentioned in text marked with a star.

marl beds (Plate 3). Much of the non-carbonate material
is probably derived from the underlying strata, and it is
noticeable that the member becomes significantly more
sandy in the eastern part of the district, perhaps due to
incorporation of material from the Bridport Sand
Formation (see Mudge, 1978) which is no longer
preserved in this area. The member attains its maximum
thickness in the centre of the district (Figure 12), being
9.8 m thick in the Stowell Park Borehole (112.45 to
122.28 m, see below). More typically, however, it is 2 to
6 m thick, and is about 5 m thick at its type section,
Limekiln Quarry [SO 9490 1853] on Leckhampton Hill,
300 m to the west of the district (Mudge, 1978; Cox and
Sumbler, in prep).

The member is generally poorly exposed in the
district, although its full thickness (3.5 m) is visible in a
railway cutting at Northfield Farm [SP 0305 1747]
(Morigi, 1995a; Richardson, 1933). At outcrop, it
weathers to a yellow or orange-brown colour, and

commonly decalcifies to yellowish or reddish brown
sand. This resembles the Bridport Sand, and indeed the
greater part of the 'Cotteswold Sand' (the Ammonite
Sands of Hull, 1857) indicated on the previous (1933)
edition of Sheet 235 is now interpreted as the Leckhampton Member (see Richardson, 1933). Similarly, in
the Stowell Park Borehole, the base of the Leckhampton
Member is now taken at 122.28 m (Table 8; Sumbler and
Barron, 1995), and not 118.62 m (389 ft 2 in) as quoted
by Green and Melville (1956, p.16) who drew the base
(of the 'Scissum Beds') at an essentially arbitrary level
within a continuous run of fairly uniform sand, the
lower part of which they regarded as 'Cotteswold Sand
of the Upper Lias'. The revised classification includes all
of these sands in the Leckhampton Member; at 122.28 m
they rest sharply on mudstones, a level which may correspond with the considerable non-sequence to be
expected at this horizon. This classification is consistent with the limited macropalaeontological and

**Plate 3** Limekiln Quarry, Leckhampton Hill [SO 9488 1856].

Rubbly beds of the Leckhampton Member in the lower part of the face (of which this is the type section) are overlain by more massive limestones of the Crickley Member. The junction lies about 0.4 m below the top of the graduated staff, which is marked in 0.5 m increments (A 15415).

palynological evidence (summarised by Sumbler and Barron, 1995).

The member is the most laterally extensive part of the Birdlip Limestone Formation, extending from Horton, Avon, to near Chipping Norton, Oxfordshire, where it passes into the Northampton Sand Formation (Barron et al., 1997). It is the only member to extend east of the Vale of Moreton Axis, where it is overlain directly by the Salperton Limestone Formation. In this situation, as seen for example at Clapton-on-the-Hill [SP 156 177], its upper part is generally altered to an intensely hard, brownish grey quartzite, surmounted by a planed, bored and oyster-encrusted hardground. Very locally, in the north-eastern part of the district, is it cut out entirely by the Salperton Limestone (Figure 13).

The Leckhampton Member is one of the more fossiliferous parts of the Birdlip Limestone, commonly containing brachiopods and large myacean bivalves. The basal bed may contain abraded fossils derived from the underlying Lias. Belemnites and ammonites such as *Leioceras* (Figure 15) are not uncommon, the latter indicating the lower Aalenian Opalinum and/or Scissum zones. Of note are a *Leioceras,* recovered from a depth of 117.60 m in the Stowell Park Borehole, and Hull's (1857, p.30) record of a large ammonite from the 'Ammonite Sands' near Clapton-on-the-Hill, probably a *Pachylytoceras phylloceratiodes* from the Leckhampton Member (Buckman, 1905b).

**Crickley Member**

The Crickley Member (Barron et al., 1997) corresponds to the Lower Limestone plus the overlying Pea Grit of previous accounts (e.g. Richardson, 1933), i.e. the 'Pea Grit Series' of some authors (but see discussion of Cleeve Cloud Member below), or to the combined Crickley Limestone and overlying Crickley Oncolite members of Mudge (1978), as identified at the type section (Crickley Hill [SO 929 163]) and Leckhampton Hill (Table 10).

The Crickley Member is present only in the western half of the district (Figures 12, 13), where it is typically 2 to 5 m but locally up to about 8 m thick. The lower part is dominated by pale grey to yellow-brown, medium- to coarse-grained, peloidal, ooidal and shell-fragmental grainstone, comprising the Lower Limestone of previous accounts. This passes rapidly downwards into the underlying Leckhampton Member, and grades upwards into rubbly, poorly sorted, shelly, shell-detrital, more or less pisoidal grainstones and packstones with thin marl beds, constituting the distinctive Pea Grit. The pisoids that characterise the latter are large (up to 10 mm) subspherical or disc-shaped grains, in which a shell-fragment nucleus is surrounded by layers of micrite. Thin-section examination reveals microbial tube structures, for example of carbonate secreting algae such as *Girvanella* (Wethered, 1891), and so the pisoids appear to be true oncoids, i.e. carbonate-coated grains formed largely as a result of microbial activity. Such pisoids may occur sporadically within the lower part of the Crickley Member, and so the Lower Limestone and Pea Grit cannot be separated consistently.

Generally, the member is not well exposed in the district, although the lower part of the member is well exposed in Limekiln Quarry on Leckhampton Hill, just to the west (Plate 3), and over 6 m of strata showing the upward passage from ooidal to pisoidal grainstone can be seen in the railway cutting near Northfield Farm (Morigi, 1995a). The member was also proved in the Stowell Park Borehole where it is nearly 7 m thick (105.51 to 112.45 m, Table 8). At outcrop, the member weathers to yellowish brown, very coarse-grained limestone rubble, and the pisoids may be found loose in the soil. The member is commonly moderately fossiliferous, particularly in the upper part, notably with brachiopods, bivalves, gastropods, echinoids and corals. A number of ammonites indicating the Murchisonae Zone are known from the Cotswolds, including *Ancolioceras* from a depth of 111.20 m in the Stowell Park Borehole.

Near Colesbourne [SO 979 140], pale grey, rubbly, micritic and highly coralliferous limestone occurs within the Crickley Member. This lithology is up to about 5 m thick, and is traceable for about 250 m along the outcrop before passing into more typical Crickley Member lithologies. It is interpreted as a reef-knoll. Similar coralliferous limestone associated with the 'Pea Grit' has also been described from Crickley Hill and the Painswick area to the west of the district (the 'Fourth Coral Bed' of Tomes, 1886, and the 'Crickley Coral Bed' of Lucy, 1890).

The typical lithologies of the Crickley Member are absent in the eastern part of the district (Figure 13) and over much of the Moreton-in-Marsh district to the north. Richardson (1904, 1929, 1933) accounted for the member's disappearance by claiming that it (his 'Pea Grit Series') was replaced by ooidal limestones comprising the 'Yellow [Guiting] Stone' or 'Pea Grit Equivalent', strata that are herein included in the Cleeve Cloud Member (see below). There is very little evidence to support Richardson's hypothesis, and it could not be confirmed by the present survey, although the relationships at this level remain somewhat uncertain. Whilst it is possible that the Crickley Member may pass laterally into the lower part of the Yellow [Guiting] Stone, there is evidence from mapping to the north of the district suggest that it may be overstepped by the latter towards the Vale of Moreton Axis (Figure 12; Barron et al., 1997).

## Cleeve Cloud Member

The Cleeve Cloud Member is essentially equivalent to the Lower Freestone of previous accounts (Table 10), and to the combined Cleeve Hill Oolite and Devil's Chimney Oolite members of Mudge (1978). It is the thickest unit of the Birdlip Limestone Formation, reaching 50 m at Cleeve Common, just north of the district, and is typically 25 to 30 m thick within the western part of the district. From there, it thins eastwards, initially due to progressive

overstep by the succeeding Scottsquar Member, and farther east because of overstep by the Salperton Limestone Formation which ultimately cuts it out entirely, so that it is absent to the east of Sherborne (Figures 12, 13).

The Cleeve Cloud Member is dominated by well-bedded, well-sorted, medium- to coarse-grained ooidal grainstone. It is poorly exposed in the Cirencester district, although there are many quarries on its outcrop elsewhere in the north Cotswolds, illustrating its former importance as a building stone (see Chapter 2). It is, for example, well displayed at the type section, Devil's Chimney Quarry [SO 9474 1842] on Leckhampton Hill, immediately west of the district (Plate 4; Cox and Sumbler, in prep.). There, the upper and greater part of the succession (corresponding to the Devil's Chimney Oolite of Mudge, 1978) is an off-white to pale brown, markedly cross-bedded oolite, with a well-developed, bored and oyster-encrusted hardground at the top. At outcrop within the district, these strata produce an angular brash of white to pale brown limestone, and the topmost hardground has been noted at a number of localities. In the west, the basal boundary with the Crickley Member appears to be gradational, but there is local evidence of erosion at this level (Richardson, 1929; Mudge, 1978). Where the Crickley Member is absent in the east, the junction with the underlying Leckhampton Member may also be a non-sequence, although this remains unconfirmed.

The lower part of the member at Leckhampton and in the western part of the district (e.g. Withington railway cutting [SP 033 153]; Woodward, 1894) includes yellowish brown, rather sandy oolites with burrows (the Cleeve Hill Oolite of Mudge, 1978). These strata are better developed farther north, at Cleeve Hill, where they were included in the 'Pea Grit Series' by Richardson (1929, 1933), although originally excluded from it by Buckman (1892). Farther east and north, this sandy

**Plate 4**   Devil's Chimney Quarry, Leckhampton Hill [SO 947 184].

This substantial quarry in the Inferior Oolite Group yielded large quantities of stone for the building of Cheltenham. The lower part of the face shows about 10 m of the uppermost part of the Cleeve Cloud Member, of which this is the type section. The section shows large-scale cross-bedding, and the notable plane of parting about half way up is a hardground. The upper part of the face includes beds of the Scottsquar Member; its lower part comprises pale, rubbly 'Oolite Marl' facies, which can be seen just above the main bench. In the highest part of the face, beds of the Aston Limestone Formation crop out (A 15419).

oolite facies dominates the Cleeve Cloud Member (Figure 12), becoming more ferruginous and of a markedly orange-yellow hue. It was termed the 'Yellow Stone', 'Yellow Guiting Stone' or 'Pea Grit Equivalent' by Richardson (1929, 1933), and corresponds essentially to the Jackdaw Quarry Oolite Member of Mudge (1978). The lateral passage between the lower part of the 'Yellow Stone' and the sandy beds assigned by Richardson (1929, 1933) to the top part of the 'Pea Grit Series' at Cleeve Hill accounts to some extent for his misleading claim that the Pea Grit passes into the 'Yellow Stone' (see discussion of Crickley Member above), and for his use of the term 'Pea Grit Equivalent' for the latter.

At outcrop to the east of Cold Aston and Farmington, the Cleeve Cloud Member ('Yellow Stone' facies) weathers to a brownish yellow colour, with some layers strongly stained yellow, orange or brown with limonite. Locally, the beds decalcify to a loose sand, similar to that produced by the Leckhampton Member. In a few places in this area [e.g. SP 1490 1666; SP 1470 1789; SP 1533 1780], the hardground at the top of the member, and the immediately subjacent beds, show signs of decalcification, solution and limonitisation, characteristics that are suggestive of subaerial emergence. At one locality [SP 1393 1746], this possible palaeokarst is developed on top of a mound-like, coralline 'reef' which, although formerly included in the Scottsquar Member (Sumbler, 1995b), is now regarded as part of the Cleeve Cloud Member; a possible paleokarst at a locality [SP 103 289] near Temple Guiting in the Moreton-in-Marsh district to the north, affects a similar coralline reef at the top of the 'Yellow Stone', some 12 m below the top of the Cleeve Cloud Member there.

The 'Yellow Stone' facies is well exposed at Bourton Hill Quarry [SP 1570 1975] on the northern margin of the district, where the strata contain abundant and conspicuous *Skolithos* burrows, suggestive of very shallow water (Plate 5). In the past, similar burrows at Leckhampton and elsewhere have been described as rootlets (e.g. Ager, 1969).

Apart from shell debris, which varies greatly in proportion, the member is largely unfossiliferous. Locally in the sandy lower part and in the 'Yellow Stone' facies, bivalves, notably the small pectinacean *Propeamussium pumilum* (Figure 15), are abundant, and echinoids and brachiopods such as *Plectoidothyris plicata* also occur. Ammonites are rare, although a specimen (MGS 2200) found near Sherborne may be a *Ludwigia*, indicating the mid Aalenian Murchisonae Zone.

### Scottsquar Member

The Scottsquar Member (Barron et al., 1997) is equivalent to the combined Oolite Marl (Buckman, 1842) and Upper Freestone (Hull, 1857) (Table 9). It has long been recognised that the distinction between these two units is arbitrary (Woodward, 1894; Buckman, 1895; Richardson, 1904; Baker, 1981). For this reason, Mudge (1978) introduced the term Scottsquar Hill Limestone Member, from which the present name is adapted.

Across most of the Cirencester district, the Scottsquar Member is the highest unit of the Birdlip Formation. Its extent is slightly less than that of the Cleeve Cloud Member because of overstep by the Salperton Limestone Formation (Figures 12, 13). The member is dominated by pale grey and brown, medium- to coarse-grained, peloidal and ooidal packstone and grainstone ('Upper Freestone'), in which beds of lower energy, white to mid-grey micrite and shell-detrital, peloidal, silty marl ('Oolite Marl') occur. The 'Oolite Marl' facies tends to predominate in the lower part, and 'Upper Freestone' facies in the upper, but the succession is extremely variable from place to place (Baker, 1981), and the two facies commonly interdigitate in a complex manner. The Scottsquar Member is typically 5 to 15 m thick, but thickens markedly to 25 m or perhaps 30 m around Norbury [SO 990 150], near Colesbourne, probably due to channelling, but possibly because of syndepositional faulting.

**Plate 5** Bourton Hill Quarry [SP 157 197].
This quarry, in the Cleeve Cloud Member, yielded a brownish yellow oolite which may be seen in many of the buildings of nearby Bourton-on-the-Water. The distinctive, near-vertical, rootlet-like structures are burrows; this facies suggests deposition in very shallow water. The hammer is 30 cm long (GS533).

Small exposures of the member occur in a number of old quarries within the district, for example near Kilkenny [SP 0057 1863], where 0.2 m of fine-grained sand separate 3.4 m of packstone, wackestone and marly limestone below, from 2.4 m of peloidal grainstone above. It is also well exposed at Notgrove Station railway cutting [SP 0939 2129], 1.3 km north of the district, and at the top of the Devil's Chimney Quarry, Leckhampton Hill, just to the west (Plate 4). At outcrop, it has generally proved possible to separate the Scottsquar Member from the rest of the Birdlip Limestone Formation. The 'Oolite Marl' commonly produces a slight hollow in the hill-slopes, and the pale and often highly fossiliferous marls may be conspicuous in the soil. This facies has long been known for the richness and excellent preservation of its fauna (Hull, 1857, p.38; S S Buckman, 1895, pp.458–460; Mudge, 1978; Baker, 1974, 1981), which is dominated by brachiopods, including the distinctive terebratulid *Plectothyris fimbria* (Figure 15). Corals, serpulids and bryozoa may also occur, and at the Frith Quarry [SO 867 082], near Painswick, to the west of the district, ammonites of the Bradfordensis Zone have been found (Parsons, in Cope, 1980b; Cox and Sumbler, in prep.). In the absence of the 'Oolite Marl', the 'Upper Freestone' facies may generally be distinguished from the underlying Cleeve Cloud Member by its less well-sorted character and the presence of an oyster-encrusted hardground beneath, and in more easterly parts of the district, by a marked colour contrast with the 'Yellow Stone' facies of the Cleeve Cloud Member.

### Harford Member

The Harford Member (Barron et al., 1997) is the uppermost member of the Birdlip Limestone Formation. It has a very limited extent in the Cirencester district (Figure 13), being confined to a few small outcrops in the north-west. Originally, it may have been more widespread, but was removed by erosion prior to the deposition of the Aston Limestone Formation. The member is more fully developed in the Moreton-in-Marsh district to the north, where it is up to 14 m thick. Based on exposures there, it has been subdivided into Naunton Clay, Harford Sands, Snowshill Clay and Tilestone (Buckman, 1897, 1901; Richardson, 1929), but mapping shows that the succession is laterally highly variable, and that these units are of little stratigraphical value (Parsons, 1976; Mudge, 1978). Apart from the so-called 'Tilestone', the member is dominated by mudstones and sandstones containing a sparse fauna of bivalves and gastropods which suggest a shallow-water, land-marginal environment. The facies is strikingly similar to that of the Grantham Formation of the east Midlands, and the two units are probably broadly contemporaneous. Although no ammonites are known from the member (see Parsons, 1976), the stratigraphical position of the unit suggests that it belongs to the upper Aalenian Concavum Zone. Generally, it appears to rest conformably on the Scottsquar Member (Parsons, 1976), although there may locally be a non-sequence, as at Leckhampton Hill, where a lens of marl which probably represents the feather-edge of the Harford Member rests on a hardground at the top of the Scottsquar Member (Buckman, 1895, 1897; Cox and Sumbler, in prep.).

Within the district, the Harford Member comprises up to 2 m of grey and brown, silty, variably sandy or shell-detrital mudstone, with sandstone beds in places. Outcrops are differentiated on the map in only three places. That on Wistley Hill [SO 9764 1800] comprises brown silty clay and is less than 200 m long, but despite being undetectable elsewhere at outcrop, the member may be present along a greater length of the escarpment, as it was reported by Buckman (1895, pp.412–414) to be 0.25 m thick on Charlton Kings Common [SO 9582 1852] and 0.79 m in a quarry on Wistley Hill [SO 9710 1787]. It is currently visible in a quarry on Ravensgate Hill [SO 9826 1844], where it is 0.1 m thick. Two outcrops on the slopes of the Turkdean valley [SP 092 183, SP 097 177] are characterised by brown and greenish grey clay or sandy clay, up to 2 m thick, and Richardson (1933, p.29) described 0.46 m of 'Snowshill Clay' from the nearby Newtown Quarry, Turkdean [SP 1116 1670]. In the 'Tumulus' railway cutting in Chedworth Woods [SP 0500 1404], 0.22 m of shell-fragmental, sandy clay belonging to the Harford Member are exposed. Evidence from boreholes, and the presence of springs such as that which supplied the nearby Roman villa [SP 052 135] (see Chapter 2), suggest that the member may be present over a wider area hereabouts, but it has not proved possible to map the outcrop.

## ASTON LIMESTONE FORMATION

The Aston Limestone Formation (Barron et al., 1997) comprises the strata of the Middle Inferior Oolite of Buckman (1905a), also termed the 'Ragstones' (Arkell, 1933a). It comprises up to 15 m of grey and brown, rubbly, variably shelly, ooidal, sandy, shell-detrital limestone, with sandy and marly beds in parts. It is present only in the north-western part of the district (Figure 14), cropping out along valley sides and as small outliers. It is thickest in the Withington–Chedworth Woods area, thinning to the south and east, partly because of attenuation of the individual members but, more importantly, because of erosion of the topmost beds beneath the Salperton Limestone Formation. The latter ultimately cuts out the Aston Limestone Formation entirely (Figure 12; Richardson, 1929, p.80, 1933, pp.17–18). The absence of the formation near Cowley [SO 95 15], on the north side of a fault, appears to suggest penecontemporaneous fault movements, prior to deposition of the Salperton Limestone Formation.

Where complete, the formation is divisible into the Lower Trigonia Grit, Gryphite Grit, Notgrove and Rolling Bank members, in ascending order (Table 10; Figure 12), but due to narrowness of the outcrops and poor exposure, it has not been possible to distinguish them consistently on the map.

### Lower Trigonia Grit Member

The Lower Trigonia Grit Member is the lowermost and most extensive unit of the Aston Limestone Formation.

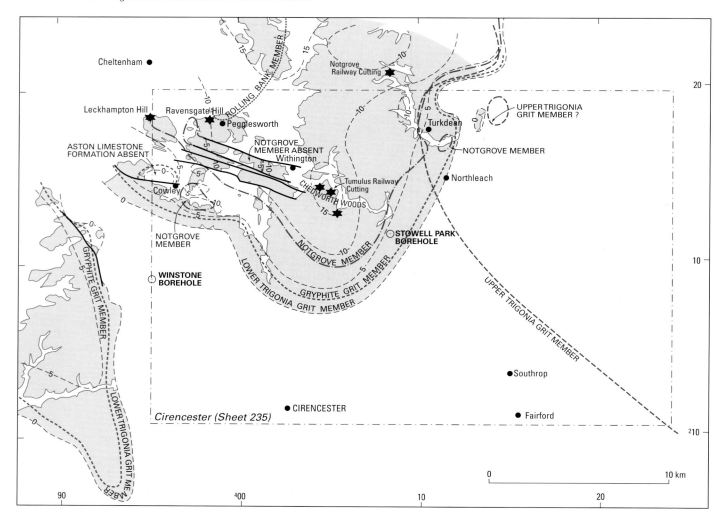

**Figure 14** Thickness of Aston Limestone Formation and extent of component members in the district and adjoining areas.

Outcrop and subcrop shown shaded. Contours in metres. Possible penecontemporaneous faults, across which thickness apparently changes, are shown by heavy lines. Extent of Upper Trigonia Grit Member of Salperton Limestone Formation also shown. Sections mentioned in text marked with a star.

In the Cirencester district, it comprises 1 to 2 m, and locally up to 3 m, of grey, very shelly and shell-detrital, moderately sandy, peloidal, ooidal wackestone, packstone and grainstone, with thin marl and sandstone beds, some shelly. It rests sharply and non-sequentially on the Birdlip Limestone Formation, and commonly contains pebbles of derived material from that formation at the base. Many of the abundant peloids are ferruginous, producing a distinctive orange-brown speckled 'ironshot' appearance. The member thins and becomes more marly, ironshot and conglomeratic northwards (Moreton-in-Marsh district). The lateral extent of the Lower Trigonia Grit Member is shown in Figure 14, although within this area it may be absent very locally beneath the Gryphite Grit Member.

The member is fully exposed in the Tumulus railway cutting (Sumbler and Barron, 1995, locality A), where it is about 1.8 m thick. Formerly, nearly 3 m of beds were

visible at Ravensgate Hill (Buckman, 1895, pp.415–416), but the currently exposed thickness is about 1.8 m. The member is 1.15 m thick in the Stowell Park Borehole (Table 8). It is now only moderately exposed at the type section on Leckhampton Hill [SO 9477 1847 to SO 9498 1847], 200 m west of the district. It weathers to brown, rubbly, shelly limestone debris in a moderately sandy soil.

The fauna includes the bivalves *Trigonia* (Figure 15), *Liostrea, Pinna, Astarte, Entolium corneolum* and *Gervillella acuta,* brachiopods such as *Aulacothyris meriani,* and the distinctive colonial serpulid *Sarcinella.* Corals such as *Isastraea, Thamnasteria* and *Thecosmilia* are locally common at the base; this coralliferous facies includes the so-called 'Second Coral Bed' of the Cheltenham area (Richardson, 1904). The Lower Trigonia Grit is one of the more ammonitiferous parts of the Inferior Oolite, and faunas indicating the Discites Zone are known from localities in adjoining districts (Buckman, 1895; Parsons, 1976, 1980, in Cope, 1980b).

## Gryphite Grit Member

The Gryphite Grit Member (Barron et al., 1997) includes both the Gryphite Grit and Buckmani Grit of Buckman (1895). In the Cirencester district, the member comprises 3 to 5 m, and rarely up to 7 m, of grey and brown, hard, rubbly, shelly, coarsely shell-detrital, sandy, peloidal grainstones, packstones and wackestones, with thin mudstone, marl and sandstone beds. It grades up from the underlying Lower Trigonia Grit Member, which it resembles in lithology, although it is generally more sandy, particularly in the lower part, and less ferruginous than the latter. At outcrop, both members weather to similar grey-brown, shelly rubble in a sandy clay soil, and so are not shown separately on the map. The thicker marl and sandstone beds may locally form slight topographic hollows associated with sparsely stony soils.

The type section of the Gryphite Grit is on Leckhampton Hill [SO 950 184], immediately beyond the western boundary of the district, where it is between 5.1 and 6.4 m thick (Buckman, 1895; Richardson, 1906). Within the district, it is exposed in the Tumulus railway cutting, where it ranges from 3.6 to 4.0 m in thickness, and includes two thin clay beds. In the Stowell Park Borehole, the member is 3.17 m thick (Table 8), although it is incomplete, being unconformably overlain by the Upper Trigonia Grit.

The fauna of the Gryphite Grit is distinctive, with abundant *Gryphaea bilobata* (Figure 15) and pachyteuthid belemnites in the upper part, and *Sarcinella* and *Lobothyris buckmani* (the eponymous brachiopod of the Buckmani Grit) in the lower part. Ammonites occur sporadically; specimens from adjoining districts indicate that the member belongs largely to the Ovalis Zone (Parsons, 1976, 1980, in Cope, 1980b).

## Notgrove Member

The Notgrove Member (Barron et al., 1997), corresponding to the Notgrove Freestone of Buckman (1887), comprises pale brownish grey, well-bedded and commonly cross-bedded, medium- to coarse-grained, moderately peloidal, ooidal grainstone. It commonly appears bimodal, with large, white superficial ooids in a finer-grained matrix. Shells and shell debris are rare, except in the lowest beds, which pass up from the underlying Gryphite Grit Member. The member has a less extensive distribution than the Gryphite Grit because of overstep by the Salperton Limestone Formation (Figures 12, 14). Beneath the latter, the top of the member is typically a well-developed, planed and oyster-encrusted hardground with abundant borings, the most conspicuous being narrow, subvertical annelid borings which may penetrate as much as 0.3 m below the hardground surface. In some places a similar hardground occurs at the top of the Notgrove Member beneath the Rolling Bank Member, e.g at Cold Comfort Quarry [SO 9961

1854] (Buckman, 1895) and nearby, where debris of intensely bored, shelly ooidal limestone was seen during the recent survey.

At outcrop, the Notgrove Member produces a distinctive blocky brash of pale grey oolite, in which pieces of the heavily bored and oyster-encrusted hardground from its top may be conspicuous. This lithology distinguishes it from other parts of the Aston Limestone Formation and from the succeeding Salperton Limestone Formation. Consequently, it has proved possible to map the member throughout most of its outcrop. It attains its maximum thickness of perhaps 10 m in the Withington–Chedworth Woods area, with almost 9 m of beds exposed in the Tumulus cutting (Plate 6; Sumbler and Barron, 1995), but it is overstepped rapidly towards the east (Figure 14), being absent in the Stowell Park Borehole (Green and Melville, 1956). Surprisingly, where the Aston Limestone Formation is more complete and the Rolling Bank Member succeeds the Notgrove Member, the latter is less than 3 m thick, probably because of erosion at the nonsequence at its top. The member is no longer well exposed elsewhere in the district, but a number of sections occur in the old railway cuttings just to the north, including the type section at Notgrove cutting [SP 0845 2090] (Buckman, 1887), about 1 km north of the district.

The fauna of the Notgrove Member is generally very sparse, although the small bivalve *Propeamussium* (Figure 15) may occur. Ammonites are particularly rare, but from its overall stratigraphical position, the member is inferred to belong to the Laeviuscula Zone (Parsons, in Cope, 1980b).

## Rolling Bank Member

The Rolling Bank Member (Barron et al., 1997), the youngest unit of the Aston Limestone Formation, comprises the combined Witchellia Grit, Bourguetia Beds and Phillipsiana Beds of Buckman (1895, 1897). It is named after the quarry on Cleeve Hill [SO 9871 2668] (Moreton-in-Marsh district) where it was once fully exposed and is possibly 8 m or more thick (Buckman, 1897; Cox and Sumbler, in prep.). Only the lowest beds (Witchellia Grit) are preserved in the Cirencester district, being confined to the Pegglesworth area [SO 99 18] (Figure 14) where they form three very narrow, faulted outcrops, of which it has been possible to depict only two on the map. The beds there comprise up to about 1 or 1.5 m of grey, brown and yellowish, rubbly, shelly, sandy ooidal, partly 'ironshot' limestone. They contain a fauna of brachiopods with relatively common ammonites, including *Witchellia* species such as *W. laeviuscula* (Figure 15), indicative of the Laeviuscula Zone. A specimen of *W.* cf. *platymorpha* (identified by Professor J H Callomon) was found during the recent survey. Higher parts of the member, not present within the district, are thought to extend into the succeeding Sauzei Zone (Parsons, in Cope, 1980b). At Cold Comfort Quarry [SO 9961 1854], Buckman (1895, pp.417–418) recorded 1.22 m of fossiliferous limestones. The section there is now obscured, but about

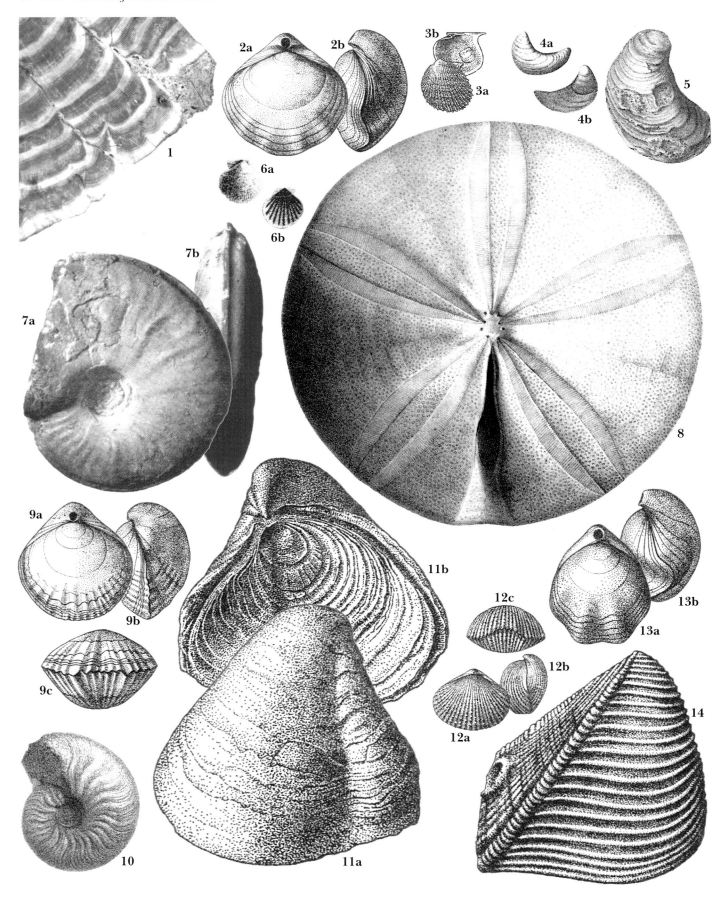

0.9 m of the member are still exposed in a nearby quarry [SO 9944 1845].

## SALPERTON LIMESTONE FORMATION

The Salperton Limestone Formation (Barron et al., 1997) corresponds to the Upper Inferior Oolite of the Cotswolds. It comprises between 8 and 20 m, but more typically 10 to 15 m, of ooidal, peloidal, shelly and shell-fragmental limestones. In the north-west of the district, the formation rests unconformably on the Rolling Bank Member, but it progressively oversteps lower parts of the Inferior Oolite towards the east and south to rest on the uppermost beds of the Lias Group (Figures 12, 13). The upper surface of the underlying limestone strata is generally a hardground, with borings and encrusting epifauna. Except for the Leckhampton Member of the Birdlip Limestone Formation, the Salperton Limestone Formation is the only part of the Inferior Oolite Group to extend eastwards across the Vale of Moreton Axis; indeed this structure appears to have had little effect on sedimentation during deposition of the Salperton Limestone Formation.

The Salperton Limestone Formation is well exposed at the type section, Notgrove railway cutting, near the village of Salperton, about 1 km to the north of the district. It can also be seen in disused railway cuttings in Chedworth Woods (Morigi, 1995b, locality P [SP 0450 1443 to 0462 1438]; Sumbler and Barron, 1995, localities

**Figure 15** Some characteristic fossils of the Inferior Oolite and Great Oolite groups (all approximately × 1); only main horizons of occurrence listed.

1. *Solenopora jurassica*; Great Oolite Group, White Limestone Formation
2a, b. *Epithyris oxonica*; Great Oolite Group, White Limestone Formation
3a, b. *Meleagrinella echinata*; Great Oolite Group, Fuller's Earth Formation
4a, b. *Praeexogyra acuminata*; Great Oolite Group, Fuller's Earth Formation
5. *Praeexogyra hebridica* ; Great Oolite Group, uppermost Fuller's Earth Formation–Forest Marble Formation
6a, b. *Propeamussium pumilum*; Inferior Oolite Group, principally Birdlip Limestone Formation, Cleeve Cloud Member and Aston Limestone Formation, Notgrove Member
7a, b. *Witchellia laeviuscula*; Inferior Oolite Group, Aston Limestone Formation, Rolling Bank Member
8. *Clypeus ploti*; Inferior Oolite Group, Salperton Limestone Formation, Clypeus Grit Member
9a–c. *Plectothyris fimbria*; Inferior Oolite Group, Birdlip Limestone Formation, Scottsquar Member
10. *Leioceras* sp.; Inferior Oolite Group, Birdlip Limestone Formation, Leckhampton Member
11a, b. *Gryphaea bilobata*; Inferior Oolite Group, Aston Limestone Formation, Gryphite Grit Member
12a–c. *Acanthothyris spinosa*; Inferior Oolite Group, Salperton Limestone Formation, Upper Trigonia Grit Member
13a, b. *Stiphrothyris tumida*; Inferior Oolite Group, Salperton Limestone Formation, Clypeus Grit Member
14. *Trigonia costata*; Inferior Oolite Group, Aston Limestone Formation, Lower Trigonia Grit Member and Salperton Limestone Formation, Upper Trigonia Grit Member

**Plate 6** Chedworth Woods railway cutting [SP 0523 1320].

The card rests upon the bored top of the Notgrove Member (Aston Limestone Formation), which is succeeded by massive shelly limestones of the Upper Trigonia Grit (Salperton Limestone Formation). The graduated pole is 2 m long (A 15430).

C, D and E [SP 0509 1381 to SP 0510 1375, SP 0523 1320 and SP 0539 1290]).

The Salperton Limestone Formation is divisible into two members, the Upper Trigonia Grit Member overlain by the Clypeus Grit Member. It has generally proved possible to map these two members separately, and they are both indicated on the map where possible (see below).

### Upper Trigonia Grit Member

In the Cirencester district, the Upper Trigonia Grit Member consists of very hard grey and brown, very shelly, shell-detrital, moderately ooidal grainstone and packstone, in rubbly, medium to thick beds. At outcrop, it weathers to orange-brown, and commonly forms large, uneven slabs. Due to its hardness, it may give rise to a prominent topographic feature. The fauna is dominated by bivalves, including large myaceans and trigoniids (Figure 15), commonly preserved as empty moulds; these are conspicuous and distinctive on weathered slabs. Other fossils include brachiopods such as *Acanthothyris spinosa* (Figure 15), *Rhactorhynchia* and *Stiphrothyris* (Figure 15). An extensive fauna of ammonites is known from the member, and indicates the Upper Bajocian Garantiana Zone (Parsons, 1980, in Cope, 1980b).

The member is typically 1 to 3 m thick, but very locally may be as much as 5 m, perhaps because of channelling into the underlying beds. It is generally absent north-east of a line from Turkdean to Southrop (Figures 12, 14), probably because of overstep by the Clypeus Grit Member, although remnants have been noted at several localities e.g. to the east of Cold Aston [SP 129 198]. Nevertheless, the member does not occur east of the Vale of Moreton Axis. It is fully exposed in some of the disused railway cuttings in Chedworth Woods (Plate 6; see above), and was penetrated by a number of boreholes, being 1.58 m thick in the Stowell Park Borehole (Table 8) and 1.6 m in the BGS Winstone Borehole. The top of the Upper Trigonia Grit is generally sharp, and is commonly marked by a hardground, which is oyster-encrusted at many localities.

## Clypeus Grit Member

The Clypeus Grit Member is the youngest and most laterally extensive unit of the Inferior Oolite Group in the Cotswolds. It forms broad spur and plateau outcrops in the northern half of the district, and is present at depth throughout the remainder. It is generally about 9 to 12 m thick, but is rather variable, with perhaps up to 16 m of beds west of Colesbourne [SO 98 13] and near Turkdean [SP 12 18], and as little as 7 m in the extreme north-west, near Hartley Farm [SO 95 17]. Up to 8.4 m of Clypeus Grit may be seen in the disused railway cuttings in the Withington–Chedworth Woods area (e.g. Sumbler

and Barron, 1995), but the member is not well exposed elsewhere in the district. Its full thickness is visible at its type section (Notgrove railway cutting) in the district to the north, where it is between 10.5 and 12.0 m thick (Cox and Sumbler, in prep.).

The member comprises pale grey to yellowish or pinkish brown, fine to coarse-grained, shell-detrital, ooidal and peloidal packstone and grainstone with subordinate wackestone. Characteristically, it contains sporadic, orange-skinned pisoids and aggregate grains, the latter suggesting reworking of partially cemented sediment. At outcrop, the Clypeus Grit weathers to rubble, producing a stony soil that commonly contains loose fossils. The abundant fauna includes large myacean bivalves, terebratulid brachiopods such as *Stiphrothyris* ('*Terebratula globata*' of authors; Figure 15) and, most characteristically, the eponymous large echinoid *Clypeus ploti* (Figure 15). The latter is particularly common in the uppermost part of the formation, and is probably largely responsible for the pervasive burrowing and consequent rubbly character of these beds. Ammonites are also relatively common, and show that the member belongs largely to the Upper Bajocian Parkinsoni Zone but extends into the Lower Bathonian Zigzag Zone.

No formal subdivision of the Clypeus Grit Member is possible within the Cirencester district or at the nearby type section; the tripartite succession identified by Richardson (1910b) in the south Cotswolds cannot be recognised, although the 'Rubbly Beds', at the top of his succession may be represented in the more rubbly upper part of the member in this district (see Richardson, 1933). Where overlain by the Chipping Norton Limestone (Chapter 6) in the north-east of the district, the top of the Clypeus Grit Member is commonly marked by a planed and oyster-encrusted surface. However, where the Chipping Norton Limestone is absent (Figure 17), no such hardground has been found beneath the succeeding Fuller's Earth Formation, although the junction is seldom well exposed because of landslipped and downwashed material from the latter. Nevertheless, a non-sequence is inferred at this level (see Chapter 6).

# SIX

# Middle Jurassic: Great Oolite Group

Like the underlying Inferior Oolite Group, the Great Oolite Group is made up largely of shallow marine carbonate rocks, but it also includes substantial units of mudstone in its lower and upper parts (Figure 16). The outcrop of the group dominates the geological map of the Cirencester district, occupying some three quarters of its area, and forming a broad tract trending from west-south-west to east-north-east across the central part, with scattered outliers to the north. The greater part of the outcrop is open, plateau-like upland formed by the White Limestone and Forest Marble formations in the upper part of the group, with underlying formations cropping out mainly in the narrow valleys which dissect this terrain.

The Great Oolite Group of the district is divisible into seven formations which, for the most part, can be recognised throughout (Table 12; Figure 16). As used herein, the formations are defined in terms of their lithofacies as developed in their type areas, and by their overall stratigraphical position, independent of any diachronism. As such, they correspond to units that have been traditionally recognised, e.g. by Woodward (1894), Richardson (1933) and Arkell (1933a). The nomenclature used differs in certain respects from that favoured by Wyatt (1996), who defined certain formational boundaries at supposed isochronous horizons, with less emphasis on lithofacies (Sumbler, in press).

Ammonites are even rarer in the Great Oolite than in the Inferior Oolite Group (Chapter 5). Whilst sufficient specimens have been found in and around the district to indicate the presence of some of the standard zones (Table 12, see Torrens in Cope, 1980b), the precise positioning of zonal boundaries is, in most cases, highly uncertain. For long-range, detailed correlation, recognition of regionally developed, quasi-isochronous event horizons (Wyatt, 1996) offers the potential for the development of a

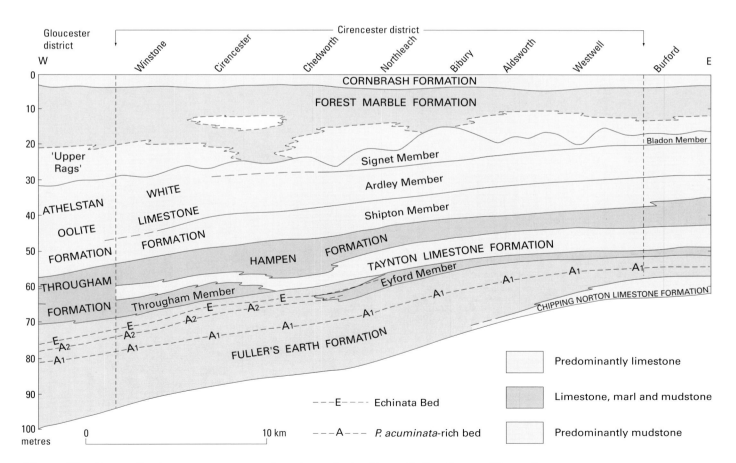

**Figure 16** Generalised west-east cross-section through the Great Oolite Group, illustrating lithostratigraphical relationships and thickness variation.

**Table 12** Lithostratigraphical classification of the Great Oolite Group, and relationship to the standard chronostratigraphical framework. Not to scale.

Vertical ruling indicates nonsequence. Ammonite symbol indicates that unit has yielded zonally indicative ammonite fauna at outcrop within the district or in adjacent areas. The ammonite-based zonation follows Torrens (in Cope, 1980b) as modified by Callomon (in Callomon and Cope, 1995) and Page (1996).The zones marked with an asterisk are those used in continental Europe for the interval previously assigned in Britain to the Hodsoni and Orbis Zones. There are sufficient subzones in common between the two areas that, following Page (1996), the continental European scheme can also be used as the standard zonation in Britain.

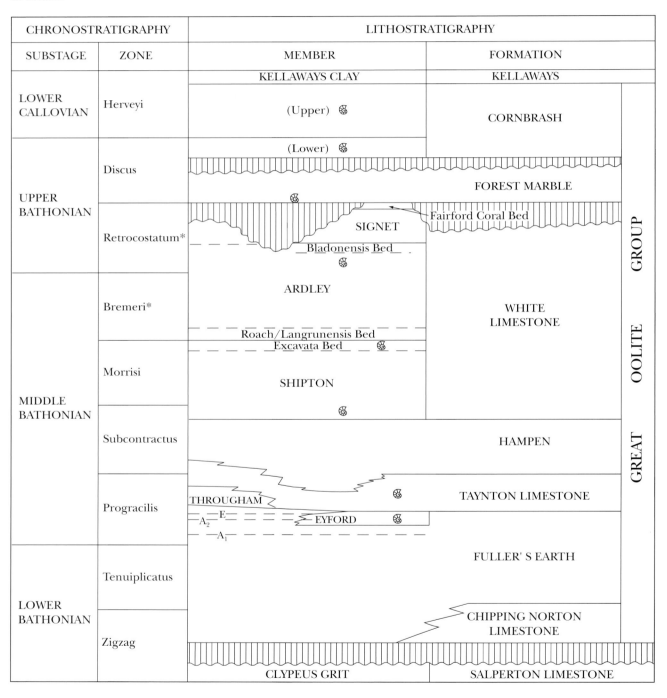

reliable chronostratigraphical framework into which the scattered ammonite occurrences may be placed. The most important of these event horizons in the Cirencester district are the Acuminata and Echinata beds in the Fuller's Earth Formation, the Excavata, Langrunensis and Bladonensis beds in the White Limestone Formation, and the bases of the Forest Marble Formation and Cornbrash Formation (Table 12; Figure 16).

Within the Cirencester district, the thickness of the Great Oolite Group expands from about 60 m in the east to about 100 m in the west (Figure 16), illustrating continued differential subsidence between the London Platform and Worcester Basin. However, the scale of subsidence was much less than in earlier Jurassic (and Triassic) times, and there is no definite evidence that any unit of the Great Oolite is overstepped across the Vale of Moreton Axis (see below), in contrast to the situation in the Inferior Oolite Group. Combined with the thickness changes, there are some instances of diachronism, particularly in the lower part of the group (Table 12). These relate variously to a westward replacement of shallow shelf facies by deeper or more open water facies, and to a gradual westward progradation of facies belts into the basin.

## CHIPPING NORTON LIMESTONE FORMATION

The Chipping Norton Limestone, at the base of the Great Oolite Group, is present only in the north-eastern part of the district, where it is up to about 5 or 6 m thick (Figure 16). It thickens towards its type area, 10 km to the north-east, where it reaches about 10 m in thickness (Horton et al., 1987). The limits of the formation are well defined at outcrop; it dies out along a north-west to south-east-trending line through the villages of Windrush [SP 192 131] and Little Barrington [SP 207 127] (Figure 17). Its limits beneath younger beds are poorly known, as it is generally impossible to distinguish the formation from the underlying Inferior Oolite in the records of those few boreholes that penetrate this level. However, the same south-eastward trend probably continues, as the formation is apparently absent in the BGS Harwell Borehole some 30 km south-east of the district (Gallois and Worssam, 1983), but is present farther north, e.g. in the Oxford area (Horton et al., 1995). Its presence in the Southrop Borehole has been inferred from downhole geophysical logs (Barron, 1986; Wyatt, 1996), but the evidence is far from conclusive, and given the regional pattern described above, it is more probable that the formation is absent (Figure 17).

The most extensive outcrops of the formation cap the high ground to the east of the Vale of Bourton, between Great Rissington [SP 199 173] and Fifield [SP 240 188], where the formation is typically 5 m thick. Most of the outcrop, representing the upper and greater part of the formation, is characterised by off-white to pale yellowish brown, flaggy, medium- to fine-grained, well-sorted ooidal grainstone, commonly with a minor proportion of shell debris. This facies has been quarried extensively, principally for walling stone. It produces a flaggy brash in the fields, although the soil is commonly rather clayey;

for the most part, this clay is probably residual material from the succeeding Fuller's Earth Formation.

The lower beds of the formation are of a different lithology. These strata have been noted along the margins of the outcrop near Great Rissington, and make up the entire thickness of the formation to the west of the Vale of Bourton where, although only 1 to 2 m thick, they form extensive dip slopes to the south-east of Cold Aston [SP 129 198]. They comprise unevenly flaggy, grey to brown, fine-grained sandy and ooidal limestones, containing a variable proportion of shell debris and, very commonly, small fragments of black lignite. The limestones commonly have a 'dirty' appearance due to the inclusion of argillaceous material, and there are probably interbeds of clay; the presence of clay clasts suggests intraformational erosion. The limestones are typically intensely burrowed, and in some cases brown clay fills the burrows. Locally, grey, more or less sandy limestones with abundant small oysters (*Praeexogyra acuminata*; Figure 15) occur. These shelly limestones are developed particularly at the base of the formation, where they are commonly interbedded with greenish grey clay and marl, which has been traced at outcrop at a number of localities between Great Rissington and Taynton [SP 234 137]. Richardson (1907a, 1933) recorded the clay as 0.3 m thick (including a 0.15 m oyster-rich limestone) in a quarry [SP 2019 1733] at Great Rissington, and as 0.15 m thick in a quarry [SP 2337 1865] near the Merrymouth Inn. Elsewhere, however, it is absent, as in the Pinchpool Farm Quarry, Windrush [SP 2007 1321] (Worssam and Bisson, 1961), where limestones rest directly on the Clypeus Grit of the Inferior Oolite Group.

The contact with the underlying Clypeus Grit is invariably sharp; a bored and in some cases oyster- and serpulid-encrusted hardground at this level has been found in field brash at several localities, and seems to be particularly well developed in the area around Sweetslade Farm [SP 141 182], near Cold Aston, and south-east of Great Rissington [SP 201 164].

The brown, sandy, argillaceous, lignite-bearing limestone facies at the base of the formation is strongly reminiscent of the Hook Norton Member, which forms the lower part of the formation in its type area, whilst the cleaner oolites in the upper part of the formation in the Great Rissington–Burford area are more like the succeeding Chipping Norton Member (e.g. Horton et al., 1987; Sellwood and McKerrow, 1974). The boundary between these members is defined by the top of the *Trigonia signata* Bed which, in places, is developed as a hardground (Sellwood and McKerrow, 1974). An oyster-encrusted hardground, approximately in the middle of the formation, in a quarry [SP 2413 1437] about 1 km north-east of Taynton (Richardson, 1933, p.38; Worssam and Bisson, 1961), may represent this bed. The clay bed present locally at the base of the formation occupies the same stratal position as the so-called Roundhill Clay of Roundhill railway cutting [SP 125 221], 2 km north of the district (Richardson, 1929). Arkell and Donovan (1952, p.249) implied that the Roundhill Clay lay above the Hook Norton Member, contradicting the correlation implied above, but the lateral continuity and relationships of both the Roundhill Clay and *Trigonia signata* Bed

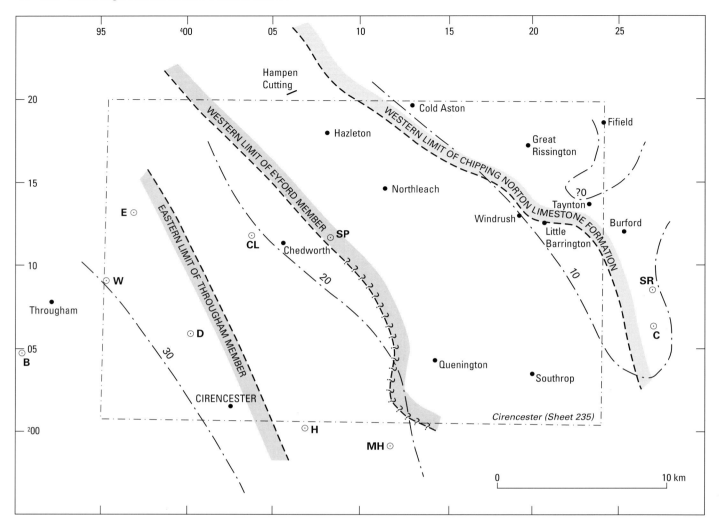

**Figure 17** Thickness variation of the Fuller's Earth Formation, and inferred limits of the Eyford and Througham members and of the Chipping Norton Limestone Formation.

remain unproven, and the validity of subdividing the Chipping Norton Limestone Formation has been questioned by Horton et al. (1987, p.65).

The top of the formation is seldom visible at outcrop because of downwashed material from the succeeding Fuller's Earth Formation. However, a bored surface at or near the top of the formation has been noted in field brash south-east of Great Rissington [SP 203 165; SP 209 166]. Despite the presence of a non-sequence at this locality, the thinning and disappearance of the Chipping Norton Limestone to the south-west is probably due to condensation and lateral passage into the Fuller's Earth Formation, rather than overstep by the latter (see Fuller's Earth Formation, below).

The fauna of the Chipping Norton Limestone is dominated by bivalves with subordinate terebratulid and rhynchonellid brachiopods. A *Parkinsonia* found in field brash derived from the basal beds of the formation [SP 1452 1846] is consistent with an early Bathonian age, as known from the type area (Torrens, in Cope, 1980b).

## FULLER'S EARTH FORMATION

The Fuller's Earth Formation is the basal unit of the Great Oolite Group throughout the district, except where the Chipping Norton Limestone is developed in the north-east. The formation takes its name from the occurrence of commercial fuller's earth (clay rich in the mineral smectite or calcium montmorillonite) in the upper part of the formation (Upper Fuller's Earth), in its type area around Bath. The Fuller's Earth of the present district corresponds only with the Lower Fuller's Earth of the type area, and does not contain smectite in significant quantities (see Chapter 2). The formation corresponds essentially to the clay unit mapped within the 'Fuller's Earth' of the adjoining Gloucester district (1:50 000 Sheet 234).

The Fuller's Earth Formation is dominated by grey mudstones of marine origin which weather to produce a dark brown clay soil. The formation also contains sporadic thin beds and lenses of calcareous sandstone or sandy limestone ('tilestone') which are particularly common in the upper part of the formation, most notably within the Eyford and Througham members (see below). Where possible, these limestone-rich strata are distinguished on the map. In addition there are several shelly limestone beds which are thought to be isochronous markers, and which help to constrain the regional correlation (Figure 16); these include blue-hearted, creamy yellow-weathering, oyster-rich limestones which have been found in field brash at many localities.

The Fuller's Earth Formation crops out principally on steep valley slopes in the north-western part of the district, and so outcrops are generally narrow. The formation is largely responsible for the steep-sided profile of these valleys, as the mudstones, being highly susceptible to erosion, weather back more rapidly than the overlying limestones. In this situation, the formation is very prone to landslipping (Chapter 2), and slipped material, with associated mudflows, commonly obscures the basal boundary. This factor, and the associated cambering of overlying limestone formations, makes thickness estimates from outcrop unreliable. However, sufficient data are available from wells and boreholes to show a pronounced north-eastward thinning, from more than 35 m in the south-west, to less than 10 m in the north-east (Figure 17). It is only about 5 m thick in the Windrush valley to the east of Little Barrington [SP 210 127] and earlier workers thought that the Fuller's Earth wedged out there (Richardson, 1933; Arkell, 1947b, fig 27; Arkell and Donovan, 1952; see 1933 edition of One-Inch Geological Sheet 235). However, it is now known to extend eastwards into the adjoining Witney district (1:50 000 Sheet 236), where it passes into the Sharp's Hill Formation, which is transitional to the non-marine Rutland Formation of the east Midlands (Bradshaw, 1978). The Fuller's Earth may, however, be absent in a small area between Taynton [SP 232 137] and Fifield [SP 240 187], although severe cambering of succeeding beds makes this difficult to confirm; indeed, the cambering suggests that a certain thickness of Fuller's Earth mudstone is present (see Chapter 2).

The best information on the internal stratigraphy of the formation (Figure 16) comes from cored boreholes (Figure 17), supplemented by downhole gamma-ray logs from these and other boreholes. In the west of the area, the basal 0.5 to 1 m of the formation comprises shell-fragmental marls and argillaceous limestone, in some cases (e.g. in the Stowell Park and Meysey Hampton boreholes) containing coarse-grained ferruginous peloids. These strata, the 'Passage Beds' of Green and Melville (1956), commonly resemble the underlying Clypeus Grit Member of the Inferior Oolite Group and have generally been mapped with that unit. However, they rest with a sharp contact and evident non-sequence on the limestones of the Clypeus Grit, in places containing limestone pebbles derived from them, much as the Chipping Norton Limestone rests on a planed, hard-ground surface of Clypeus Grit at localities in the north-east (see above). The 'Passage Beds' are probably the lateral equivalents of the Chipping Norton Limestone, as implied by Richardson (1933, p.27) in his record of Chedworth Wood (Tumulus) cutting [SP 0508 1391], the only exposure in the district where the junction between the Fuller's Earth and Clypeus Grit can be seen. There, the section currently shows about 1.6 m of 'Passage Beds', comprising mainly greyish orange, more or less shell-fragmental, 'ironshot', peloidal wackestone. These beds may equate with the basal unit of the Fuller's Earth in the Bath type area (i.e. Unit 1 of Penn and Wyatt, 1979; Wyatt, 1996). In the north-eastern part of the district, thinly fissile, grey to brown, fine-grained, sandy, laminated calcareous sandstone beds are developed locally at the base of the formation.

Above these basal beds, the lower part of the formation is dominated by dark greenish grey mudstone and silty mudstone, with scattered bivalves such as *Bositra*, *Gervillella*, *Modiolus* and *Oxytoma*, and sporadic specimens of the brachiopod *Lingula*.

A bed of marly or micritic limestone packed with specimens of the small oyster *Praeexogyra acuminata* (Figure 15), roughly in the middle of the formation, has been recognised in several boreholes; in those at Harnhill, Meysey Hampton and Sandpool Farm, just to the south of the district, it is associated with marls bearing coarse-grained, ferruginous peloids or pisoids. This marker bed (A1 of Table 12, Figure 16) may equate with Unit 4 in the Bath type area (Penn and Wyatt, 1979). Partly on the basis of downhole gamma-ray log interpretation, this oyster-rich bed appears to be present throughout the district, and also in the Shilton Road Borehole, just to the east.

Above this marker bed, a substantial unit of soft, massive, fine-grained, argillaceous sandstone or sandy mudstone is developed in boreholes in the western part of the district, although it has not been detected at outcrop in this area. This arenaceous unit, which passes into the lower part of the Eyford Member in more easterly parts of the district (see below), is succeeded by a second oyster-rich limestone or marl (A2 of Table 12 and Figure 16) that probably corresponds to the so-called Acuminata Bed, Unit 6 of the type area (Penn and Wyatt, 1979; Wyatt, 1996). Generally about 2 m or so higher in the succession, a marl or limestone yielding the small bivalve *Meleagrinella echinata* (Figure 15) as well as oysters has been recorded in boreholes in the west and southwest of the district. This bed (E of Table 12 and Figure 16) is the the Echinata Bed, Unit 8 of the type succession (Penn and Wyatt, 1979; Wyatt, 1996). The oysters in the Acuminata Bed and Echinata Bed are mainly typical *P. acuminata*, but also include larger, more wedge-shaped forms akin to *P. hebridica* (Figure 15). The association of *P. acuminata* and *P. hebridica* seems to be characteristic of the upper part of the Fuller's Earth in the region (1:50 000 Sheets 235 and 217) (Arkell, 1933b). Oyster beds yielding both these species are found within the Eyford Member of the easternmost part of the district, implying that the thin succession there is essentially complete, and that the thinning is due to condensation. This interpretation differs from that of Wyatt (1996), who considered the thinning to result from overstep by the Taynton Limestone Formation, such that much of the lower part of the formation (including the oyster-rich marker bed A1 of Table 12 and Figure 16) is cut out in the immediate area of the Vale of Moreton Axis.

In the east, the Eyford Member is the highest unit of the Fuller's Earth Formation, but in the west, the Echinata Bed is succeeded by mudstones which pass upwards into arenaceous beds of the Througham Member (see below).

## Eyford Member

The Eyford Member crops out in the area around Cold Aston [SP 130 198], in the north of the district, forming broad outcrops south of the village, as indicated on the 1:50 000 map. It also extends into the Hazleton [SP 080 180] area to the west, and similar limestones occur in the Great Barrington–Fifield area [SP 240 187] to SP 210 137]. The unit may reach up to 5 m or so in thickness, as in Hampen cutting [SP 060 203], immediately north of the district (Cox and Sumbler, in prep.). An exposure [SP 1168 1975] west of Cold Aston showed 1.3 m of pale grey, platy and fissile, finely ooidal grainstone with mudflakes, interbedded with grey, laminated, fissile, calcareous sandstone ('tilestone'), resting on clays with *P. acuminata*. The fine-grained ooidal grainstones resemble lithologies found within the overlying Taynton Limestone of this area, hinting at some degree of passage between the two units, so that the mapped junction of the Fuller's Earth and Taynton Limestone is poorly defined in places.

The Eyford Member appears to be thinly represented in cored boreholes near Northleach, and also in the Stowell Park Borehole, where the succession is similar to that at Hampen. Based largely on borehole correlation (Figure 16), oyster-rich limestones within the member at these localities are inferred to correspond to the Acuminata Bed and Echinata Bed developed farther west, so that the Eyford Member would appear to be at a slightly lower horizon than the lithologically similar Througham Member (see below). 'Tilestones' associated with oyster beds assigned to the Eyford Member occur at the top of the Fuller's Earth Formation at several localities in the Windrush valley, in the eastern part of the district. The southward extent of the Eyford Member at depth is somewhat uncertain; it may be present in boreholes in the Quenington area [SP 144 043], but is probably absent farther south.

The Eyford Member is better developed in the Moreton-in-Marsh district (Sheet 217) to the north, where it has traditionally yielded tilestones known as Cotswold Slates, widely used for roofing throughout the north Cotswolds (Chapter 2; see *Cover* photograph). The strata were assigned to the Stonesfield Slate Series (or Beds) by Richardson (1929) and Arkell (1933a), but this name is inappropriate, as the Stonesfield Slate of the type locality [SP 393 173] in Oxfordshire lies within the succeeding Taynton Limestone (Boneham and Wyatt, 1993). The strata were named the Eyford Member (or Eyford Sandstone Member) by Ager et al. (1973, p.7), based on the type section at Huntsman's Quarry [SP 126 252] near Eyford Hill, about 5 km to the north of the district (Cox and Sumbler, in prep.). Although originally defined as a subdivision of the Sharp's Hill Formation, into which the Fuller's Earth Formation passes eastwards, the member is herein included in the Fuller's Earth, as

the type Sharp's Hill Formation is characterised by a more marginal marine facies than is developed at Eyford. The inclusion of the beds of the Eyford Member in the Charlbury Formation (Boneham and Wyatt, 1993; Wyatt, 1996) is inappropriate, as the Charlbury Formation in its the type area near Stonesfield is of different facies, and is not contiguous with the Eyford Member, failing westward towards the Vale of Moreton Axis.

An extensive fauna is known from the Eyford Member at Eyford (Savage, 1961); it includes reptiles, fish and insects, and the ammonites *Procerites progracilis* and *P. mirabilis*, indicative of the Middle Bathonian Progracilis Zone (Torrens, 1969). During the recent survey of the district, a large *Procerites* was collected from a trench [SP 0655 1904] north-west of Hazleton. The fossils, collected mostly in the 19th century, have generally been misleadingly recorded as being from the 'Stonesfield Slate', although the fauna from the latter is rather more diverse, including important forms such as early mammals.

## Througham Member

A unit of grey, fissile, sandy limestones and very fine-grained ooidal grainstones is developed at the top of the Fuller's Earth Formation in the western part of the district (Figures 16, 17). Although it is very similar in facies to the Eyford Member, it is not contiguous with that unit, and occurs at a higher stratigraphical level, above the Echinata Bed. For these reasons, it is given a new name, the Througham Member. The member has not been separated on the map (Sheet 235) because of poor exposure. It has been included within the outcrop of the succeeding Taynton Limestone on the face of the map or, where that cannot be recognised (see below), with the Hampen Formation.

The member is currently exposed in the floor of Daglingworth Quarry [SP 001 061], where boreholes show it to have a total thickness of about 6 m. It is absent only a few kilometres to the east, however, e.g. in the Harnhill and Chedworth Laines boreholes, where the Taynton Limestone lies on mudstones just above the Echinata Bed. The westward thickening of the Througham Member takes place at the expense of the succeeding Taynton Limestone (Figure 16), implying a process of lateral passage. Immediately west of the district, the member passes into the lower part of the 'Througham Tilestones' of 1:50 000 Sheet 234. The 'Througham Tilestones' are herein renamed the Througham Formation. In its type area around the village of Througham [SO 921 079], this unit apparently incorporates equivalents of the attenuated Taynton Limestone together with the Hampen Formation above (Figure 16; see discussion of Hampen Formation, below).

## TAYNTON LIMESTONE FORMATION

The Taynton Limestone Formation succeeds the Fuller's Earth throughout virtually all of the district. It forms narrow outcrops in the steep-sided valleys of the central area, such as those of the rivers Churn, Coln and Leach, but has more extensive outcrops in the north-east, in the valley of the Windrush and its tributary the Sherborne Brook, particularly near Northleach [SP 114 146], Farmington [SP 136 154] and Taynton [SP 234 137].

The Taynton Limestone Formation takes its name (introduced, as Taynton Stone, by Woodward, 1894) from Taynton Down, to the north of the village of Taynton, where there is an extensive area of quarries dating back to medieval times (Chapter 2; Arkell, 1947a). Most are now heavily overgrown but Lee's Quarry [SP 236 152], still worked sporadically, has good exposure and may be regarded as the type section (Plate 2). It shows over 7 m of highly cambered Taynton Limestone, with some clay and marl seams up to 0.2 m thick (Sumbler and Williamson, 1999). The limestone is a cream to brownish buff, coarse- to very coarse-grained, moderately well- to very poorly sorted ooidal and shell-fragmental grainstone, with pale cream to white ooids in a colourless to yellowish brown spar cement. The ooids generally have a relatively large, shell-fragment nucleus, with a thin, white coating of soft, chalky, accreted carbonate; they commonly appear in marked colour contrast to the darker groundmass of the rock, particularly in weathered brash. The presence of these large, pale, 'superficial' ooids is a particular characteristic of the formation. The rock is well bedded, and is cross-bedded throughout, commonly with abundant shells (including small oysters, pectinids and echinoid debris) and sporadic mudflakes concentrated on foresets. Cross-bedding is seen in all exposures; at Farmington Quarry [SP 130 169], cosets are more than 5 m thick (Plate 7); foreset azimuths here, at Taynton, and at several other localities in the district, indicate currents flowing predominantly from the north and east.

Because of its position immediately above the Fuller's Earth, the outcrop of the Taynton Limestone is almost invariably affected by cambering (Chapter 8), making estimates of thickness from outcrop unreliable. Thicknesses recorded in borehole logs are often unreliable too, because of the difficulty in distinguishing the formation from limestones in the Fuller's Earth and Hampen formations, except where cores are available. However, taking all the available information, the formation is generally some 6 to 8 m thick in the type area and throughout the greater part of the district, and the maximum thickness is probably about 10 or 11 m.

Farmington Quarry (Plate 7) is one of the more westerly large-scale workings in the Taynton Limestone; the beds exposed there were wrongly regarded as belonging to a lower horizon by Richardson (1933) (the so-called Farmington Freestone, within his 'Stonesfield Slate Series', i.e. a part of the Fuller's Earth Formation; see Sumbler, 1995b). To the west, commencing in the Northleach area, the proportion of good freestone in the formation diminishes due to the development of interbeds of pale brown, fine- to very fine-grained, ooidal grainstone and, more rarely, greyish brown, finely sandy 'tilestone' with ooid wisps and coarsely shelly, oyster-rich limestone. These lithologies, typical of the Througham Member (Fuller's Earth Formation) and the succeeding Hampen Formation (see below), gradually replace the typical Taynton Limestone from the top and base respectively, by interdigitation (Figure 16). Regionally, the principal cause of thinning appears to be the passage of the basal part into facies of the Througham Member, and for this reason, the formation averages only about 4 m in thickness in the western part of the district (e.g. Winstone Borehole). This thickness may be maintained some 7 km to the south-west of the district, where the Minchinhampton Beds (Wyatt, 1996) of the Minchinhampton Borehole constitute some 4.5 m of typical Taynton Limestone facies. The formation is also thin in the north and north-western parts of the district, for example in the Stowell Park and Chedworth Laines

**Plate 7** Large-scale cross-bedding in the Taynton Limestone Formation, Farmington Quarry [SP 130 169], 1994.

The face is approximately 5 m high and constitutes part of a single coset. Layers of shell-debris on the foresets form planes of parting which enable blocks of stone to be easily extracted (GS534).

boreholes, where it is only about 2 m thick. There, its thinness results from a replacement of the upper part of the formation by Hampen Formation lithologies. Locally in the north-west, the Taynton Limestone Formation may be replaced altogether, or at least is impossible to detect at outcrop, so that the Hampen Formation is shown resting directly on Fuller's Earth Formation on the 1:50 000 map. The Taynton Limestone is also particularly thin at Daglingworth Quarry [SP 001 061], where it is represented by only 0.6 m of coarsely ooidal limestone with proportionately thick developments of both the Througham Member and Hampen Formation.

Fossils from the Taynton Limestone include bivalves such as *Camptonectes*, *Placunopsis*, *Plagiostoma*, *Pteroperna*, *Radulopecten* and the oysters *Praeexogyra acuminata* and *P. hebridica* (Figure 15). Brachiopods, notably species of *Kallirhynchia*, are also quite common. Ammonites are extremely rare, but a *Procerites* cf. *tmetolobus* has been found at Farmington Quarry, probably from the lower part of the formation. The species is generally assigned to the Lower Bathonian. The Taynton Limestone at Slade Quarry [SP 070 217], just to the north of the district, has yielded *Procerites mirabilis*, indicating the Progracilis Zone (Torrens, in Cope, 1980b). The Minchinhampton Beds are in part, at least, somewhat younger, extending into the Subcontractus Zone (though probably not the Morrisi Zone as suggested by Torrens, in Cope, 1980b and Wyatt, 1996), giving evidence for the diachronous relationship shown in Table 12.

## HAMPEN FORMATION

The Hampen Formation (formerly Hampen Marly Beds or Formation) forms narrow outcrops along the river valleys of the district, and broader outcrops on the interfluves in the north-west. The formation is present down dip from the outcrop throughout the district. Based on sections and cored boreholes, the thickness of the formation varies from about 4 to 11 m, with a general thickening towards the west. Apparently greater formational thicknesses in the extreme west of the district, where the Taynton Limestone cannot be separated, include strata that equate with the underlying Througham Member of the Fuller's Earth Formation (see below).

The type section of the formation, at Hampen Cutting SSSI [SP 062 205], 0.5 km north of the district, has been described by Sumbler and Barron (1996). There, the formation comprises 9 m of limestones with interbedded marls, the latter dominating the upper part of the section but otherwise subordinate to the limestones. Within the district, exposures at Oxpens Barn [SP 087 144] (Plate 8) and Daglingworth Quarry [SP 001 061] (Plate 9), displaying 8.94 m and 6.74 m respectively, show lithologies similar to those of the type section, and confirm the lateral persistence of the marly upper part. Claims (Arkell, 1933a; 1947b; Arkell and Donovan, 1952; Green and Melville, 1956; Palmer, 1979) that the Hampen Formation dies out in the Chedworth area, by south-westward passage into an expanding White Limestone

**Plate 8**  A rare exposure of the Hampen Formation, Oxpens Barn [SP 087 145] near Northleach.

The section shows the typical thinly bedded fine-grained, slightly sandy ooidal limestones, with lenticular beds of marl and clay. The staff is 2 m long (A 15437).

Formation, are incorrect. This view was based on a faulty interpretation of Richardson's (1911) record of the Stony Furlong [SP 060 109] and Chedworth Station [SP 055 115] railway cuttings. In fact, the Hampen Formation is about 10 m thick there, comprising Richardson's (1911) beds 33 to 36 as well as underlying, undescribed strata. Similarly, although Green and Melville (1956) considered the formation to be absent in the Stowell Park Borehole, re-examination of core specimens has established its presence, with a thickness of 9.57 m (Sumbler and Barron, 1995, 1996; Cox and Sumbler, in prep.).

The dominant and characteristic lithology of the Hampen Formation at the type locality, and throughout most of the district, is a grey to brown, thinly bedded, fine- to very fine-grained, well-sorted, ooidal grainstone to packstone. These limestones are commonly slightly sandy or silty, with the sand typically concentrated in paler laminae or lenticles. The limestones generally have

**Plate 9** Daglingworth Quarry.
The section shows nearly 30 m of strata in the middle part of the Great Oolite Group. Most of the lower part of the face belongs to the Hampen Formation; its top bed is the marl band which forms the recess in the face, one-third of the way up the photograph, i.e. about 8 m above the base of the section. The succeeding beds belong to the Shipton and Ardley members of the White Limestone Formation; the Excavata Bed, at the junction of the two members, forms the narrow ledge about 10 m above the base of the White Limestone Formation (A 15440).

a faint bituminous smell when freshly broken, and contain rare carbonaceous plant fragments. Small-scale cross-bedding is ubiquitous, and the limestones produce a platy or unevenly flaggy brash commonly displaying burrows and trails on the bedding surfaces. These flaggy limestones were quarried extensively for walling and perhaps to produce tilestones for roofing. The limestones commonly contain wisps of relatively coarse-grained white ooids, like those of the Taynton Limestone, and lenses of coarse, shell-fragmental ooidal grainstone, of Taynton Limestone type, occur quite commonly in the lower part of the Hampen Formation. In the north-west of the district, similar grainstones also occur in the middle and at the top of the formation, for example in the Elkstone and Stowell Park boreholes, making separation of the Hampen and Taynton Limestone formations problematic. Locally, in the absence of a consistently mappable Taynton Limestone, the Hampen Formation and the superficially similar Througham Member of the Fuller's Earth beneath cannot be distinguished. In these areas, the entire package of up to 20 m of strata between the mudstones of the Fuller's Earth and the base of the White Limestone Formation has been mapped as Hampen Formation. In the Gloucester District (1:50 000 Sheet 234), to the west and south-west, the equivalent unit constitutes the Througham Tilestone (the Througham Formation of Figure 16).

The marls of the formation are typically grey, clayey and, in some cases, sandy or silty. They weather to yellowish brown and, at outcrop, contribute to a brownish clayey soil. The marls are generally well bedded or laminated and commonly contain abundant shell debris, with oyster shells being particularly common. At Hampen, marls make up some 45 per cent of the formation (Sumbler and Barron, 1996), but in the western and central parts of the district, a figure of 20 to 30 per cent is more typical. As seen in sections, many of the marl beds tend to pass laterally into shaly limestones,

but those at the top of the formation are more persistent, and occur in beds up to about 1 m thick. This marl-dominated unit at the top of the formation can be recognised at outcrop (e.g. Plate 9) and in cored boreholes throughout much of the district, and is a useful marker in downhole geophysical logs of boreholes for which no cores are available. Its relationship to isochronous markers in the Fuller's Earth and White Limestone formations suggests that it occurs at a more or less constant horizon, except perhaps in the easternmost part of the district. In the south-west of the district and beyond, however, the marly strata tend to fail: in the Harnhill and Bisley boreholes (Figure 17), for example, the formation is almost entirely composed of fine-grained ooidal limestones. These persist westwards, and probably pass into the lithologically similar Dodington Ash Rock (Wyatt, 1996) of the Minchinhampton area.

The thickness variation within the Hampen Formation is believed to be mainly a manifestation of a diachronous relationship with the Taynton Limestone Formation, with the lower beds of the Hampen Formation, as developed in the central parts of the district, passing laterally into the upper part of the Taynton Limestone Formation to both west and east (Figure 16). The thickness change is most marked in the central part of the district, in a zone extending from Bibury [SP 115 068] to Sherborne [SP 175 144], and corresponding approximately to the Vale of Moreton Axis. To the east of this zone, the formation is generally only 4 to 6 m thick and typically comprises about 50 per cent marl. These beds represent the marly upper part of the formation as developed to the west. Within this thinner succession, there is a progressive eastwards change in lithological character, with a reduction in the proportion of grainstones and grey marly clays, which are replaced, from the top of the formation downwards, by lower energy, bioturbated, rubbly-weathering micritic limestones and greenish white marls. For example, in the section at Lee's Quarry,

Taynton [SP 236 152], in the easternmost part of the district, much of the Hampen Formation is made up of pale grey and fawn marls interbedded with rubbly, poorly sorted, peloidal wackestones and packstones (Plate 2). These lithologies are similar to those of the White Limestone Formation, and suggest a lateral interdigitation of the two formations in this area (Figure 16), a relationship that is more definitely established still farther east (Palmer, 1979; Sumbler, 1984). Rootlet beds, indicative of very shallow waters, appear immediately east of the district near Burford [SP 252 121] and, with other non-marine characters, become progressively more common eastwards, so that in the Oxford–Brackley area, some 30 km to the north-east, the strata are better classified as Rutland Formation. The latter formation was laid down in land-marginal areas of the London Platform and East Midlands Shelf (Bradshaw, 1978; Horton et al., 1995).

The fauna of the Hampen Formation (see also Palmer, 1979) is dominated by bivalves such as *Camptonectes*, *Modiolus*, *Myophorella*, *Protocardia* and particularly oysters, notably *Praeexogyra hebridica* (=*Ostrea sowerbyi* of Richardson, 1933; see Figure 15). The latter may occur abundantly in the marls, or may be cemented into lumachelles that superficially resemble the oyster beds of the Fuller's Earth, although the smaller *P. acuminata*, common in the Fuller's Earth, does not seem to occur within the Hampen Formation. Brachiopods (e.g. *Kallirhynchia*) and echinoids (e.g. *Nucleolites*) occur sporadically, and gastropods (e.g. *Natica*, *Pseudomelania*) become increasingly common in the more easterly parts of the district. A specimen of the ammonite *Procerites* (private collection) was obtained from the basal part of the formation during construction of the shallow cuttings along the Northleach bypass during the 1980s [probably from a point between SP 100 162 and SP 114 155]. The only other ammonite known from the formation is the holotype of *Procerites imitator* from near Fritwell in Oxfordshire (Torrens, in Cope, 1980b). These ammonites are not zonally diagnostic, but from its position in the sequence, the formation is deduced to belong mainly to the Subcontractus Zone in the Cirencester district. The inferred equivalent to the west of the district (the Dodington Ash Rock) extends into the younger Morrisi Zone (Wyatt, 1996), illustrating a westward younging of the lithofacies association, as seen with the Taynton Limestone Formation.

## WHITE LIMESTONE FORMATION

The outcrop of the White Limestone Formation forms a dissected plateau (a modified dip slope), occupying an extensive tract of country across the central part of the district, and extending into the valleys of the south-east. In addition, there are a number of outliers in the north. The formation varies considerably in thickness, from an estimated 15 m or less to perhaps more than 25 m. To a large extent, this variation results from channelling at the base of the succeeding Forest Marble Formation, which locally removes the upper part of the White Limestone, but there also appears to be a general thickening of constituent units of the formation towards the west (Figure 16).

The White Limestone Formation is divisible, in ascending order, into the Shipton, Ardley and Signet members (Sumbler, 1984, 1991), each member representing a shallowing-upward sedimentary cycle (Barker, 1976; Palmer, 1979). The Shipton and Ardley members together comprise the greater part of the White Limestone, typically totalling some 20 m or so in the central part of the district. The strata are characterised by pale grey to white micritic limestones (wackestones and packstones) that form a characteristic brash of white sub-angular fragments in the soil of arable fields. Flaggy weathering ooidal and shell-fragmental grainstones also occur, particularly in the upper part of the succession. At some levels, partial cementation has taken place around burrows to give a cavernous-weathering 'Dagham Stone' (Woodward, 1894, p.286); such beds are generally lenticular, but in some cases they are surmounted by cemented hardgrounds that can be traced over large areas. These hardgrounds form the basis of the subdivision of the formation, and are crucial in regional correlation (Sumbler, 1984; Wyatt, 1996). Despite some overall lithological differences, the Shipton and Ardley members cannot be readily distinguished in the absence of good sections, and so are shown undifferentiated on the map. However, the two members can generally be separated in exposures and borehole cores mainly by recognition of various distinctive marker beds (Figure 16 and see below), and can also be tentatively identified on gamma-ray logs of uncored boreholes. Recognition of these markers becomes increasingly uncertain towards the south-western part of the district and, with the gradually increasing dominance of ooidal grainstones in that direction, the White Limestone Formation is replaced by the Athelstan Oolite of the Malmesbury district (Cave, 1977; Wyatt, 1996). Over most of the district, the Signet Member is of markedly different lithology and has been distinguished on the map wherever possible. However, as with the underlying members, it becomes increasingly difficult to recognise towards the west because of an increased development of ooidal grainstones.

### Shipton Member

The Shipton Member is typically about 8 m thick within the district. There is some indication of westward or

**Figure 18** The White Limestone succession in the Cirencester district.

Section 1 from Sumbler MS (BGS files).

Section 2 from Richardson, 1911; beds 3 to 12 based on the Wiggold [SP 045 057], Stow Road [SP 048 071], Folly Barn [SP 055 083] and Aldgrove [SP 057 090] cuttings; Beds 18 to 32 based on Stony Furlong cutting [SP 063 107].

Section 3 from Sumbler (1995b).

Section 4–5 based on mapping (Sumbler, 1994a, b).

Section 6 based on Whitehill [SP 270 108], Stonelands [SP 278 097], Eton College [SP 298 102] and Worsham [SP 300 118] quarries (Sumbler, 1984, fig. 3).

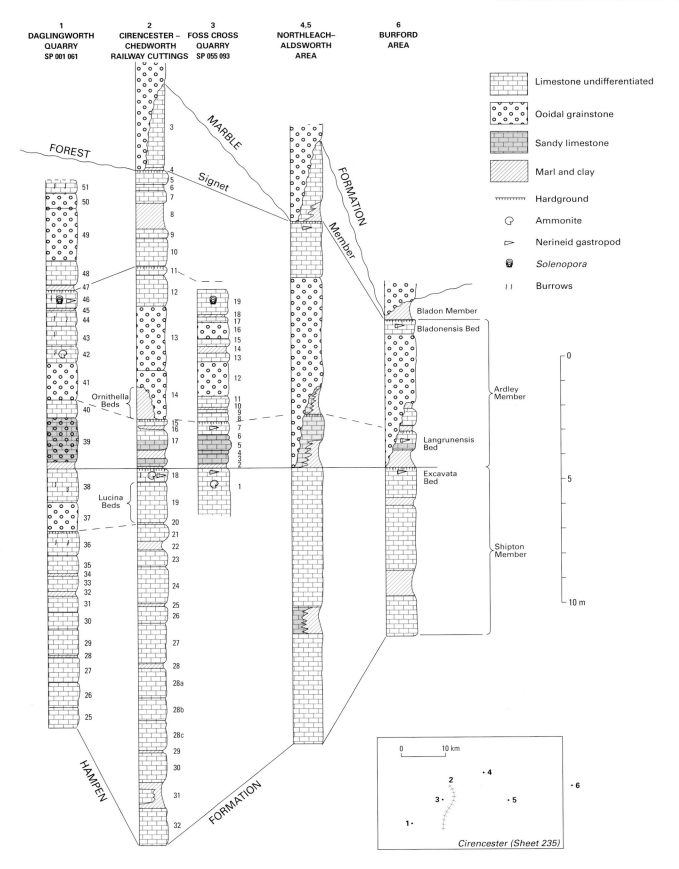

south-westward thinning, with thicknesses of about 10 m in the central and eastern parts of the district (Figure 18), but only 6.6 m in the Harnhill and Winstone boreholes in the south and west. The member is also known to thin to the east, with about 6 m in the Burford area just outside the district, and only 4 m at the type locality, Shipton-on-Cherwell Quarry [SP 477 175], some 24 km to the east. This eastward thinning is the result of progressive lateral passage of the lower beds of the formation into facies of the Hampen Formation (Figure 16; Sumbler, 1984). A specimen of *Tulites mustela*, from 'near the base of the White Limestone' (and with a matrix consistent with this level) from a quarry 'about half a mile NW by W of Salperton Church' (Richardson, 1929, p.119), just to the north of the district [c. SP 07 20], is indicative of the Middle Bathonian Subcontractus Zone (Torrens, in Cope, 1980b).

The Shipton Member is dominated by wackestones and packstones containing a greater or lesser proportion of large (often 1 mm or more) peloids. Typically, these limestones lack clear bedding structure, with peloids and shells scattered throughout the rock, as a result of intense burrowing. The peloids, commonly slightly ferruginous and yellowish in colour, include faecal pellets, intraclasts and true ooids. Marl seams are common, and ooidal grainstones also occur particularly in the south-west and to a minor degree elsewhere, mainly in the upper part of the member. The top bed of the member is a peloidal packstone known as the Excavata Bed, from the occurrence of *Aphanoptyxis excavata*, which often occurs with other nerineid gastropods. It is capped by a non-sequence, locally marked by a planed and bored hardground surface. This hardground bed has been mapped in places in the eastern part of the district, and is known from boreholes and quarries in the west, where gastropods are generally less common.

Grainstones occur locally at the base of the member, but the lowest beds are more usually peloidal packstones which contrast markedly with the lithologies of the underlying Hampen Formation. At several localities [e.g. SP 134 141; SP 110 122; SP 049 127; SP 078 150], the basal beds yield abundant oysters (of *P. hebridica* type), as well as large lumps of compound corals such as *Isastraea limitata*. The echinoid *Clypeus muelleri* also occurs sporadically at this level, in some cases in association with the corals.

In the eastern part of the district, a bed of white marl and silty marl, up to 1 m or more thick, and about 3 to 5 m above the base of the formation, has been traced for a considerable distance along the southern lip of the Windrush valley (Figure 18). Farther west, around Northleach, this bed is represented by a brown marly clay interbedded with fine-grained, more or less fissile, grey to brown sandy limestone, much like those of the Hampen Formation. This unit forms a notable marker in gamma-ray logs of boreholes in the central and eastern parts of the district. Farther east, it passes into the Hampen Formation (see above; Figure 16).

The whole of the Shipton Member was exposed in the Stony Furlong railway cutting [SP 061 109] at Chedworth (Richardson, 1911, 1933, plate 3; Sumbler and Barron, 1995; Cox and Sumbler, in prep.; Figure 18), but much of the section is now obscured. A peloidal grainstone with micritic clasts at the base of the formation is still poorly visible at the top of Chedworth Station cutting [SP 0547 1162]. This bed is inferred to be Richardson's Bed 32 (the highest of his section there), giving a total of 13.4 m for the Shipton Member (beds 18 to 32). However, data from elsewhere in the district (see above) suggest that this thickness is excessive, and there may be some errors in Richardson's record.

The upper 3 m or so of the Shipton Member (Richardson's beds 18 to 21) are still exposed in Stony Furlong cutting, near the road bridge [SP 0628 1063] (Figure 18). The lowest bed seen (Bed 21) is a brown, rather sandy marl that may equate with the marl/sandy limestone bed within the member farther east. Bed 19, 1.4 m of peloidal wackestone, with ooidal grainstones in the lower part, corresponds to Richardson's 'Lucina Beds', which have yielded an extensive fauna including corals, gastropods, numerous bivalves (such as the eponymous *Lucina*) and echinoids (*Clypeus*, *Nucleolites*). Bed 18, the Excavata Bed, is a buff, poorly sorted, peloidal packstone, recrystallised to a very hard, pinkish fawn, microcrystalline limestone in its upper part. It is very fossiliferous in parts, yielding nerineid gastropods, *Lucina*, *Tancredia*, trigoniids and corals. Richardson (1911) found a loose specimen of the ammonite *Morrisiceras*, probably from this bed; the specimen indicates the Middle Bathonian Morrisi Zone.

At Foss Cross Quarry [SP 055 093], 1.5 km to the south-west of Stony Furlong, the upper part of the 'Lucina Beds' and the succeeding Excavata Bed are exposed (Figure 18; Plate 10); again, the upper part of the latter is recrystallised and is developed as a cavernous-weathering 'Dagham Stone'. The Excavata Bed contains abundant fossils including *A. excavata* (Barker, 1976), and has also yielded the ammonite *Morrisiceras comma* (Morrisi Zone) recorded by Torrens (in Cope, 1980b). In the nearby Aldgrove cutting [SP 0563 0874 to SP 0580 0947], the Excavata Bed is no longer exposed, but from Richardson's (1911, Bed 17) description, it is capped by a hardground with 'a waterworn surface' and '*Lithophagus* crypts'.

At Daglingworth Quarry [SP 001 061] in the south-west of the district, the Shipton Member is 9.3 m thick (Figure 18; Plate 9), and consists almost entirely of buff to white peloidal packstones; there is noticeably less marl in the succession than is the case farther east. The Excavata Bed (Bed 38), which forms an extensive bench in the quarry, is hard and crystalline in the upper part, but there is no sign of a hardground at this level. Some 2.2 m lower in the succession, the top of Bed 36 (incorrectly identified as the Excavata Bed by Wyatt, 1996), is a planed hardground with borings and adhering oysters which probably equates with the 'waterworn' top surface of Bed 20 in Stony Furlong cutting, as described by Richardson (1911).

## Ardley Member

The Ardley Member includes packstones and wackestones, but the middle part of the succession is

**Plate 10**  White Limestone Formation, Foss Cross Quarry.

This photograph was taken in 1966, but the face shown is still preserved. The lowest bed in the face, being examined by the geologists, is the Excavata Bed (Bed 1) which marks the top of the Shipton Member; the highest bed is the Solenopora or Beetroot Bed (Bed 19) in the Ardley Member (see Figure 18) (A 10527).

dominated by buff, ooidal and shell-fragmental grain-stones. At some localities, these make up the greater part of the member. Cavernous 'Dagham Stone' horizons are particularly common, and several hardgrounds of more or less regional extent occur; one of these caps the Bladonensis Bed at the top of the member. The Ardley Member is typically 9 to 10 m thick where fully developed, and there is some indication of thickening to the west, with about 12 m in the Cirencester–Chedworth area (Figure 18). However, it is substantially less in places, with only about 7 m in some boreholes (based on gamma-ray logs) and an apparent 5.5 m in the cored Meysey Hampton Borehole, just south of the district (although this thickness may be unreliable due to erroneous core depth-markings). To some extent, these thinner successions may result from channelling at the base of the succeeding Signet Member.

In the easternmost part of the district, the succession is much like that in the Burford area of Oxfordshire (Figure 18; Sumbler, 1984, fig. 3). There, the basal bed of the member, overlying the Excavata Bed, is a greenish grey clay which passes upwards into a sandy limestone. A little farther west, near Sherborne, the clay is gradually replaced by intercalations of fine-grained, grey to brown, sandy limestone, so that near Northleach [SP 114 147], the basal unit of the Ardley Member is a hard, compact, grey, sandy limestone up to 2 m thick (Figure 18). This limestone, generally surmounted by a planed, bored and oyster-encrusted hardground, is exposed in a number of old quarries [e.g. SP 1358 1190; SP 1697 1317] and has been mapped out locally. It corresponds to the sandy Roach Bed and the overlying Langrunensis Bed which, in Oxfordshire, is characterised by the gastropod *Aphanoptyxis langrunensis* (Sumbler, 1984; Barker, 1994). Locally, in the Sherborne-Burford area, the hardground is overlain by a bed of fossiliferous marl with *Epithyris*

*oxonica* (Figure 15), commonly accompanied by corals such as *Isastraea* and *Thamnasteria,* and bivalves such as *Modiolus* and *Plagiostoma subcardiiformis,* a facies and fauna very similar to that of the basal Signet Member. This unit equates with the so-called Ornithella Beds of Richardson (1911) (see below). In many places, it is replaced by brown, unfossiliferous clay or, in the North-leach area, by hard, greyish brown, sandy limestone, much like that at the base of the Ardley Member there.

Over large areas, the succeeding part of the Ardley Member is dominated by buff to white, flaggy, cross-bedded, variably shell-fragmental, medium– to coarse-grained, ooidal grainstones (Figure 18). These oolites were extensively quarried, most notably at Quarry Hill [SP 099 058] (probably the source of Arkell's (1947b) 'Bibury Stone') where the workings include under-ground galleries. The bases of these oolite units are commonly erosive; locally they cut down into the Lan-grunensis Bed or even into the upper part of the Shipton Member. Oolites become increasingly dominant over micritic rocks westwards, reflecting progressively higher energy and more open marine conditions farther offshore, as envisaged by Worssam and Bisson (1961), although the change is neither as sudden nor as pro-nounced as they implied.

The highest part of the Ardley Member comprises a few metres of strata dominated by white micritic limestone (carbonate mudstone), generally almost devoid of peloids or shell debris. At the top, just below the Signet Member, it contains nerineid gastropods at some localities, and may be capped by a bored hardground. This gastropod-bearing unit represents the Bladonensis Bed, charac-terised in Oxfordshire by *Aphanoptyxis bladonensis* (Barker, 1976, 1994; Sumbler, 1984). In places, it is absent because of channelling at the base of the Signet Member or Forest Marble Formation.

The whole of the Ardley Member was formerly exposed in the railway cuttings between Cirencester and Chedworth, described by Richardson (1911), although not in one continuous section (Figure 18). After allowance is made for probable errors in Richardson's (1911) section of Stony Furlong cutting [SP 061 109] (see above), the thickness of the member there is about 12 or 13 m. To the south, by combining the information from the Wiggold [SP 045 057], Stow Road [SP 048 071; SP 051 075], Folly Barn [SP 055 083] and Aldgrove [SP 057 090] cuttings, and the extant Foss Cross Quarry section [SP 055 093], the succession (Richardson's (1911) beds 5 to 16) may be a little thinner, totalling 10.3 to 10.5 m (Sumbler, 1995c).

The basal 5.44 m or so of the member (Richardson's beds 13c to 17) are still exposed in Stony Furlong cutting [SP 0628 1063] (Figure 18; Sumbler and Barron, 1995; Cox and Sumbler, in prep.). Beds 15 to 17, resting on the Excavata Bed, represent the Roach and Langrunensis beds. They contain crumbly, fissile, rather sandy seams of limestone and marl, and according to Richardson (1911) are capped by a planed, oyster-encrusted hardground. Richardson (1911) stated that the succeeding ooidal and peloidal packstone-grainstone of Bed 14 passed laterally (southwards) into the 'Ornithella Beds', fossiliferous marls that contain corals, bivalves and brachiopods, including the eponymous 'Ornithella', now *Digonella digonoides*. In fact, photographs of the section (e.g. Richardson, 1911, plate 19; Richardson, 1933, plate 3b) show that the Ornithella Beds underlie the limestones and are cut out by the latter, which infill a channel that cuts down to the underlying Bed 15 (Figure 18). The highest beds now exposed are buff, cross-bedded, ooidal grainstones of Bed 13, also exposed in a nearby quarry [SP 0657 1055].

The lower 6.58 m of the member are exposed in Foss Cross Quarry (Figure 18; Plate 10; Sumbler, 1995c; Cox and Sumbler, in prep.); the beds now exposed correspond to Richardson's (1911) beds 12 to 16 of the Aldgrove cutting. The lower part of the section is substantially similar to that at Stony Furlong. The highest bed seen (Bed 19) is the so-called Beetroot or Solenopora Bed, characterised by pink-banded stromatolites formed by the red alga *Solenopora jurassica* (Figure 15; Harland and Torrens, 1982). The Solenopora Bed was recorded by Richardson (1911) in Aldgrove and Folly Barn cuttings, and has been found in field brash to the south of Foss Cross Quarry. A hardground surface formerly exposed in the quarry a short distance south of the present section, was described by Kershaw and Smith (1986). They equated it with the hardground developed upon the Langrunensis Bed, but more probably it caps the Solenopora Bed which, as developed in Aldgrove and Stony Furlong cuttings (Richardson, 1911, Bed 11) and at Daglingworth Quarry (see below), is likewise surmounted by a bored, oyster-encrusted surface.

From Richardson's (1911, 1933) data, the higher beds of the Ardley Member, formerly exposed in railway cuttings nearer Cirencester, vary considerably in thickness and internal stratigraphy from place to place. The Bladonensis Bed, at the top of the Ardley Member,

is Richardson's Bed 5 (Figure 18), which he termed the Gervillia Bed. This bed was formerly exposed in the Wiggold [SP 045 057] and Stow Road [SP 048 071] cuttings. Amongst Richardson's fossil collection from these two cuttings (held by BGS) are specimens of the eponymous '*Gervillia*', i.e. the bivalve *Bakevellia waltoni*. As elsewhere in the district, the top surface of this bed is a hardground, described by Richardson (1911) as hard and waterworn, and (at Stow Road) with annelid borings and adhering oysters.

Almost the whole of the Ardley Member is represented in Daglingworth Quarry [SP 001 061] (Figure 18; Plate 9). Some 10.8 m of strata are exposed, and are capped by remnants of Forest Marble clay; beds equivalent to the Signet Member do not appear to be present. At the base of the member, the Roach Bed (39) is a sandy shaly marl which passes upwards into hard, grey, fine-grained, thinly bedded, silty limestone with local signs of herring-bone cross-stratification. The overlying peloidal packstone-grainstone of Bed 40 is probably the Langrunensis Bed; it has a planar top, but there is apparently no hardground developed at this locality. The overlying few metres of strata are mainly peloidal packstones and grainstones, containing several beds of Dagham Stone (most notably Bed 44). Dagham Stones are particularly well developed at this locality; indeed, the term derives from the old name for Daglingworth (Woodward, 1894). A specimen of the ammonite *Procerites quercinus* from this part of the succession indicates the Upper Bathonian Retrocostatum Zone (Torrens, in Cope, 1980b); according to Barker's (1976) section, the specimen came from a level about 4 m above the base of the member (Bed 42 of Figure 18). Some 6.55 m above the base, a well-developed hardground, with borings and encrusting epifauna at the top of Bed 46, forms an extensive bench in the north-western part of the quarry. The presence of *Solenopora jurassica* (Figure 15) in the underlying limestone of Bed 46 (Barker, 1976, Bed 7) suggests correlation with the Solenopora Bed of the Foss Cross area. The overlying 4.2 m of beds, to the top of the section, are mainly well-sorted, cross-bedded peloidal and ooidal packstones and grainstones. According to the quarry workers, these beds commonly yield fragmentary reptilian fossil material. In this connection, it is interesting to note Buckman's (1860) record of a cluster of reptile (probably turtle) eggs from a quarry near Hare Bushes [SP 034 029], Cirencester (Cox, Sumbler and Milner, 1999). The matrix of the specimen (no. R1809, The Natural History Museum, London) is a wackestone-packstone typical of the Ardley Member, and given the locality of the find, most probably came from its upper part.

## Signet Member

The Signet Member constitutes the highest part of the White Limestone Formation in the area west of Burford, including the Cirencester district (Sumbler, 1991). It is the equivalent of the Bladon Member of Oxfordshire (Sumbler, 1984), but the facies are sufficiently different for an alternative name to be appropriate. The type section is at Job's Lane, Signet [SP 245 102], a few hundred metres beyond the eastern boundary of the district. There, the member is up to about 6 m thick, but 2 to 3 m are more usual. It reaches a maximum of about 11 m near Fairford, whilst at many localities it is absent altogether. This patchy distribution is largely the effect of erosion at the base of the Forest Marble, which has removed the member in many places, as indicated schematically in Figure 16. However, in its sedimentary facies, the member is transitional between the White Limestone (Ardley Member) and Forest Marble, including lithologies which may be matched in either of these formations. For this reason, the member is difficult to trace consistently, and its depiction on the geological map may not be fully comprehensive. The upper boundary is particularly problematical in the central and eastern parts of the district where some outcrops now recognised as Signet Member were originally mapped as Forest Marble by Hull (c. 1856; see the 1933 edition of Sheet 235). Conversely, with the development of oolites in the west, it becomes increasingly difficult to separate the Signet Member from the underlying Ardley Member and, west of the River Churn, they become indistinguishable. The transitional nature of the beds also proved a problem for Richardson (1933) who classified them as 'Kemble Beds' at many exposures, variously of 'Great Oolite facies' or of 'Forest Marble facies'. Worssam and Bisson (1961) also included the strata in the 'Kemble Beds', but much confusion attaches to this term which is now abandoned (Torrens, in Cope, 1980b; Sumbler, 1984, 1991; Cox and Sumbler, in prep.).

The most typical lithology of the Signet Member, dominating the succession in the type area and in the east, is a brownish grey wackestone, with a slightly sandy or clayey micrite matrix that contains scattered peloids and, characteristically, small fragments of bluish grey shell material and black lignite. The rocks are strongly bioturbated and poorly bedded, producing a rubbly brash. Commonly, the rocks are recrystallised and may be bored, indicating penecontemporaneous cementation. Other limestone facies include greyish blue to buff, cross-bedded, shell-fragmental, ooidal grainstones and brown sandy limestones, much like those of the Forest Marble. Locally, in the type area and perhaps elsewhere, these grainstones cut out the Bladonensis Bed as a result of channelling. Farther west, in the Quenington–Barnsley area, such higher energy facies become dominant, with a major part of the succession being made up of compact, uniform, rubbly to platy, pale grey to buff or brown, slightly sandy, fine- to medium-grained ooidal packstone/grainstone with lignite specks. One of the most westerly localities at which the Signet Member has been noted is the Wiggold cutting [SP 045 057], where Richardson (1911, beds 3 and 4; Figure 18) recorded 3.14 m of 'coarse oolitic limestone', containing bored pebbles of the Gervillia (=Bladonensis) Bed at the base, and with an oyster-encrusted top.

Lenses of green and brown clay and marl, in some cases associated with white carbonate mudstones (micrites), occur in many places, particularly at the base of the member. These basal clayey beds are commonly very fossiliferous, notably with *Plagiostoma subcardiiformis* and *Praeexogyra hebridica*, often associated with large forms of the brachiopod *Epithyris oxonica* (Figure 15) and locally with corals such as *Chomatoseris porpites*, *Isastraea limitata*, *Stylina babeana* and *Thamnasteria lyelli*.

At a number of localities in the Bibury–Fairford area, pure white carbonate mudstones (micrites) and coralliferous marls occur in the topmost 2 m or so of the Signet Member; these beds constitute the Fairford Coral Bed (Sumbler, 1991), the type locality of which is in a field [SP 133 023] to the north-west of Fairford. At many localities, the coralliferous rocks stand up as low knolls, surrounded by lower ground of the Forest Marble outcrop, and occurrences invariably coincide with unusually thick (over 5 m) developments of the Signet Member (e.g. about 11 m, the maximum known, at the bed's type locality). From the distribution and field relationships of the deposits, it seems likely that the Fairford Coral Bed represents small, isolated patch reefs which grew on areas of hard substrate developed on shoals, whilst other facies of the Signet Member accumulated concurrently in the surrounding, slightly deeper water. Numerous species of corals have been recorded from the Fairford Coral Bed (Negus and Beauvais, 1975; Sumbler, 1991); the most abundant are species of *Isastraea*, *Thamnasteria* and *Thecosmilia*. The corals typically occur as large lumps, generally bored to some extent and encrusted by oysters, but often with the external structure exquisitely preserved. At most localities, the corals are associated with an abundant fauna dominated by *Modiolus imbricatus*, ostreids, *Plagiostoma subcardiiformis* and large *Epithyris oxonica* (Figure 15). A similar fauna was recorded from the 'Reef Bed' of the Kemble area, south-west of Cirencester, which is undoubtedly equivalent (Cox and Sumbler, in prep.), although there it has been regarded as the basal unit of the Forest Marble (Cave, 1977).

Another notable fossil from the Signet Member is Worssam and Bisson's (1961) record of an ammonite from near Westwell [SP 2335 1078], identified by Arkell (1958 p.228) as *Siemiradzkia* sp., possibly *S. pseudorjaza-nensis*, a species also recorded from the Forest Marble (see below).

## FOREST MARBLE FORMATION

The outcrop of the Forest Marble Formation occupies an extensive tract of country in the south and south-east of the district, with many small outliers to the north-west. Overall, the formation is dominated by mudstone (indexed FMb on the map), but lenticular beds of limestone (ls) occur throughout and generally dominate the lower part (Figure 16). However, there is no consistent internal stratigraphy, and the succession is laterally very variable. The thickness of the formation is also highly variable from place to place. Overall, the formation thickens from a mean of about 15 m in the east to 25 m or more in the west and south-west, but additional local variations occur, so that the total thickness range within the district is probably between about 10 and 30 m. These local variations are a consequence of channelling at the base of the formation. Locally, the channels have depths of over 10 m amplitude and completely remove the Signet Member at the top of the White Limestone Formation (shown schematically in Figure 16). A good example of this occurs at Stow Road cutting [SP 048 071] (Richardson, 1911), where the Forest Marble infills a channel (described by Richardson as a 'syncline') which cuts down some 2.1 m into the Ardley Member of the White Limestone. At Sunhill Quarry North [SP 1166 0304], near Quenington, channels 10 to 20 m wide and several metres deep were formerly visible, cutting down through the basal Forest Marble and about 1 m into the underlying Signet Member. The sea-floor topography of late Signet Member times may have had a controlling influence on the distribution of the channels at the base of the formation, with channelling concentrated in existing lows (Sumbler, 1991). Where the Signet Member is particularly thick, for example in the Quenington area, it is commonly succeeded by mudstone higher in the Forest Marble succession (Figure 16), and not by channel limestone.

The limestones of the Forest Marble are typically cross-bedded, and characteristically weather to form large slabs in the soil, contrasting with the underlying White Limestone. They have been worked extensively, mainly for field walls and paving stones, and also locally for roofing tilestones. Richardson (1933) described many quarries, but most are now infilled. Small sections remain in many places, however, as detailed in the relevant BGS technical reports for the district; notable examples, illustrating large-scale cross-bedding, occur near Quenington [SP 145 042] and Betty's Grave, Poulton [SP 102 021]. The most common rock-type is a coarse- to medium-grained, shell-fragmental and ooidal grainstone, commonly containing scattered large shells of pectinaceans and oysters, together with intraformational mud-flakes and small pieces of lignite. A white to cream or pale grey limestone of this type, rather similar to Taynton Limestone in general appearance, is widely developed at the base of the formation. It probably infills the deepest channels, being associated with the thinnest developments of the Signet Member. This distinctive unit probably equates broadly with the limestones at the base of the Forest Marble in the Malmesbury district to the south-west, which have been variously termed Upper Rags or Acton Turville Beds (excluding the Reef Bed, see Signet Member above) (Cave, 1977; Penn and Wyatt, 1979). Higher in the formation, the shell material is dominated by broken oyster shells of a bluish tint, and lumachelles of unbroken oysters (*Praeexogyra hebridica*) also occur locally. Such rocks may be partly recrystallised, and the nature of the rock matrix obscure. The limestones are commonly interbedded with mudstone and are highly lenticular, with individual limestone units several metres thick commonly wedging out within a few hundred metres. As well as channel-filling units, some of these limestones may have been deposited as banks and shoals, flanked by deeper water where mud accumulated (Allen and Kaye, 1973; Holloway, 1983). Similar compact limestones with bluish shell fragments also occur locally at the base of the formation; these rocks may resemble lithologies in the underlying Signet Member, in which case separation of the White Limestone and Forest Marble formations is problematical.

The mudstones of the Forest Marble are generally greenish grey when fresh, but weather to a fawn or orange-brown clay, commonly containing tiny calcareous concretions ('race'). They may contain lenticles of brown or bluish grey, recrystallised, shell-fragmental grainstone, or grey to brown, fissile, fine-grained sandy limestone. Larger bodies of sandy limestone occur also, and these may weather to a sandy loam containing slabs of brown, rippled, sandy limestone, or with little or no brash at all. Examples occur at The Sands [SP 084 053] near Barnsley, around Donkeywell Farm [SP 135 039] near Quenington, at Upper Chedworth [SP 074 104] and near Eastleach Martin [SP 200 057].

The fauna of the Forest Marble Formation is dominated by oysters and other robust bivalves. Rhynchonellid brachiopods also occur, and debris of bryozoa and echinoderms is often a minor but conspicuous component of the limestones. Ammonites are very rare, but the type specimen of *Clydoniceras hollandi* indicating the lower part (Hollandi Subzone) of the Upper Bathonian Discus Zone, was obtained from the basal Forest Marble near Thames Head [ST 972 987], about 2 km to the south of the district (Buckman, 1925; Arkell, 1933a, p.270). *Siemiradzkia pseudorjazanensis* has been recorded from an apparently higher level in the Forest Marble at Blue House Quarry [SU 016 993] just south of Cirencester, but whether this indicates the Discus or Retrocostatum Zone is uncertain (Arkell, 1958; Torrens, 1974; Page, 1996).

## CORNBRASH FORMATION

In southern and eastern England, the Cornbrash Formation is the oldest deposit associated with the marine transgression that heralded a long period of marine deposition during Callovian and later Jurassic times. It consists of a complex succession of limestones, interbedded with marls, and is well known for local intraformational non-sequences; evidence for erosion includes pebble beds, hardgrounds, and reworked, bored and epifauna-encrusted fossils.

The Cornbrash has traditionally been divided into Lower Cornbrash and Upper Cornbrash, of latest Bathonian and earliest Callovian age respectively (Douglas and Arkell, 1928), and distinguished most readily by their ammonite and brachiopod faunas (see below). These two divisions form the basis of Page's (1989) Berry and Fleet members, which he endeavoured to define using modern lithostratigraphical criteria. However, they cannot be separated unequivocally by lithology alone.

The Cornbrash outcrop occupies about 20 km$^2$ in the south-east of the district, extending from the outskirts of Cirencester eastwards to Fairford [SP 15 01], and forming a well-developed but dissected dip slope north-eastwards from there. A number of small, faulted outliers occur to the north-west of the main outcrop, notably at Cirencester Park [SP 019 019] and in the Barnsley–Bibury area.

The Cornbrash is made up mainly of pale greyish, purplish or olive-brown, slightly argillaceous, micritic limestones, containing fine-grained shell debris and peloids (packstones and wackestones). Characteristically, the rock is heavily bioturbated, the burrows often being marked by paler marly micrite patches. Marl beds also occur throughout the formation. Generally, the limestones give rise to a rubbly brash and weather to a distinctive golden-brown colour. In many places, brown to purplish brown platy limestones with a rather sandy appearance occur in the upper part of the formation; this facies is probably restricted to the Upper Cornbrash (Douglas and Arkell, 1928, p.132). Over large areas of the dip slope, the soil comprises a brown loam with little limestone debris. This is probably composed largely of residual material from the Kellaways Formation.

In many areas, the Cornbrash produces a scarp feature rising above the Forest Marble outcrop, although in some places the mapped base of the formation, determined from field brash and augering, is set back from this feature by up to 150 m. Cryoturbation of the limestones into the underlying clays of the Forest Marble may make it difficult to position the basal Cornbrash boundary precisely. Generally, the Cornbrash outcrop is not significantly affected by cambering because of the relatively low amplitude of the topography in the south-east of the district, although minor cambering has been noted in the valleys near Southrop and Broughton Poggs [SP 235 039].

Within the district, the thickness of the Cornbrash is estimated to range from about 3 to 4.5 m, but there is little confirmation of this; although many wells penetrate the Cornbrash, reliable data are sparse. The best thickness data come from two boreholes [SP 1434 0061; SP 1304 0042] sited on the outcrop near Fairford, immediately to the south of the district, each proving Cornbrash to a depth of 4.2 m. The Meysey Hampton cored borehole, about 1.5 km beyond the southern boundary of the district, proved a total thickness of 4.4 m of Cornbrash. Elsewhere in England, the Cornbrash ranges from less than 0.5 m up to a maximum of about 10.5 m (Page, 1989). Within the district, the Lower and Upper Cornbrash are inferred to be of approximately equal thickness (see below).

Fossils are common at some levels in the Cornbrash; brachiopods and bivalves are the most common, and are locally abundant amongst the brash in ploughed fields. Ammonites occur much more rarely; only one (a *Choffatia*? from field brash near Fairford) was found during the recent survey. Some genera (mainly perisphinctids such as *Choffatia* and *Homoeoplanulites*) are common to both divisions of the Cornbrash, but other forms underpin the stratigraphical subdivision of the formation. The oppeliid *Clydoniceras* occurs only in the Lower Cornbrash (Discus Zone), and the sphaeroceratid *Macrocephalites* only in the Upper Cornbrash (Herveyi Zone). According to Page (1989), three successive *Macrocephalites* assemblages can be recognised in the Upper Cornbrash. The brachiopods, because of their relative abundance, are generally of more practical value for sub-

division (Douglas and Arkell, 1928). Four brachiopod biozones are recognised based on respective abundances of the index species; these are (from below) *Cererithyris intermedia* and *Obovothyris obovata* in the Lower Cornbrash, and *Microthyridina siddingtonensis* (named from Siddington [SU 03 99], immediately south of Cirencester town) and *Microthyridina lagenalis* in the Upper Cornbrash.

In the past, the limestones of the Cornbrash were dug for road-metal from extensive shallow quarries, and a number of sections were recorded by Blake (1905) and Woodward (1894). Many of these were obscured by the time that the countrywide review of the Cornbrash by Douglas and Arkell (1928; 1932) was published, and exposures are now very rare. Localities with diagnostic brachiopod faunas include a quarry [SP 0597 0189] south of Ampney Park, showing 1.5 m of pale brownish grey, rubbly wackestone of the Lower Cornbrash, in which Richardson (1933, p.80) recorded *Ornithella* [=*Obovothyris*] *obovata*. A quarry [probably SP 130 007] 'close to the Three Magpies Inn' (now demolished) showed 1.37 m of Lower Cornbrash, yielding fossils that included both *Cererithyris intermedia* and *Obovothyris obovata* as well as numerous *Clydoniceras* from near the base of the section (Douglas and Arkell, 1928, p.133). Richardson (1933, p.80) mentioned a quarry [probably SP 121 011] in the Lower Cornbrash (*O. obovata* Zone), '1¼ miles E 15° N of Poulton Church', and near Farhill Farm [SP 169 029], he recorded 1.45 m of Lower Cornbrash including a marl with *C. intermedia* and *O. obovata*. At Southrop Quarry [SP 201 029], Douglas and Arkell (1928, p.133) recorded 0.86 m of limestone with both these brachiopods. *Clydoniceras discus* (var. *hochstetteri*) from Fairford, indicative of the Lower Cornbrash, was figured by Buckman (1924), and another specimen from the Filkins [SP 249 043] area was figured by Arkell (1951).

The whole of the Cornbrash, about 4.0 m thick, was penetrated by the 1924 Lewis Lane Waterworks Borehole at Cirencester. The Upper Cornbrash yielded a *Homoeoplanulites*? (Page, 1988), erroneously recorded as a *Proplanulites* from the Kellaways Rock by Richardson (1925, 1933). *Homoeoplanulites* is also known from Fairford, again probably from the Upper Cornbrash (Buckman, 1924; Arkell, 1958; Page, 1989). Douglas and Arkell (1928, p.134) mentioned a section showing 0.91 m of 'very hard, purplish grey, flaggy limestone' of the Upper Cornbrash 'half a mile south-west of Poulton'. However, there is no sign of any quarry at this location [about SP 095 003], and the site in question is more likely to be an old roadside quarry south-east of Poulton [SP 106 008]. At Milton End Quarry [SP 1460 0078], Fairford, Douglas and Arkell (1928) recorded 2.08 m of Upper Cornbrash, comprising limestone with two beds of marl making up about half of the succession. The lowest 0.45 m of the section belong to the *M. siddingtonensis* Biozone, and the remainder to the succeeding *M. lagenalis* Biozone. A number of zonally (and sub-zonally) diagnostic ammonites are known from the Upper Cornbrash of Fairford (Page, 1988). In a quarry [SP 228 032] near Broughton Poggs, Douglas and Arkell (1928) noted 1.3 m of Upper Cornbrash, the lower 0.9 m comprising grey to purplish flaggy limestones. Marly rubble at the top of the section yielded fossils including *M. siddingtonensis*, with *M. lagenalis* in the overlying soil.

SEVEN

# Middle Jurassic: Kellaways and Oxford Clay formations

On the 1933 edition of Sheet 235, the Kellaways and Oxford Clay formations were not differentiated (being shown together as Oxford Clay), but the two formations are now mapped separately.

## KELLAWAYS FORMATION

The Kellaways Formation crops out to the south-east of the Cornbrash dip slope, near the southern margin of the district, where it forms a very low, discontinuous escarpment, e.g. to the west and east of Fairford [SP 137 007; SP 183 007] and south of Broughton Poggs [around SP 225 028]. Between these two areas, it is largely concealed beneath drift. In addition, downfaulted outliers occur near Southrop [around SP 210 040], Ampney St Peter [around SP 086 013] and Barnsley [around SP 093 061]. Boreholes prove that another outlier, entirely concealed by river terrace deposits, occurs beneath the town of Cirencester [around SP 023 020].

In the eastern part of the district, the Kellaways Formation is estimated to be about 10 to 13 m thick, and about 13 m has been proved in several boreholes just to the south of the district (e.g. at Down Ampney; Figure 19; Horton et al., 1989). Farther west, boreholes to the south of Cirencester show a much thicker succession, for example about 22 m near Ashton Keynes [SU 0637 9318], and about 25 m in the Sandpool Farm Borehole and in the formation's type area near Chippenham, some 25 km to the south of the district (Cave and Cox, 1975; Figure 20). The narrow zone of thickening coincides with the buried margin of the Worcester Basin which evidently still influenced sedimentation in the Mid to Late Jurassic. The formation is divisible into the Kellaways Clay and Kellaways Sand members.

### Kellaways Clay Member

In the type area, the Kellaways Clay is divisible into two parts, a lower unit of smooth mudstones, and an upper and thicker unit of silty and finely sandy mudstones. The latter unit is restricted to the Worcester Basin (Figure 20), so that throughout most of the Cirencester district, only the lower unit, corresponding to the Cayton Clay of Page (1989), is present. It consists of dark grey, smooth-textured, slightly silty, poorly fossiliferous mudstone with scattered pyritic traces. As elsewhere in southern England, the boundary with the underlying Cornbrash is marked by a coarsely shell-detrital marl, typically 0.4 m thick. This is taken herein as the basal bed of the Kellaways Clay, although in other accounts (e.g. Horton et al., 1989), it has been included in the Cornbrash. Its contact with the latter is gradational.

At outcrop, the Kellaways Clay is seen as a bluish grey to brown clay, producing heavy soils which contrast markedly with those of the underlying Cornbrash. Within the district it is estimated to be 3 to 4 m thick, and 3.7 to 3.9 m were proved at Down Ampney (Figure 19; Horton et al., 1989), about 4 km to the south. It appears to be substantially thicker beneath Cirencester, with some 7.3 m of 'dark blue clay' (base at 15.85 m (52 ft)) being recorded between river terrace deposits and Cornbrash in the 1924 Lewis Lane Borehole, illustrating the thickening of the succession into the Worcester Basin. Richardson's (1925, 1930, 1933) classification of this borehole is erroneous: there is no Oxford Clay at the site, and the unit classified by him as 'Kellaways Beds' is part of the Cornbrash. The occurrence of *Macrocephalites* ['*Ammonites macrocephalus*'] in an earlier borehole at the site (Harker, 1891; Woodward, 1895), together with other ammonite records from adjoining areas, indicates that the Kellaways Clay belongs to the Kamptus Subzone of the Lower Callovian Herveyi Zone (Page, 1989). Other fossils are generally restricted to bivalves, such as *Corbulomima*, *Modiolus* and nuculaceans, serpulids and procerithiid gastropods.

### Kellaways Sand Member

The Kellaways Sand consists of pale grey to orange and ochreous, fine-grained sand and argillaceous sand, patchily cemented into hard, lenticular masses of calcareous sandstone; the beds are commonly intensely bioturbated. At outcrop, it gives rise to a pale brown loam or light sandy soil, rarely containing small corroded fragments of sandstone. In a few places, the basal boundary with the Kellaways Clay Member is marked by a line of seepage. In boreholes at Down Ampney (Horton et al., 1989), the member is 10.1 to 10.5 m thick, but within the district it appears to be slightly thinner, probably about 7 to 9 m. Farther to the south and west, at the margin of the Worcester Basin, the lower part of the Kellaways Sand expands by intercalations of silty and finely sandy mudstone to form the sandy upper unit of the Kellaways Clay of the type area, where it makes up the greater part of the formation (Figure 20).

Generally, the member is poorly exposed, but has been sporadically revealed by gravel extraction. In 1994, drains [SP 185 001] in the bottom of the ARC Lechlade Quarry, immediately south of the district, showed up to 1 m of bluish grey silt and fine-grained clayey sand, containing sporadic small *Gryphaea*. Also present amongst excavated debris were pieces of hard, grey to pale brown, calcareous sandstone and large (typically 0.7 × 0.4 m), septarian, silty, argillaceous limestone ('cementstone') nodules. The sandstone yielded the ammonites *Cadoceras*, *Kepplerites* and *Proplanulites*, and bivalves including

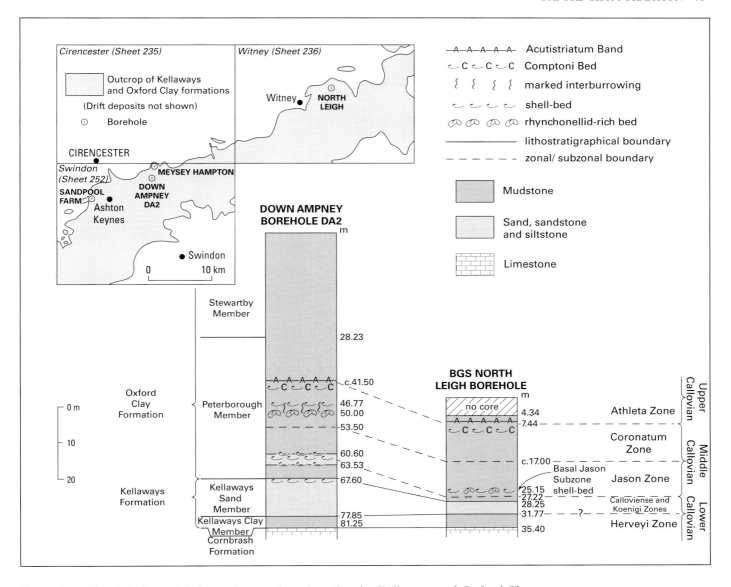

**Figure 19**  Simplified graphic logs of control sections for the Kellaways and Oxford Clay formations; Down Ampney Borehole DA2 (Horton et al., 1989) and BGS North Leigh Borehole (BGS files).

*Chlamys*, *Pleuromya alduini* and *Gryphaea* (*Bilobissa*). Some of the limestone nodules were very fossiliferous, with abundant bivalves, particularly *Anisocardia tenera* and/or *Rollierella minima* as well as *Neocrassina?*, *Nicaniella phillis*, *Pleuromya* and *Protocardia*, and rare ammonites including *Proplanulites*. Similar lithologies, comprising large bodies of calcareous sandstone with richly fossiliferous concretions, are better developed to the south-west of the district, including the formation's type area. Known as the 'Kellaways Rock', they are exposed in a disused railway cutting just south of Cirencester [SU 045 980] (Harker, 1884), and in the floor of gravel pits in the South Cerney area [SU 05 97]. Ammonites from the latter area indicate that the member belongs to the Koenigi and Calloviense zones (Page, 1989).

## OXFORD CLAY FORMATION

The Oxford Clay crops out only in the south-eastern corner of the district. Only the basal part of the formation is present, comprising about 30 m of strata that belong to the Peterborough Member (formerly known as the Lower Oxford Clay). The total thickness of the member was proved to be 39.4 m in Borehole DA2 at Down Ampney (Figure 19; Horton et al., 1989).

Where the outcrop is not concealed by river terrace deposits, the Oxford Clay produces a brown clay soil, and ditches commonly show smooth, pale yellow-brown and bluish grey mottled clay, containing small crystals and aggregates of selenite that result from the weathering of pyrite in the presence of calcium carbonate. At greater

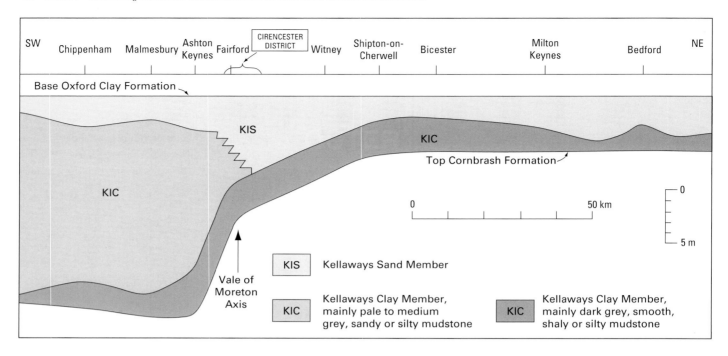

**Figure 20** Thickness and facies variation in the Kellaways Formation in the region around the Cirencester district, illustrating the influence of the Vale of Moreton Axis.

depths, where the formation is less weathered, as in borehole cores, medium to pale grey mudstone is interbedded with olive to brownish grey, shaly, moderately fissile, shelly bituminous mudstone with pyritic shell beds and thin ammonite-rich layers. The member is highly fossiliferous with abundant ammonites (mainly *Kosmoceras* on which the standard zonation is based) and bivalves. The latter, particularly nuculaceans and *Melea-*

*grinella*, commonly occur in abundance in thin shell beds. A thin, pale olive-brown argillaceous limestone ('cementstone') that has been traced for a short distance on the hill [SP 228 019] north-east of Little Faringdon, is though to be the Acutistriatum Band, marking the base of the Upper Callovian Athleta Zone. At Down Ampney, this bed occurs 26.1 m above the base of the Oxford Clay (Figure 19; Horton et al., 1989).

# EIGHT

# Quaternary

## NORTHERN DRIFT FORMATION

Scattered pebbles and cobbles of quartz, quartzite and other exotic lithologies (including small quantities of flint) have been recorded on high ground at various localities in the north Cotswolds (Hull, 1855, 1857; Lucy, 1872; Dines in Richardson, 1929, 1933). For the most part, these pebbles are remnants of the Northern Drift, deposits of clayey sand and gravel and gravelly clay which occur principally to the east and north-east of the Cirencester district, in areas adjoining the valley of the River Evenlode. Because of the presence of far-travelled rocks, the Northern Drift was generally thought to be of glacial origin. However, it is now understood that most of its deposits are ancient river terrace sediments, commonly much modified by post-depositional effects such as leaching, cryoturbation and solifluction (Hey, 1986). The deposits were laid down in early and mid Pleistocene times, by an ancestral Thames–Evenlode river with headwaters in the English Midlands and Welsh Borders, far beyond the present source of the Evenlode at Moreton-in-Marsh [SP 206 114] (Whiteman and Rose, 1992). Most of the pebbles can be matched with material in the conglomerates of the Triassic Kidderminster Formation ('Bunter Pebble Beds') and Devonian Old Red Sandstone which crop out in these areas.

Within the district, remanié Northern Drift deposits are best preserved on the watershed ridge between the rivers Evenlode and Windrush. There, in fields bordering the A424 road between Fifield and Taynton, rounded pebbles of white to yellow vein quartz, with subordinate quartzite and rarer chert, gritstone and Lias ironstone, are common in the soil which is derived principally from the local White Limestone Formation bedrock. The pebbles occur mainly higher than 180 m above OD, reaching 206 m above OD at Blackheath Clump [SP 241 154], just beyond the eastern margin of the district. In a quarry [SP 2398 1713] at Tangley cross-roads, now largely infilled and completely overgrown, Callaway (1905), Richardson (1907b, 1927) and Dines (in Richardson, 1933, p.84), described pebbly soil and subsoil overlying White Limestone, the latter containing fissures infilled with yellowish brown clay with erratic pebbles of the types mentioned above (see Richardson, 1933, pl. 6). The clay was interpreted as a 'boulder clay' (i.e. till), reinforcing the glacial hypothesis for the Northern Drift. More probably, however, the fissure-filling clay is derived from a bed in the White Limestone, with an admixture of Northern Drift gravel. Several clay and marl beds occur in the White Limestone in the neighbourhood of the quarry, and give rise to a rather clayey soil in which Northern Drift pebbles are conspicuous. From its elevation (about 192 m above OD) and

composition (with a particularly high ratio of quartz to quartzite pebbles), the Tangley deposit is assigned to the Waterman's Lodge Member, of early Pleistocene age (Table 13; Hey, 1986; Whiteman and Rose, 1992). Younger members of the Northern Drift association are not preserved within the district but occur just to the north and east.

Elsewhere in the district, scattered exotic pebbles and cobbles, mainly of quartzite, are widespread, even on the highest ground, well away from the Evenlode valley. Some of the pebbles have undoubtedly been transported by man, perhaps having seen use as pot-boilers, sling or hammer-stones, or brought in more recently with manure or animal feeds. However, their distribution is so widespread that it seems likely that in many cases they derive from a former drift cover. To the north of the district, they have been recorded at elevations up to and above 300 m above OD (Richardson, 1929), and so may be older than the earliest (Waterman's Lodge) terrace unit recognised so far in the Northern Drift succession.

One such high-level drift remnant, at 250 m above OD, was found during archaeological work at Hazleton Long Barrow [SP 073 189], where pebbles of quartzite, quartz and subordinate Lias siltstone and ironstone were found at a concentration of one per 9.5 m$^2$ (Worssam, 1987). Partly because the pebble suite differs from that typical of the Northern Drift as described by Hey (1986), notably in its higher quartzite:quartz ratio, Worssam (1987) suggested a glacial origin for these deposits. In the past, such remnants of the most ancient parts of the Northern Drift were presumably more widespread, and are probably the source of the exotic pebbles found in the younger terrace gravels of the Thames and its tributaries (see below).

## RIVER TERRACE DEPOSITS

River Terrace deposits, comprising ancient fluvial sediments, occur chiefly along the rivers in the south-eastern part of the district. Four separate aggradations have been recognised from the height distribution of the deposits (Figure 21), but all are lithologically similar, being composed principally of pebbles of local Middle Jurassic limestone.

The oldest deposits, those of the Fourth and Third terraces, occur as dissected remnants on low hills in the south-east. These appear to relate to former courses of the River Thames, which now flows a few kilometres outside the district, illustrating the gradual south-eastward migration of that river concurrent with down-cutting through Quaternary time. The younger Second

**Table 13**
Quaternary
deposits of the
Cirencester
district in their
chronological
context.

| System/Series | | | British Stage | Representative deposits in the Cirencester district | Oxygen Isotope Stage | Age (ka) |
|---|---|---|---|---|---|---|
| QUATERNARY | PLEISTOCENE | | HOLOCENE — FLANDRIAN | Alluvium    Tufa | 1 | |
| | | Upper | DEVENSIAN | Northmoor Member (1st Terrace deposits)    Rissington Member    Cheltenham Sand and Gravel    Head | 2 | |
| | | | | | 3 | |
| | | | | | 4 | |
| | | | | | a | |
| | | | | | c    5 | 100 |
| | | | IPSWICHIAN | Summertown-Radley Member (2nd Terrace deposits)    ?Sherborne Member | e | |
| | | | | | 6 | |
| | | Middle | WOLSTONIAN | | 7 | 200 |
| | | | | Wolvercote Member (3rd Terrace deposits) | 8 | |
| | | | HOXNIAN | | 9 | 300 |
| | | | ANGLIAN | Hanborough Member (4thTerrace deposits) | 10 | |
| | | | | | 11 | 400 |
| | | | | | 12 | |
| | | | CROMERIAN COMPLEX — NORTHERN | | 13 | 500 |
| | | | | | 14 | |
| | | | DRIFT | | 15 | 600 |
| | | | | | 16 to ?21 | |
| | | Lower | FORMATION | | ?22 | not to scale |
| | | | | Waterman's Lodge Member | | |
| | | | | | to c.63 | 1600 to c.2000 |

Chronostratigraphical framework from Sumbler (1996). The ages of the various deposits are very
poorly known in detail, and there are major gaps within the Quaternary record of the district;
these are of unknown extent and consequently are not indicated on this diagram. The even-
numbered oxygen isotope stages are cold or glacial phases; the odd-numbered ones are temperate
or interglacial phases.

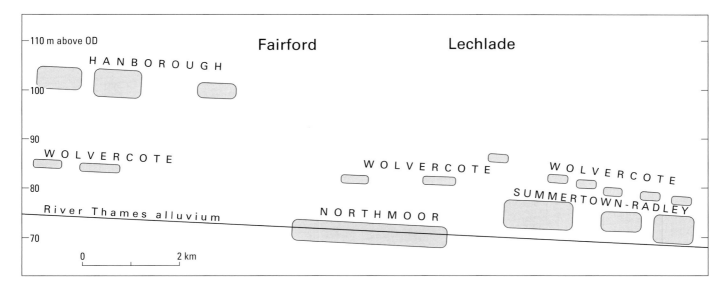

**Figure 21**   Long profile illustrating the height ranges and mutual relationships of the terrace deposits of the River Thames in the south-eastern part of the district.

and First terrace deposits relate more obviously to the modern drainage system. They are particularly extensive in the lower reaches of the valleys of the rivers Coln and Leach, where they include important commercial resources of sand and gravel; the resource potential of these deposits was assessed by Robson (1975, 1976; see Chapter 2). Less extensive river deposits occur in the Churn valley at Cirencester, and along the River Windrush at the southern end of the Vale of Bourton. Preservation of terrace deposits in the steep-sided valleys of streams elsewhere is very localised, but is most common on the inside bends (slip-off slopes) of incised meanders. More generally, the valleys seem to have been flushed clean of gravel deposits during downcutting episodes.

Correlation of the deposits in the south-east of the district with the well-established succession of the River Thames (Bridgland, 1994) is fairly certain, but the same cannot be said of the more isolated deposits in the tributary valleys, where the deposits of different aggradations are not readily distinguished. For these, assignment to either the First or Second Terrace is of purely local significance, and no correlation with the terraces of the River Thames is implied, unless explicitly stated in the following account.

### River Thames and lower Coln and Leach valleys

FOURTH TERRACE DEPOSITS (HANBOROUGH MEMBER)

Apart from the Northern Drift, the oldest river terrace deposits occur on the southern margin of the district, west of Fairford [SP 122 008; SP 139 006]. These form parts of hill-top plateaux at elevations of about 105 m above OD, as seen around Meysey Hampton [SP 121 003] and Waiten Hills [SP 136 003]. From their location, they appear to relate to a former course of the River

Thames, which has now migrated 3 to 4 km southwards and cut down some 30 m, the level of the modern flood-plain being about 75 m above OD at Castle Eaton [SU 145 960] (Figure 21). On the basis of their elevation, these deposits are equated with the Hanborough Member of the Oxford area, which is probably mainly of early Oxygen Isotope (OI) Stage 10 age (Table 13; Bridgland, 1994; Sumbler, 1995d), herein regarded as part of the Anglian Stage.

The deposits consist of gravel, overlain by a loamy soil. The gravel is made up largely of limestone pebbles, generally 20 to 50 mm in diameter, with sparse quartz and quartzite (about 1 per cent) and rarer brownish flints or cherts. These exotic lithologies are probably derived from the older Northern Drift (see above), but sporadic grey or white flints are probably artefacts brought in by man and are younger than the gravel deposit itself. Locally, lenses within the gravel are cemented by calcium carbonate into a conglomerate (calcrete), which may be brought to the surface by ploughing. The gravels were formerly exposed to a depth of 1.5 m in a small gravel pit [SP 1227 0092], and boreholes just south of the margin of the district show that the deposits reach 4 to 5 m in thickness.

North-west of Fairford [SP 139 015], quartzite pebbles are quite common in a loamy soil, which also contains sparse rounded limestone pebbles as well as debris of the Cornbrash bedrock. The deposits reach an elevation of 105 m above OD, and are probably a remnant of the Hanborough Member. The relative abundance of quartzite pebbles may be due to loss, through leaching, of most of the limestone pebbles. It is possible that pockets of less altered gravel occur in places, but a 'gravel pit' [SP 1402 0145] marked on early editions of the Ordnance Survey topographic map appears to be a Cornbrash quarry, and 2.2 m of gravel noted at this locality by Robson (1975, map) was not confirmed during the recent survey of the district. Similar, partly decalcified remanié gravel occurs on a hill top [SP 230 024] north-east of Little Faringdon.

### THIRD TERRACE DEPOSITS (WOLVERCOTE MEMBER)

The Third Terrace of the River Thames is represented by a line of small outliers of gravel that cap low hills in the south-eastern corner of the district [e.g. SP 182 006; SP 198 010; SP 208 020; SP 225 015; SP 239 022]. These remnant deposits have surface levels typically around 82 m above OD, but range up to 87 m or more, lying some 10 m to 15 m above the present level of the Thames floodplain (Figure 21). On this basis, they appear to equate with the Wolvercote Member of the Thames terrace suite, of which the deposits in this area probably date mainly from the latter part of OI Stage 10 (late Anglian; Table 13; Sumbler, 1995d). The deposits comprise sandy, clayey, limestone-rich gravel with some flints, and probably do not exceed 2 m in thickness.

### SECOND TERRACE DEPOSITS (SUMMERTOWN–RADLEY MEMBER)

Extensive gravel terraces occur in the south-eastern corner of the district, and have been worked extensively between Lechlade [SP 205 000] and Little Faringdon [SP 225 015] (Chapter 2). These terrace deposits, typically 4 to 6 m in thickness, apparently relate to both the ancestral River Thames, and to its tributaries, the rivers Coln and Leach. At Lechlade, close to the modern Thames which flows some 2 km beyond the corner of the district, the terrace surface lies at 76 to 78 m above OD, some 7 m or so above the modern floodplain (Figure 21). Consequently, it is assigned to the Second Terrace of the Thames, formed upon gravels of the Summertown–Radley Member. This member is known to be a composite unit that includes sediments of various ages, probably ranging from OI stages 8 (early 'Wolstonian') to possibly 5a (early Devensian) (Table 13; Bridgland, 1994).

Near Lechlade, the base of the Second Terrace deposits is generally slightly higher than the surface of the younger First Terrace deposits, so that there is a 'rock-step' (bedrock outcrop) between them as also seen in places within the district [e.g. SP 189 008]. When traced upstream along the River Leach and other Thames tributary valleys, such as the Broadwell Brook, however, the terrace surfaces rise less steeply than the floodplains of the rivers. Thus, near Southrop [SP 213 030] and Broughton Poggs [SP 235 037], the terrace is only 1 to 2 m above the adjoining modern floodplain, and gravel pits there [e.g. SP 213 028], formerly showed the gravels to extend beneath the level of the alluvium. This fact led Briggs et al. (1985, p.26; fig. 12) to assign the terrace gravels around Lechlade to the younger Northmoor Member, but the apparent continuity of the Second Terrace surface suggests that their classification is incorrect. Along the River Coln, convergence with the modern floodplain is less pronounced, with the Second Terrace at Fairford [SP 146 008] standing some 1.5 m higher than the First Terrace.

The Second Terrace deposits are composed of limestone gravel, overlain by a brown loam soil. Flints occur rarely, as do sporadic quartz and quartzite pebbles, presumably reworked from older deposits. In addition, silty material has been noted at some localities, probably filling channels in the gravels.

### FIRST TERRACE DEPOSITS (NORTHMOOR MEMBER)

First Terrace gravels, contiguous with those of the River Thames, occur on either side of the River Coln downstream from Fairford [SP 151 010], on the southern margin of the district. They are assigned to the Northmoor Member, mainly of Devensian (OI Stages 4 to 2) age (Table 13; Bridgland, 1994). Near Fairford, the terrace, designated 1Na on the 1:50 000 map, stands 1 to 2 m above the Coln floodplain, and it maintains this height relationship when traced downstream to the Thames (see Figure 21). Boreholes and pits sited on the terrace have proved the deposits to average about 3 m in thickness, but they exceed 7 m locally (Robson, 1975), and are also known to underlie the alluvium of the modern floodplain. The gravels have been extensively exploited in the past, and are currently (1996) being extracted in the ARC Lechlade Quarry [around SP 184 000], just beyond the southern margin of the district (Plate 11). In 1994, a section there [SP 1864 0007] showed up to 5 m of white to pale brown, moderately well-bedded, poorly sorted gravel, with cryoturbation festoons in the top metre or so, overlain by 0.4 m of pale brown, calcareous loam and dark brown, humic topsoil. The gravel, composed mainly of flat limestone pebbles with rare quartzite and quartz pebbles and brown flints, contains sporadic ferruginous bands and, locally at the base, lenses of humic and peaty silt and fine sand.

Deposits at the margins of the First Terrace outcrop, designated 1Nb on the 1:50 000 map, occur to the north of the A417 road, near Thornhill Farm [SP 181 006]. The pattern of the outcrop indicates that they relate to a channel passing around the north and east sides of Thorn Hill. The deposits, consisting of yellowish brown, clayey limestone gravel, are probably up to about 2 m thick and form a bench about 1 m above Terrace 1Na (see above). Thus, their base is several metres higher, and presumably substantially older, than that of the thick deposits of Terrace 1Na. The two facets of the first terrace, which are widely developed along the Thames, may relate to two aggradations recognised within the Northmoor Member (Briggs et al., 1985); these are of Mid Devensian and Late Devensian age.

Gravels that probably belong to the Northmoor Member are present beneath the alluvium of the lower River Leach; they were worked from an extensive pit [SP 217 015] near Little Faringdon during the 1970s. The pit is now partly backfilled and restored, but up to 3.5 m of limestone gravel were formerly visible beneath alluvial silts. A radiocarbon date of 28 400 ± 1000 years BP was obtained from silty peat in the lower part of the deposits at this locality (Briggs et al., 1985, table 2), but significantly younger dates of 9510 ± 120 and 2770 ± 100 years BP from organic material at higher levels may relate to the alluvium.

**Plate 11**   Sand and gravel working in the Northmoor Member (First Terrace deposits) of the River Coln, immediately south of the district (1995) [SU 182 998].

The deposits here are approximately 5 m thick and are composed chiefly of limestone pebbles (GS535).

## River Churn

Terrace deposits composed of limestone gravel and calcareous sand form a broad bench on the west bank of the River Churn at Cirencester, on which the older central part of the town is built [SP 026 018]. The terrace surface is generally little more than 1 m above the adjacent floodplain. The thickness of the deposits appears to be highly variable; boreholes and trial pits indicate that the deposits may be up to 4.75 m thick locally, but elsewhere may be very thin or absent, perhaps suggesting that the deposits lie in channels. More restricted terraces occur at Stratton [SP 018 032], Baunton [SP 024 042] and upstream as far as Perrott's Brook [SP 019 061]. They have been worked on a small scale in the past at several localities. A trial pit [SP 017 031] proved gravel to a depth of 4.5 m without bottoming the deposits, and so these gravels evidently extend beneath the alluvium, like those in Cirencester town.

Being the only terrace developed along the Churn, the deposits are assigned to the First Terrace by default. They probably correspond to the Northmoor Member of the Thames but may include older units (cf. the River Leach).

## Upper River Coln

Apart from the deposits in the lower reaches of the Coln, below Fairford (see above), river terraces occur in only three places along the River Coln. At Hutnage [SP 056 139], a deposit with an upper surface up to 4 m above the modern floodplain comprises subangular, very poorly sorted limestone gravel. A pit there formerly exposed 1.8 m of buff-coloured, partially cemented limestone gravel (Dines, in Richardson, 1933, p.88). At Stowell Mill [SP 082 128], a similar gravel deposit lies at about the same level above the alluvium and, on the opposite side of the valley a little farther downstream [SP 082 125], a tract of gravelly sand lies about 1 m above the floodplain. None of these deposits is likely to exceed more than 3 to 4 m in thickness.

## Upper River Leach

Terraces made up of platy limestone gravel, ranging from 1.5 to 2 m above the floodplain, occur in the Leach valley near Eastleach Martin [SP 203 052]. The deposits have been worked from small pits at two localities. Although assigned to the First Terrace, correlation with the Thames succession is uncertain. Given the convergence of the Second Terrace with the alluvium when traced up the Leach valley (see above), it is possible that the deposits may equate with the Summertown–Radley Member rather than the younger Northmoor Member (First Terrace deposits) of the Thames.

## River Windrush

Two gravel terraces have been recognised along the River Windrush and its tributary the Sherborne Brook, on the Lias outcrop in the Vale of Bourton. They are absent downstream, where the valley narrows as it cuts through the Middle Jurassic limestone succession, and so correlation with the Thames succession downstream is uncertain. The two terraces are assumed to represent two separate aggradations; the deposits beneath the First Terrace are herein named the Rissington Member, and those beneath the higher and older Second Terrace are named the Sherborne Member. Recent BGS work suggests that both units are represented within the 'Bourton Terrace' of Briggs (1973, pp.336–344, and in Roe, 1976), which is extensive just beyond the northern margin of the district.

### SECOND TERRACE DEPOSITS (SHERBORNE MEMBER)

Within the district, the Sherborne Member occurs as a small remanié outcrop [SP 1880 1690] near Great Rissington, and as thicker and more extensive deposits immediately north of the confluence with the Sherborne Brook. The deposits form sloping spreads that grade gently towards the river, but where the terrace top surface is best preserved [SP 184 153; SP 184 157], it lies approximately 5 m above the modern floodplain. At their riverward margin, the deposits are separated from the alluvium by a rock-step, 3 to 4 m high.

The deposits, probably no more than 1.5 to 2 m thick, comprise limestone gravel, overlain by a reddish, decalcified loam. The gravels have been worked on a small scale in the past; Dines (in Richardson, 1933, p.88) noted a pit [SP 1852 1506] which showed 0.9 m of compact limestone gravel, with sand lenticles and rare small pebbles of quartz and quartzite. He also recorded 'Neolithic' worked flints, which were also noted on the surface during the recent survey; these artefacts are probably younger than the gravel itself.

### First Terrace deposits (Rissington Member)

The Rissington Member is best developed at Bourton-on-the-Water [SP 175 203], just beyond the northern margin of the district, where it has been extensively worked. Within the district, small outcrops adjoin the floodplain on the west bank of the Windrush [SP 176 193; SP 177 187], a more extensive outcrop with a well-developed terrace form lies on the east bank [SP 184 176], and small outcrops occur on the south bank of the Sherborne Brook [SP 150 151; SP 185 147]. The deposits of the Rissington Member comprise gravel of sub-rounded limestone pebbles, generally of 10 to 40 mm grade, much like those of the Sherborne Member. The surface of these deposits extends up to about 2.5 m above the floodplain, but slopes gently towards the river, where there is typically a step of about 1.5 m down to the floodplain. The gravels extend beneath the alluvium, so there is no rock-step between the alluvium and the terrace, contrary to the depiction on the previous (1933) edition of Sheet 235. The extensive Santhill gravel pit [SP 179 192], now flooded, worked these suballuvial gravels; there, and in the Bury Barns Pit [SP 177 205] to the north, they may be up to 5 m thick. Their upper part is probably reworked, and as such can be regarded as contemporaneous with the alluvium (see below).

A lens of silt in the gravels at Bury Barns [SP 177 208] has yielded molluscs and pollen indicative of cold interstadial conditions (Gilbertson in Roe, 1976, p.18; Brown et al., 1980). The overlying gravels showed ice-wedge casts and cryoturbation involutions, presumably dating from the Late Devensian glacial maximum, suggesting that the organic silt layer may be of mid-Devensian age (?OI Stage 3), compatible with a radiocarbon age of 34 500 ± 800 years BP, obtained from the tusk of a woolly mammoth (*Mammuthus primigenius*) found in the gravels at Little Rissington Sewage Works [SP 181 200] (O'Neil and Shotton, 1974; Briggs in Roe 1976, p.13; Briggs et al., 1985, p.32; Brown et al., 1980). Mammoth remains have also been recorded from the Rissington Member at Santhill [SP 179 192] and Bury Barns (O'Neil and Shotton, 1974). On the basis of these data, it seems likely that the Rissington Member equates with the Northmoor Member of the Thames (Table 13), into which the

Windrush flows near Standlake [SP 403 013]. The older Sherborne Member may therefore include representatives of older parts of the Northmoor Member, the Summertown–Radley Member, or indeed older units such as the Hanborough Member. At Chessels pit [SP 174 226], 2.5 km to the north of the district, gravels probably belonging to the Sherborne Member have yielded bones and teeth of both woolly mammoth and woolly rhinoceros (*Coelodonta antiquitatis*) (Richardson and Sandford, 1960; O'Neil and Shotton, 1974). These species are typical of mid and late Pleistocene cold stages in general.

## ALLUVIUM

An alluvial floodplain is present along the course of all the principal rivers and streams of the district. Generally, the floodplains are very narrow because the streams are constrained within steep-sided valleys cut through the limestones of the Inferior Oolite and Great Oolite groups. The floodplains are broader where the rivers cross the outcrops of less resistant mudstone rocks. Thus, the broadest expanses of alluvium occur along the course of the River Windrush in the Vale of Bourton, where the floodplain is over 500 m wide in places. There, the alluvium is a brown, silty clay looking much like weathered Lias, from which it is probably in large part derived. It is overlain by a dark brown, humic, loamy clay soil. This loam and clay seldom exceeds 0.8 to 1.2 m in thickness, and deep ditches almost invariably enter limestone gravel below, probably representing the reworked upper part of the Rissington Member (see above). These reworked gravels, down to the level of the base of the river channel, may be regarded as contemporaneous with the overlying alluvial clay, which is inferred to be wholly of Holocene age. The floodplain is still building up to a minor extent, with thin layers of alluvial mud being left on the fields after floods.

Along the rivers Churn, Coln and Leach and their minor tributaries, the floodplain is generally less than 100 m wide, and the alluvium infills a shallow channel, probably no more than 3 m deep at maximum. Typically, the alluvium is a brown peaty loam or brownish grey clay, commonly containing a proportion of tufa, i.e. calcium carbonate precipitated from the calcareous spring water that contributes to the flow of all the rivers. This tufa may be present as both disseminated mud and discrete pellets, and is locally so abundant that it dominates the sediment. Dredgings show that the alluvial loam and clay, generally no more than 1 to 1.5 m thick, is commonly underlain by a lag deposit of gravel that is composed of small rounded pebbles of locally derived limestone, rarely more than about 1 m thick. These gravels may in part be reworked from the terrace gravels present in places along the rivers. Such gravels have been worked on a small scale in a few places, e.g. at Ablington, where a section in an old pit [SP 1081 0733] showed 0.6 m of poorly sorted gravel, with pebbles up to 70 mm in diameter. The alluvial channel of the river is generally incised into bedrock, except in the lower reaches of the rivers where it is cut into thicker sub-alluvial gravels of the Northmoor Member (see above)

Tracts of alluvium that stand slightly higher than the modern, active floodplain occur in a few places. Designated 'Older Alluvium', they represent early phases of floodplain development, and can be regarded as Holocene river terraces. Near the northern margin of the district [SP 174 194], Older Alluvium infills an abandoned loop of the River Windrush; its surface level is approximately 0.5 m above the active floodplain. It comprises reddish brown clayey loam underlain by limestone gravel which probably belongs to the Rissington Member. Small areas of Older Alluvium also occur in the valley of the River Leach, near Southrop [SP 202 035], comprising grey to reddish brown clay.

## HEAD AND DRY VALLEY DEPOSITS

Head, comprising accumulations of solifluction debris of periglacial origin, together with more recent hillwash (colluvium), occurs in most of the valleys and on the gentler slopes of the district. Only the thicker, laterally more extensive deposits are indicated on the map. Their lithology varies according to the materials from which they were derived.

The most extensive head deposits occur in broad, minor valleys on the lower slopes of the Vale of Bourton. They comprise brown silty clay, evidently made up principally of reworked Lias siltstones and mudstones, and generally contain a scatter of limestone or ironstone pebbles derived from the Marlstone Rock and Inferior Oolite upslope. Thicknesses probably seldom exceed 2 m. Ditch sections show poorly sorted clayey gravel beneath the clayey superficial layers; locally [e.g. SP 1911 1837], this gravel is composed of black ironstone fragments, at least some of which appear to be altered limestone. Other head deposits blanket some of the hill slopes in the south-

east of the district [e.g. SP 200 010; SP 238 023]. They are composed of brown silty clay commonly passing down into clayey sandy gravel, and were evidently derived mainly from the terrace gravels which cap the hills, together with the local Oxford Clay bedrock.

### DRY VALLEYS

A characteristic topographical feature of the district, and indeed of the limestone terrain of the Cotswolds in general, is the abundance of dry valleys, i.e. valleys which, because of the permeability of the bedrock, do not normally contain streams, except perhaps during wet winters when the water table is particularly high (see Chapter 2). Such valleys generally form the upper reaches of, or are 'tributary' to those occupied by more or less permanent streams. Notable examples include the upper reaches of the valley of the Ampney Brook or Winterwell, north-west of Barnsley [SP 078 051], the valley system around Aldsworth [SP 156 100], and the upper reaches of the Sherborne Brook valley above Farmington [SP 147 152]. Parts of the valley of the River Leach are also normally dry (Plate 12). Such dry valleys are typically floored by a flat, floodplain-like tract of brown loamy clay overlying limestone gravel. These deposits, probably up to 2 m thick in places, are evidently an ancient alluvium. In most cases, the margins of this alluvial fill are covered by an accumulation of solifluction material composed of angular limestone debris, and in the steeper upper reaches of the valleys, this may entirely obscure any alluvial material present. For this reason, all of the deposits of the dry valleys are indicated as head on 1:50 000 Sheet 235.

The form and distribution of these valleys, and the nature of the associated deposits, leaves no doubt that they were formed by water. They were probably initiated during cold periods of the Quaternary, when the presence of thick permafrost rendered the ground impermeable. Once a valley system was established,

**Plate 12**   Dry valley, a characteristic feature of the Cotswold landscape.

This valley [SP 195 067], cut through limestone of the Great Oolite Group north of Eastleach Martin, is dry through most of the year, but during wet seasons, forms part of the course of the River Leach. The Leach is seldom more than a small stream, but the form and scale of this valley indicates erosion by a substantial river (A15450).

downcutting would proceed even in the absence of permafrost, whenever the groundwater levels were high
enough to produce surface streams in the valleys. The
current dry state of the valleys may relate both to lower
precipitation rates than in the past, and to a gradual fall
in the groundwater levels due to landscape evolution: as
the principal rivers cut downwards, they naturally tend to
lower the water table, cutting off the water supply to
their own headwater valleys. In some cases, the disappearance of streams in certain valleys may be a relatively
recent phenomenon, perhaps in part related to current
groundwater pumping practice (see Chapter 2). In other
cases, the valleys may not have seen running water since
Pleistocene times; in such cases, 'tributary' valleys may
'hang' above the present active stream valleys, i.e. are
graded to a level somewhat higher than the present
streamway, indicating a considerable amount of down-
cutting in the main valley since the tributary stream was
last active.

## TUFA

Tufa is a calcareous deposit, precipitated from spring
water that is saturated with calcium carbonate as a result
of percolation through limestone rocks. Deposits of tufa
are present around many of the springs of the area,
commonly forming a coating around rocks, pebbles and
plant material, and in some cases forming a substantial
mound or 'apron'. Although tufa is still being deposited
today, the main period of formation was probably in
earlier Flandrian times (Table 13), when the climate was
warmer than at present. Few of the deposits are of sufficient extent to be shown on Sheet 235. In the south-
eastern part of the district, however, more extensive
outcrops of tufa are presumed to relate to former dip
slope springs that rose where the Cornbrash Formation
dips beneath the Kellaways Clay. The largest outcrop is
that north-east of Great Lemhill Farm [SP 212 022],
forming a mound up to 1.5 m high of tufaceous silt. The
deposit extends beneath the adjoining alluvium of the
River Leach, where it has probably been partially
reworked by the river. Elsewhere in the district, the
alluvium of the river floodplains may contain minor
lenses of tufa (see Alluvium). Some of the other deposits,
such as that near Common Barn [SP 219 028], extend
onto river terrace gravels, and often impregnate the
gravel itself.

## PEAT

Minor growths of peat occur in association with springs,
or on poorly drained ground such as that commonly
associated with landslip. Additionally, minor lenses of
peat may occur within the alluvium of the floodplains in
some places. The only area of peat large enough to
depict on Sheet 235 is that near Southrop [SP 207 027].
The deposits, up to 1.5 m thick, overlie tufa and river
terrace gravels adjoining the floodplain of the River
Leach.

## CHELTENHAM SAND AND GRAVEL

Deposits in the north-western corner of the district are
part of an extensive spread of sand and gravel which
underlies much of Cheltenham. Within the district, the
deposits are composed of fine- to medium-grained,
generally unbedded quartz sand, with seams of poorly
sorted limestone gravel which dominate the lower part.
Except where dissected by streams, the surface of the
deposits is of fairly low relief, but overall, slopes gently
westwards to the Vale of Gloucester. The Cheltenham
Sand and Gravel is very variable in thickness as a result of
channelling at the base, but reaches a probable maximum
of about 10 m. It is currently exposed in the disused
railway cutting at Little Herbert's [SO 9652 1967] where
3.5 m of yellow-brown, medium-grained sand with
limestone and ironstone gravel rest on Lias clay. Former
exposures in the area were recorded by Richardson (1913,
1929, 1933). At the former Coxhorne Pit [SO 981 199],
deposits comprised 2.7 m of subangular limestone gravel
containing a clay 'lenticle' at one point. Farther west, pits
[SO 9542 1997] bordering the railway cutting exposed
1.2 m of sand and loam resting on 4.6 m of limestone
gravel with seams of pink quartz sand (see Richardson
1929, plate 5). Remains of 'mammoth' and 'deer' were
collected here; a mammoth tooth was also obtained from
an excavation [SO 964 208] from the lower gravelly part
of the deposits at Charlton Kings, just outside the district
(Richardson and Sandford, 1961).

The deposits are evidently composite; the lower,
gravelly part (the Cheltenham Gravel, corresponding
essentially to the Fan Gravel of Worssam et al., 1989) is
composed predominantly of Middle Jurassic limestones,
together with a component of ironstone, limestone and
reworked fossils from the Lias. It is evidently of very local
origin, and probably accumulated as a solifluction apron,
possibly with some fluvial reworking, at the foot of the
Cotswold scarp. (Tomlinson, 1940; Briggs, 1975;
Worssam et al., 1989). The overlying Cheltenham Sand is
dominantly an aeolian deposit, probably derived in large
part from the terraces of the River Severn, which form
broad expanses only a few kilometres west of Cheltenham (Briggs, 1975). Again, the material has probably
been partially reworked by fluvial processes.

The age of the Cheltenham Sand and Gravel is
uncertain. From the inferred depositional environment
and limited faunal evidence, the deposits accumulated
principally during cold stages of the Quaternary, and it is
likely that the Cheltenham Sand and Gravel is very largely
of Devensian age (Table 13). From the relationships of the
deposits to local rivers, Briggs (1975) inferred correlation
with the Beckford Terrace deposits near Bredon Hill, some
15 km to the north. A radiocarbon date of $27\,650 \pm 250$
years BP was obtained from peaty material in the lower part
of the sand unit there. On this basis, the Cheltenham Sand
probably equates broadly with the Northmoor Member of
the Thames succession. In mode of formation, the underlying Cheltenham Gravel is analogous to gravels at Bourton-
on-the-Water which grade into the Sherborne Member of
the River Windrush, and which may relate to the older
Summertown–Radley Member (see above).

# NINE

# Structure

## FAULTS AND FOLDS

On a broad scale, the structure of the Jurassic rocks seen at outcrop within the district is simple, with strata dipping in a predominantly south to south-easterly direction, at angles generally between 0.5° and 1.5° (Figure 22). Locally, anomalous dip directions and values as high as 20° are encountered; these minor folds are generally associated with faults, except where caused by the superficial effects of cambering or valley bulging (see below).

### NORTH–SOUTH STRUCTURES; THE VALE OF MORETON AXIS

Although not the most numerous faults in the area, these are most significant in terms of the deep structure. They

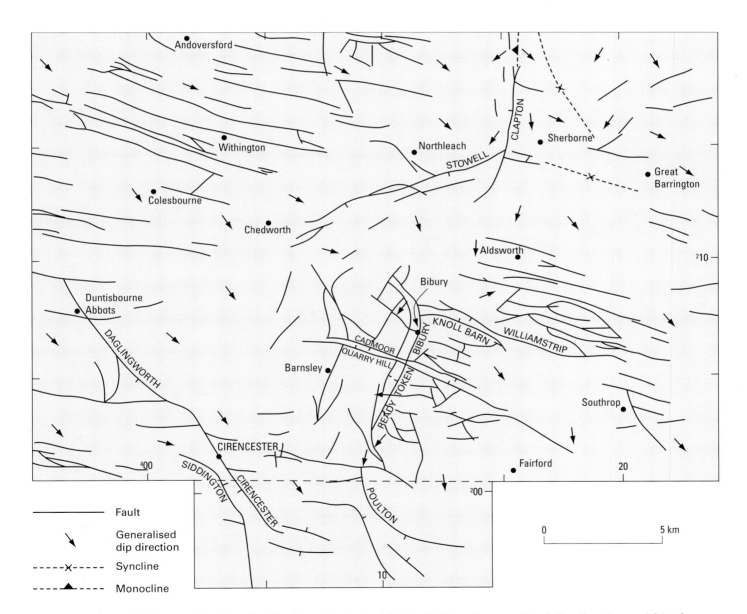

**Figure 22** Simplified map showing distribution of principal faults, folds and generalised dip directions within the Cirencester district, and adjacent area to the south.

Named faults are those mentioned in the text; crossmark, where shown, indicates downthrow side.

form a sinuous, predominantly north-north-east to south-south-west-trending fault belt made up of the Clapton, Bibury and Ready Token faults (Figure 22). Seismic surveys suggest that these are the surface expression of the eastern margin of the Worcester Basin, a major graben structure of Permian and early Mesozoic age (Chapter 3). The fault belt thus marks the Vale of Moreton Axis (Chapter 3), the name given to the zone of thinning in the Jurassic cover rocks, which is the manifestation of the basin margin. The surface fault belt is a structure of very modest scale, but gives a strong clue to fault distribution and geometry at depth.

The Clapton Fault runs along the western margin of the Vale of Bourton in the north of the district. It throws beds down to the west, with a maximum displacement of about 25 m. Towards its northern end, the beds to the west of the fault dip to the west or west-south-west at 1.5° to 2.5°. To its east, they resume their more usual south or south-eastward dip, so that the fault effectively coincides with a minor monoclinal fold. In the Inferior Oolite succession of this area, the overstep of the Scottsquar Member by the Salperton Limestone Formation corresponds closely with this fault, but this is probably coincidental. While both phenomena are related to the margin of the Worcester Basin, there is no definite evidence of fault movements during deposition of the Inferior Oolite, either here or elsewhere in the district. On the eastern side of the Vale of Bourton, south-westward dips, locally up to 3°, are seen. These opposing dips show the presence of a gentle, south-south-eastward plunging syncline along the vale (Figure 22), and not an anticline as stated by Hull (1855), Buckman (1901) and later workers; their supposed anticline relates to the Jurassic depositional effects of the Vale of Moreton Axis (see Chapter 3), and not to the present structural disposition of the rocks.

To the south, the Clapton Fault branches, one arm being the west-south-west-trending Stowell Fault, which is associated with a number of subparallel faults (Figure 22). With few exceptions, this group of faults have south-south-eastward throws, locally exceeding 25 m. A few kilometres farther south, the Bibury Fault has a westward throw of about about 15 m. It is accompanied by a subparallel fault of opposing but smaller throw a few hundred metres to the west, probably an antithetic fault analogous to, but on a smaller scale than those seen at depth on seismic sections (see below). Together, these two faults form a narrow, sinuous graben, which contains the most northerly outliers of the Cornbrash Formation in the district. The Ready Token Fault, the southward continuation of the Bibury Fault, also has a westward throw of up to 20 m. It produces a pronounced, west-facing, linear scarp feature, because of the erosional contrast between the White Limestone Formation on the eastern side, and the Forest Marble mudstones on the western (downthrow) side. As with the Clapton Fault, the strata on the western side of these structures generally dip towards the south-west, in a minor monocline (Figure 22).

Commercial seismic data acquired in connection with the exploration of the region for hydrocarbons have revealed the deep structure of the district (Chapter 3), and have enabled the faults which bound the Worcester Basin at depth to be positioned with some accuracy. However, the en-echelon distribution shown on Figure 7 is influenced by the fault pattern mapped at the ground surface, from which it is offset some distance to the west. One of the best seismic sections is shown in Figure 8. This shows a marked thinning of the Sherwood Sandstone Group, and to a lesser extent, the Mercia Mudstone Group across the boundary fault, implying intra-Triassic, syndepositional movement. However, the resolution at levels above the Penarth Group is too poor to give any indication whether there was similar movement during deposition of the Jurassic strata, and there is no definite evidence at the surface for intra-Jurassic movement. More probably, the surface faults relate to differential subsidence of the thicker sediment pile in the Worcester Basin, and may not necessarily be physically connected with the faults at depth. Nevertheless, for convenience, the deep faults are named after their presumed surface counterparts in the following account.

Seismic sections indicate that Permian strata thin eastwards to a feather edge close to the boundary fault system. On the section shown in Figure 8, this comprises the westward dipping Clapton Fault, with about 250 m of downthrow at the level of the pre-Permian basement surface. It is associated with an antithetic, eastward dipping, hangingwall fault with a much smaller throw. The fault is poorly imaged within the sub-Permian basement and its effects within the latter is unclear. To the south, the Clapton Fault is replaced en-echelon by the Northleach Fault (Figure 7) which appears to have no counterpart at the surface. It has a throw of 100 m to 150 m at the basement level, and once again an eastward dipping antithetic fault is present. A west-south-west to east-north-east fault, corresponding to the Stowell Fault at the surface, links the deep Clapton and Northleach faults, and appears to have acted as a transfer fault, accommodating some of the differential displacement. The master fault dips south-south-east and is associated with a flower-like geometry on some seismic sections.

Surface mapping suggests that the Northleach Fault continues southwards as an en-echelon fault system via the Bibury and Ready Token faults. At depth, these probably have similar geometries to the Northleach and Clapton faults, but with smaller throws.

The displacements on the marginal faults are considerably less than in the Stratford-upon-Avon district, some 40 km or so farther north; e.g. the 250 m downthrow on the Clapton Fault compares with up to 1100 m on the Inkberrow, Weethley and Clopton faults (Chadwick and Smith, 1988; Chadwick and Evans, 1995).

Chadwick and Evans (1995) have presented subsidence curves for the Worcester Basin which indicate two phases of rapid subsidence, one in late Permian and the other in early Triassic times, each followed by a period of slower subsidence. The latter evidently terminated with the deposition of the Penarth Group, which is of fairly uniform thickness across the region without any significant change across the basin margin. Renewed subsidence of the basin in the Early Jurassic is indicated by the progressive eastward overlap of successive units in the lower part of the Lias Group (Chapter 4; Figure 10). This phase of basin infill terminated with deposition of the shallow-water Marlstone Rock Formation, generally developed throughout the region, but thickest over the London Platform, and absent in a narrow zone coinciding with the Vale of Moreton Axis (i.e. the basin margin). Minor subsidence continued in the area of the Worcester Basin, accounting for a thicker and more complete Whitby Mudstone Formation (uppermost Lias Group) and Inferior Oolite succession there than over the platform to the east. The presence of many breaks in the Inferior Oolite succession (marked by hardground surfaces) accompanied by erosion of the pre-existing strata towards the Vale of Moreton Axis, has been taken to indicate that this subsidence was episodic, but these phenomena may alternatively relate to periods of lowered sea level, whilst slow subsidence continued. At the end of Inferior Oolite times, the Upper Bajocian Salperton Limestone Formation was deposited across the region, without any major influence from the Vale of Moreton Axis. In the Great Oolite too, the effects appear to have been minimal, although there is some indication of accelerated facies change in the neighbourhood of the axis. Of these, the most obvious are the thickening of the Hampen Formation immediately west of the axis, and the restriction of the Chipping Norton Limestone to areas to the east (Figure 17), although the latter relationship breaks down to the north of the district where thick Chipping Norton Limestone occurs well to the west of the axis. The final indication of influence of the Worcester Basin on sedimentation is the marked thickening of the Kellaways Formation across the axis (Chapter 7; Figure 20), demonstrating differential subsidence during early Callovian times.

WEST-NORTH-WEST TO EAST-SOUTH-EAST STRUCTURES

The predominant fault trend in the district is from west-north-west to east-south-east; such faults are particularly common in the north-west and south-east parts of the district (Figure 22). They generally have throws of a few metres, but more substantial examples with displacements of over 20 m may be traced for several kilometres, often following remarkably straight paths. Generally the largest throws are seen in the north-west part of the district, with displacements up to 45 m being commonplace, and one of about 60 m [SO 999 149] being the largest throw known at outcrop in the district. Throws in both northward and southward directions are encountered, and in some cases faults with opposing throws occur in closely spaced pairs. For example, the subparallel Quarry Hill and Cadmoor faults near Barnsley have opposing throws of up to 30 m, and the strata between them are let down into a graben a few hundred metres wide, in which the beds are folded into a gentle syncline. This graben contains the most northerly outlier of the Kellaways Formation in the district. An analogous graben, although with lesser displacement, is seen to the north of Coln St Aldwyns, between the Williamstrip and Knoll Barn faults. The converse situation is seen in

Chedworth Woods [SP 050 140], where a horst of Inferior Oolite strata, about 100 m wide, is upthrown about 25 m.

The Daglingworth–Cirencester Fault has an unusual north-west to south-east trend which is shared with the Poulton Fault, lying just outside the district (Figure 22). To the south, both faults curve round to the more usual west-north-west to east-south-east-trend. Both faults have a south-westward downthrow, generally with displacements of no more than 10 m. However, the throw of the Cirencester Fault could be greater beneath Cirencester town, where it is responsible for the presence of a subdrift inlier of the Kellaways Formation, known from boreholes (see Richardson, 1933, p.92 for an earlier interpretation of this structure). In the southern part of the town, the Cirencester Fault is joined by the subparallel Siddington Fault, which has a north-eastward downthrow. The graben between the two faults can be traced for several kilometres into the district to the south (Figure 22). A comparable graben with a similar geometry is also associated with the Poulton Fault when traced to the south of the district; the fault on the southern side of this structure has a downthrow of some 48 m (Horton et al., 1989).

Faults belonging to the west-north-west to east-south-east set are not easily resolved on the generally old and poor quality seismic data from the district, and so it remains unclear what effect, if any, they have at depth. From their trend, it may be inferred that they are associated with the latest Jurassic and early Cretaceous phase of extension, associated with further development of the Wessex Basin, although the district lies some way north of the main basin-bounding faults (e.g. the Pewsey Fault; Whittaker, 1985). However, there is some indication that faults of this trend may be responsible for local thickness variations in the Inferior Oolite Group in the north-west of the region (Figures 11, 13, 14), suggesting Mid Jurassic movements, although this is hard to confirm because of the prevalence of cambering effects (see below). It has also been suggested that structures with the same trend may have influenced Lower Jurassic sedimentation (Simms, 1990), but the evidence for this is extremely tenuous. Where these west-north-west–east-south-east faults meet the north–south structures described above (e.g. south of Bibury), relationships suggest that they are generally the older of the two sets, although there are many exceptions to this rule.

## SUPERFICIAL (NON-DIASTROPHIC) STRUCTURES

### Landslips

Landslips have occurred widely throughout the district, wherever mudstone or, to a lesser extent, sandstone formations crop out on a slope. When the strength of the deposits forming a slope is insufficient to resist the gravitational shear stress, slipping results (Chapter 2). Landslips may be triggered or reactivated by human activities such as excavation, construction and deforestation, or by natural processes such as weathering. Any such slope has potential for landslipping, but where these deposits are overlain by water-bearing strata, the probability of slipping increases considerably. This situation is common in the Cirencester district, because both the Lias Group and Fuller's Earth Formation are overlain by permeable limestones.

The largest landslips have been recorded along the Cotswold escarpment between Pilley [SO 952 195] and Dowdeswell [SP 00 19], where they principally affect the Whitby Mudstone Formation. The upper limit of the landslips is marked by a series of large, subtly arcuate scars which are generally in the basal limestones of the Inferior Oolite Group. Below the scars, rotated masses of limestone-capped mudstone form multiple terrace-like features with their tops sloping slightly towards the hillside. Further downslope, the ground is rough and broken, reflecting the complex rotational and translational processes within the landslips. Springs, which issue from the disturbed ground in many places, have provided sufficient water to generate lobate mudflows that have commonly over-ridden the Marlstone Rock Formation and descended across the Dyrham Formation slopes, to form a rough-surfaced apron low on the hillside. The most intensive landslipping probably occurred during periglacial phases of the Pleistocene, but fresh cracks in the ground, tilted trees, and buildings showing structural damage or even partial burial, attest to the current active state of some landslips.

Landslipping also occurs in the Vale of Bourton, although it is less widespread than on the main Cotswold escarpment. Again, the Whitby Mudstone is mainly affected, particularly on the western side of the valley around Clapton-on-the-Hill [SP 163 179]. The most extensive landslips have been mapped in areas of unimproved pasture where their topographical expression is clear. On arable land, ploughing may have obscured these features to the extent that they have gone unrecognised, so that landslipping may be more extensive than has been mapped.

The Fuller's Earth Formation is also widely affected by landslips, particularly in the western part of the district. They are most extensive along the Frome valley, in the Bagendon valley south-east of Elkstone [SO 967 123], around Pen Hill [SO 995 124] (Plate 1) and at Rendcomb [SP 018 098]. Landslips are also common in the Coln valley at Chedworth [SP 05 11], and in the Leach valley near Northleach [SP 114 146] and along the valley of the Sherborne Brook to the north. Indeed, the Fuller's Earth has a marked propensity for landslipping, and most outcrops on slopes exhibit this characteristic to some degree. The general morphology of the landslips is very similar to those that have affected the Lias Group. The limestone units in the lower part of the Great Oolite Group, i.e. the Eyford Member, Taynton Limestone Formation and the Hampen Formation, are commonly disrupted by landslips of the underlying Fuller's Earth, with large bodies of limestone having been carried down slope and incorporated into the landslip deposits, leaving scars in the hillside. At Chedworth, the terraced landscape produced by landslips provides an attractive setting for the village. The landslips have generally over-

ridden the Salperton Formation and locally have descended to the valley floor, both at Chedworth and more notably along the Frome valley and north-east of Rendcomb. Fresh scars in the landslips at Pen Hill, Northleach and Farmington [SP 136 154] indicate that they are still active in places.

## Cambering and valley bulging

Cambering and valley bulging are associated, non-diastrophic phenomena that can occur wherever competent beds overlie incompetent, usually mudstone strata at outcrop. The general distribution of these structures within the district is shown in Figure 23.

**Cambering** involves the collapse and downhill displacement of the competent strata, and is closely related to the landslipping phenomenon described above. It is prevalent in the Cirencester district, sometimes on a very large scale, wherever the limestones of the Inferior Oolite and Great Oolite groups overlie the mudstones of the Lias Group or the Fuller's Earth on valley slopes or escarpments. The Marlstone Rock Formation is also affected to a minor degree (see also Chapter 2: slope stability). Evidence for cambering includes extensive limestone 'dip slopes' which dip down into valleys, anomalous dips towards the valley in exposures (Plate 2), minor faults which repeat beds downslope, and apparently excessive thicknesses of limestone formations associated with a corresponding thinning of the underlying mudstones. Commonly, in the absence of good exposure, cambering effects may be difficult to distinguish from diastrophic structures; for example, on the geological map, the outcrop pattern associated with cambering replicates that of a synclinal fold whose axis follows the valley. However, the presence of 'gulls' is an unequivocal indicator of cambering. These are widened joints or fault structures developed subparallel to the slope contour, and may be seen as a step-like feature or linear depression at the ground surface. Where most strongly developed, such features may extend for several hundred metres along the valley shoulders (Figure 23). Ongoing work in the Moreton-in-Marsh district suggests that many of the larger gulls are trough-like, graben structures.

The limestones of the Great Oolite Group are markedly cambered along the Churn valley and its largest tributaries as far south as Cirencester, along the Frome valley and the Duntisbourne valley south-east of Duntisbourne Abbots [SO 970 078], along the Coln valley north of Fossebridge [SP 081 113], around Yanworth [SP 075 137] and west of Compton Abdale [SP 061 166], along the Leach valley between Hampnett [SP 100 157] and Eastington [SP 130 130], around Farmington [SP 136 156], and between Taynton [SP 234 137] and Fifield [SP 240 188]. Commonly the cambered ground extends back from the valley shoulders for 500 m or more. Vertical displacements can be considerable; for example, in the Frome valley, between Pinsbury Park [SO 955 049] and The Leasowes [SO 951 038], the base of the limestones crop out some 20 m lower than might be expected, and the underlying Fuller's Earth clays have been

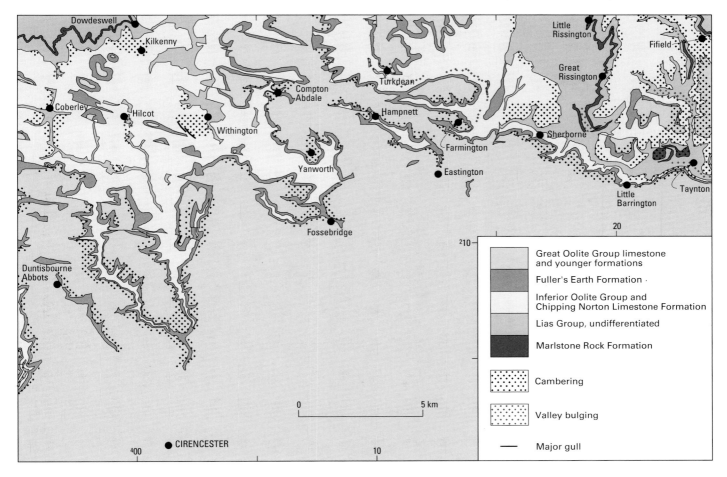

**Figure 23** Sketch map showing the approximate known extent of cambering and valley bulging within the district. Other areas may also be affected.

reduced to only 10 m in thickness, less than half their normal thickness in this area. 'Dip and fault' structures (Horswill and Horton, 1976), which are thought to be widespread in the cambered ground, are well displayed at Lee's Quarry, Taynton [SP 236 152], where the strongly cambered beds are broken up into blocks dipping in various directions and separated by debris-filled gulls (Worssam and Bisson, 1961, fig. 5; see also Plate 2).

The Inferior Oolite Group is affected by cambering along the top of the Cotswold escarpment between Seven Springs [SO 968 171] and Upper Dowdeswell [SP 007 193]: it is particularly well seen 1 km to the west of Upper Dowdeswell, where large faulted slabs from the basal part of the Birdlip Limestone Formation dip northwards towards the valley. The Birdlip Limestone Formation is cambered in the upper Churn valley around Coberley [SO 965 158] and along the small tributary valley to the north of Hilcot [SO 998 162]. West of Withington [SP 032 157], where the group is about 60 to 70 m thick, the wide outcrop of the Aston Limestone is the result of the downhill repetition of the sequence by several superficial faults. Here, gulls up to 500 m long and 30 m wide are a notable feature of the landscape (Figure 23). The Inferior Oolite slopes around the

southern part of the Vale of Bourton (north of Sherborne [SP 174 145] and between Great Rissington [SP 195 172] and Little Rissington [SP 190 198]) are extensively cambered. Locally, blocks of calcite spar are seen in the field brash, perhaps indicating the presence of infilled gulls. Between Sherborne and Little Barrington, the predominant northward dip of the strata along the Windrush valley may in part be due to a gentle synclinal fold in this area (Figure 22), but is undoubtedly accentuated by cambering.

Between Kilkenny [SP 008 187] and Foxcote Hill Farm [SP 002 176], there is a series of tilted fault blocks bounded by faults having a north to north-eastward throw (see 1:50 000 Geological Sheet 235). Within each block, the beds dip unusually steeply to the south; in a quarry [SP 0057 1863] at Kilkenny, dips of up to 24° were recorded. The genesis of these structures is uncertain, but they are thought to be related to the large-scale cambering and major landslips of the nearby Cotswold escarpment.

**Valley bulging** occurs in valleys that are floored by incompetent strata. Its effects are, to some extent, the converse of cambering; upward bulging of mudstone strata in the valley floor may impart considerable dips to the overlying limestones, replicating the effect of an anticline following the valley. Valley bulging is probably widespread in the district but, because of the paucity of exposure, it has been identified with certainty at only a few localities (Figure 23).

North of Seven Springs [SO 967 177], the unusual elevation of the Whitby Mudstone may be explained by valley bulging. In the Frome valley, the Bridport Sand at Poor's Wood [SO 9503 0790] and Pinbury Park [SO 954 047] is also affected. Valley bulging is particularly marked along the partly dry valley of the Sherborne Brook, near Turkdean [SP 105 173] and Farmington [at SP 148 168], where the Whitby Mudstone Formation and the overlying Leckhampton Member (Inferior Oolite Group) occur in the valley bottom, at elevations up to 15 m higher than might be expected from the succession seen on the adjoining slopes. In many cases, the bulging is asymmetrical with respect to the valley; this is particularly noticeable in sinuous sections, where Whitby Mudstone typically crops out on spurs on the inside of a bend, but the opposite steep bluff on the outside of the bend is made up of Inferior Oolite limestones. In places, the Whitby Mudstone stands up as a minor knoll at the foot of such spurs, and dips of up to 15° away from the valley axis have been recorded in the overlying Leckhampton Member.

Other noteworthy examples of valley bulging affecting the Whitby Mudstone have been recorded in the Vale of Bourton, upstream from the confluence of the Windrush and Sherborne Brook, along Coombe Brook between Great Rissington and Taynton, and west of Fifield [SP 228 190]. Less certainly, there is some evidence for valley bulging in the Coln valley near Withington [SP 031 156] and in the bottom of the small valley at Hilcot [SO 999 160].

The mechanisms involved in cambering and valley bulging are not well understood, but it is generally accepted that stress release in the softer deposits, following rapid incision through a rigid caprock, is the most significant initial factor. Early workers, such as Hollingworth et al. (1944), suggested that these conditions would cause deformation of the argillaceous beds, promoting an upward bulging of the valley floor and lowering of the valley sides. However, Parks (1991) considered that the scale of these features could not be explained by stress release alone and postulated that, after the initial release of stress, cambering and valley bulging could only result from mass wasting in a periglacial climate. According to this model, heave induced by the formation of ice in the incompetent beds, coupled with permafrost creep, caused their lateral displacement and the extension and consequent disruption of the overlying competent strata. The low permeability of argillaceous sediments prevented the rapid escape of meltwater during thawing, and the resultant increased pore water pressures reduced the shear strength of the sediments, allowing them to be deformed by the weight of the superincumbent strata. The upper part of the soft sediments may have behaved like a viscous fluid, allowing the disrupted blocks of rigid strata to settle and rotate. Other authors (Hutchinson, 1991; Ballantyne and Harris, 1994) have suggested that basal thawing of the argillaceous sediments may have forced soft, thawed clays upwards under still-frozen ground in the valley bottom. All workers are agreed that cambering and valley bulging occurred principally during the cold phases of the Pleistocene (Table 13).

# INFORMATION SOURCES

BGS publishes an extensive range of geoscience maps, memoirs, regional geology guides, offshore regional reports, technical reports and other publications for the United Kingdom and adjacent continental shelf. Those that relate to the Cirencester district or immediately adjoining areas are listed below. Also listed are unpublished reports, an index of selected boreholes, and other relevant information. BGS maintains a catalogue comprising over two hundred datasets, including some digital databases, which give index-level access to its large and diverse collections of material. Further information can be obtained from The Manager, Information Services Group, British Geological Survey, Keyworth, Nottingham NG12 5GG. A publicly accessible data catalogue is available at the BGS world wide web site (http://www. bgs.ac.uk).

## MAPS

* Maps are also available as digital datasets under licence

### Geological maps

*1:2 500 000*
Sub-Pleistocene geology of the British Islands and adjacent continental shelf, 2nd edition, 1979

*1:1 584 000*
Geological map of the British Islands, 5th edition, 1969

*1:1 500 000*
Tectonic map of Britain, Ireland and adjacent areas*, 1996

*1:1 000 000*
United Kingdom, Ireland and adjacent continental shelf (South). Pre-Permian geology of the United Kingdom (South), 1985

*1:625 000*
Geological map of the United Kingdom (South)* Solid, 3rd edition, 1979
Quaternary map of the United Kingdom (South)*, 1st edition, 1977

*1:250 000*
Chilterns (Sheet 51N 02W)* Solid, 1991
Bristol Channel (Sheet 51N 04W)* Solid, 1988
Bristol Channel (Sheet 51N 04W) Quaternary geology and sea-bed sediments, 1986

*1:50 000 or 1:63 360*
Tewkesbury (Sheet 216) Solid and Drift, 1988
Moreton-in-Marsh (Sheet 217) Solid and Drift, 1981
Chipping Norton (Sheet 218) Solid and Drift, 1968
Gloucester (Sheet 234) Solid and Drift, 1972
Cirencester (Sheet 235) Solid and Drift, 1998*
Witney (Sheet 236) Solid and Drift, 1982
Malmesbury (Sheet 251) Solid and Drift, 1970
Swindon (Sheet 252) Solid and Drift, 1974
Abingdon (Sheet 253) Solid and Drift, 1971

*1:10 000 and 1:10 560*
The primary survey was carried out at the one-inch (1:63 360) scale by E Hull in the 1850s as part of the Old Series Geological Sheet 44, published in1857. Part of this map, with the addition of Drift deposits surveyed at the six-inch (1:10 560) scale by H G Dines in 1931, was reissued as New Series one-inch Geological Sheet 235 (Cirencester) in 1933. A small part of the district, lying within 'county series' six-inch (1:10 560) scale maps Gloucestershire 37 SW and SE and 45 NW and NE, was resurveyed at that scale in 1952 and 1953. The remainder of the district was resurveyed at the 1:10 000 scale between 1982 and 1994, and the earlier six-inch maps were also updated to the 1:10 000 scale. These new maps, covering the whole of the district, were used to compile the new (1998) edition of 1:50 000 Sheet 235.

The 1:10 000 scale maps which, either wholly or in part, fall within 1:50 000 scale Sheet 235 are listed below, together with the surveyor's initials and the dates of the survey. The surveyors were: A J M Barron, G Bisson, A Horton, A N Morigi, M G Sumbler, I T Williamson and B C Worssam.

The 1:10 000 scale maps are available for consultation in the Library, British Geological Survey, Kingsley Dunham Centre, Nicker Hill, Keyworth, Nottingham NG12 5GG, and also at BGS Edinburgh and the London Information Office, in the Natural History Museum, South Kensington, London. Dye-line copies may be purchased from Customer Services. Corresponding Technical reports are available for most of these maps (see Books and reports).

| | | | |
|---|---|---|---|
| SO 90 NE | Duntisbourne Abbots | AJMB | 1985 |
| SO 90 SE | Coates | AJMB | 1985 |
| SO 91 NE | Seven Springs | AJMB, ANM | 1993 |
| SO 91 SE | Elkstone | AJMB | 1992–1993 |
| SO 92 SE | Cheltenham (East) | AJMB | 1982 |
| SP 00 NW | North Cerney | AH | 1985 |
| SP 00 NE | Barnsley | MGS | 1985 |
| SP 00 SW | Cirencester | AH | 1985 |
| SP 00 SE | The Ampneys | MGS | 1985 |
| SP 01 NW | Andoversford | ANM | 1993–1994 |
| SP 01 NE | Compton Abdale | AJMB, MGS | 1993–1994 |
| SP 01 SW | Colesbourne | ANM | 1992–1993 |
| SP 01 SE | Chedworth | MGS, AJMB, ANM | 1993–1994 |
| SP 10 NW | Bibury | MGS | 1984 |
| SP 10 NE | Hatherop | BCW, AJMB | 1952, 1984 |
| SP 10 SW | Quenington | MGS | 1984 |
| SP 10 SE | Fairford | AJMB | 1984 |
| SP 11 NW | Farmington | MGS | 1993–1994 |
| SP 11 NE | The Rissingtons | MGS | 1993–1994 |
| SP 11 SW | Northleach | MGS | 1993 |
| SP 11 SE | Sherborne | BCW, MGS | 1952, 1992 |
| SP 20 NW | Eastleach Martin | BCW, GB, AH | 1952, 1984 |
| SP 20 SW | Filkins | AH | 1984 |
| SP 21 NW | Fifield | ITW, MGS | 1994 |
| SP 21 SW | The Barringtons | GB, BCW, MGS | 1952–1953, 1994 |

### Geophysical maps

*1:1 500 000*
Colour shaded relief gravity anomaly map of Britain, Ireland and adjacent areas, 1997

Colour shaded relief magnetic anomaly map of Britain, Ireland and adjacent areas, 1998
Earthquakes, 1980–1994; 1995

*1:1 000 000*
Southern Britain, Ireland and adjacent areas; Bouguer gravity anomaly, 1992

*1:250 000*
Chilterns (Sheet 51N 02W); Aeromagnetic anomaly, 1980
Chilterns (Sheet 51N 02W); Bouguer gravity anomaly, 1983
Bristol Channel (Sheet 51N 04W); Aeromagnetic anomaly, 1988
Bristol Channel (Sheet 51N 04W); Bouguer gravity anomaly, 1986

*1:50 000*
Sheet 235 (Cirencester). Geophysical information map (GIM); plot-on-demand map summarising graphically the publicly available geophysical information held for the sheet in the BGS digital databases. Features include:
  Regional gravity data: Bouguer anomaly contours and location of observations.
- Regional aeromagnetic data: total field anomaly contours and location of digitised data points along flight lines.
- Gravity and magnetic fields plotted on the same base map at 1:50 000 scale to show correlation between anomalies.
- Separate colour contour plots of gravity and magnetic fields at 1:125 000 scale for easy visualisation of important anomalies.
- Location of local geophysical surveys.
- Location of public domain seismic reflection and refraction surveys.
- Location of deep boreholes and those with geophysical logs.

## Hydrogeology maps

*1:625 000*
Sheet 1 (England and Wales), 1977

*Groundwater vulnerability maps*
*(Prepared for the Environment Agency by BGS and the Soil Survey and Land Research Centre)*

*1:100 000*
Sheet 37 (Southern Cotswolds), 1996
Sheet 38 (Berkshire), 1996

## Economic geology maps

*1:1 000 000*
Britain; industrial mineral resources, 1996

*1:1 500 000*
Britain and Ireland; metallogenic map, 1996

## BOOKS AND REPORTS

### Geological notes and local details

Reports in this series are specifically related to the component 1:10 000 geological maps included within the Cirencester district. They give details of the geology of the area and records of sections and important cored boreholes. Though not widely available, they can be consulted at the BGS library, or may be purchased through BGS.

BARRON, A J M. 1986.  Geological notes and local details for 1:10 000 sheets: SP 10 SE (Fairford).  *British Geological Survey Technical Report*, WA/DM/86/12.

BARRON, A J M. 1987.  Geological notes and local details for

1:10 000 sheets: SP 10 NE (Hatherop).  *British Geological Survey Technical Report*, WA/DM/87/1.

BARRON, A J M. 1988.  Geological notes and local details for 1:10 000 sheets: SO 90 SE (Coates).  *British Geological Survey Technical Report*, WA/DM/88/41.

BARRON, A J M. 1988.  Geological notes and local details for 1:10 000 sheets: SO 90 NE (Duntisbourne Abbots).  *British Geological Survey Technical Report*, WA/DM/88/43.

BARRON, A J M. 1994.  Geological notes and local details for 1:10 000 Sheet SO 91 SE (Elkstone). *British Geological Survey Technical Report*, WA/94/13.

BARRON, A J M. 1995.  Geological notes and local details for 1:10 000 Sheet SO 91 NE (Seven Springs).  *British Geological Survey Technical Report*, WA/94/14.

BARRON, A J M. 1995.  Geological notes and local details for 1:10 000 Sheet SP 01 NE (Compton Abdale).  *British Geological Survey Technical Report*, WA/95/4.

BARRON, A J M. 1999.  Geology of the Cheltenham (East) area,.  *British Geological Survey Technical Report*, WA/99/04.

HORTON, A. 1986.  Geological notes and local details for 1:10 000 Sheet SP 20 NW (Eastleach Martin). *British Geological Survey Technical Report*, WA/DM/86/3.

HORTON, A. 1988.  Geological notes and local details for 1:10 000 Sheet SP 20 SW (Filkins).  *British Geological Survey Technical Report*, WA/DM/88/31.

MORIGI, A N. 1995.  Geological notes and local details for 1:10 000 Sheet SP 01 SW (Colesbourne).  *British Geological Survey Technical Report*, WA/95/106.

MORIGI, A N. 1995.  Geological notes and local details for 1:10 000 Sheet SP 01 NW (Andoversford).  *British Geological Survey Technical Report*, WA/95/107.

SUMBLER, M G. 1985.  Geological notes and local details for 1:10 000 sheets: SP 10 NW (Bibury).  *British Geological Survey Technical Report*, WA/DM/85/2.

SUMBLER, M G. 1994.  Geological notes and local details for 1:10 000 Sheet SP 11 SE (Sherborne).  *British Geological Survey Technical Report*, WA/94/26.

SUMBLER, M G. 1994.  Geological notes and local details for 1:10 000 Sheet SP 11 SW (Northleach).  *British Geological Survey Technical Report*, WA/94/85.

SUMBLER, M G. 1994.  Geological notes and local details for 1:10 000 Sheet SP 21 SW (The Barringtons).  *British Geological Survey Technical Report*, WA/94/92.

SUMBLER, M G. 1995.  Geological notes and local details for 1:10 000 Sheet SP 11 NW (Farmington).  *British Geological Survey Technical Report*, WA/95/3.

SUMBLER, M G. 1995.  Geological notes and local details for 1:10 000 Sheet SP 11 NE (The Rissingtons).  *British Geological Survey Technical Report*, WA/95/17.

SUMBLER, M G. 1995.  Geological notes and local details for 1:10 000 Sheet SP 00 NE (Barnsley, Gloucestershire).  *British Geological Survey Technical Report*, WA/95/66.

SUMBLER, M G. 1995.  Geological notes and local details for 1:10 000 Sheet SP 10 SW (Quenington).  *British Geological Survey Technical Report*, WA/95/68.

SUMBLER, M G. 1995.  Geological notes and local details for 1:10 000 Sheet SP 00 SE (The Ampneys).  *British Geological Survey Technical Report*, WA/95/74.

SUMBLER, M G and BARRON, A J M. 1995.  Geological notes and local details for 1:10 000 Sheet SP 01 SE (Chedworth). *British Geological Survey Technical Report*, WA/95/73.

WILLIAMSON, I T. 1995. Geological notes and local details for 1:10 000 Sheet SP 21 NW (Fifield). *British Geological Survey Technical Report*, WA/95/79.

## General geology, hydrogeology and mineral resources

Books and papers relating to the Cirencester district and adjoining areas, published by (or for) BGS.

CAVE, R and PENN, I E. 1972. On the classification of the Inferior Oolite of the Cotswolds. *Bulletin of the Geological Survey of Great Britain*, No. 38, 59–65.

CAVE, R and COX, B M. 1975. The Kellaways Beds of the area between Chippenham and Malmesbury, Wiltshire. *Bulletin of the Geological Survey of Great Britain*, No. 54, 41–66.

CAVE, R. 1977. Geology of the Malmesbury district. *Memoir of the Geological Survey of Great Britain*, Sheet 251 (England and Wales).

DINES, H G. 1928. On the glaciation of the north Cotteswold area. *Summary of Progress of the Geological Survey of Great Britain* (for 1927), Vol. 2, 66–71.

GREEN, G W and MELVILLE, R V. 1956. The stratigraphy of the Stowell Park Borehole (1949–1951). *Bulletin of the Geological Survey of Great Britain*, No. 11, 1–66.

GREEN, G W. 1992. *British Regional Geology: Bristol and Gloucester region*. (3rd edition). (London: HMSO for British Geological Survey).

HORTON, A, and POOLE, E G. 1977. The lithostratigraphy of three geophysical marker horizons in the Lower Lias of Oxfordshire. *Bulletin of the Geological Survey of Great Britain*, No. 62, 13–33.

HORTON, A, POOLE, E G, WILLIAMS, B J, ILLING, V C and HOBSON, G D. 1987. Geology of the country around Chipping Norton. *Memoir of the British Geological Survey*. Sheet 218 (England and Wales).

HULL, E. 1857. The geology of the country around Cheltenham. *Memoir of the Geological Survey of Great Britain*. (Old Series Sheet 44).

KELLAWAY, G A, HORTON, A and POOLE, E G. 1971. The development of some Pleistocene structures in the Cotswolds and Upper Thames Basin. *Bulletin of the Geological Survey of Great Britain*, Vol. 37, 1–28.

POOLE, E G. 1969. The stratigraphy of the Geological Survey Apley Barn Borehole, Witney, Oxfordshire. *Bulletin of the Geological Survey of Great Britain*, No. 29, 1–103.

RAMSAY, A C, AVELINE, W T and HULL, E. 1858. Geology of parts of Wiltshire and Gloucestershire. *Memoir of the Geological Survey of Great Britain* (Old Series Sheet 34).

RICHARDSON, L. 1930. Wells and springs of Gloucestershire. *Memoir of the Geological Survey of Great Britain*.

RICHARDSON, L. 1933. The country around Cirencester. *Memoir of the Geological Survey of Great Britain*. (Sheet 235, England and Wales).

RICHARDSON, L, ARKELL, W J and DINES H G. 1946. Geology of the country around Witney. *Memoir of the Geological Survey of Great Britain*. (Sheet 236, England and Wales).

ROBSON, P. 1975. The sand and gravel resources of the Thames Valley, the country around Cricklade, Wiltshire: Description of 1:25 000 resource sheets SU 09/19 and parts of SP 00/10. *Mineral Assessment Report of the Institute of Geological Sciences*, No. 18.

ROBSON, P. 1976. The sand and gravel resources of the Thames Valley, the country between Lechlade and Standlake: Description of 1:25 000 Sheet SP 30 and parts of SP 20, SU 29 and SU 39. *Mineral Assessment Report of the Institute of Geological Sciences*, No. 23.

SUMBLER, M G. 1996. *British Regional Geology: London and the Thames valley*. 4th edition. (London: HMSO for the British Geological Survey).

WOODWARD, H B. 1893. The Jurassic rocks of Britain. Vol. 3. The Lias of England and Wales (Yorkshire excepted). *Memoir of the Geological Survey of the United Kingdom*.

WOODWARD, H B. 1894. The Jurassic rocks of Britain. Vol. 4. The Lower Oolitic rocks of England (Yorkshire excepted). *Memoir of the Geological Survey of the United Kingdom*.

WOODWARD, H B. 1895. The Jurassic rocks of Britain. Vol. 5. The Middle and Upper Oolitic rocks of England (Yorkshire excepted). *Memoir of the Geological Survey of the United Kingdom*.

WORSSAM, B C. 1963. The stratigraphy of the Geological Survey Upton Borehole, Oxfordshire. *Bulletin of the Geological Survey of Great Britain*, No. 20, 107–156.

WORSSAM, B C and BISSON, G. 1961. The geology of the country between Sherborne, Gloucestershire and Burford, Oxfordshire. *Bulletin of the Geological Survey of Great Britain*, No. 17, 75–115.

## Biostratigraphy and petrography

The following reports are not generally available to the public, but in some cases they may be examined on application to BGS.

CALVER, M A. 1960. Report on the Coal Measures fossils from the Upton Borehole, Burford, Oxfordshire. Palaeontological Department report PDL/60/1. British Geological Survey.

COX, B M. 1993. A review of palaeontological work already undertaken for the re-survey of 1:50 000 Geological Sheet 235 (Cirencester). *British Geological Survey Technical Report*, WH/93/127R.

COX, B M. 1993. Cirencester Sheet: notes on faunal characters of the Inferior Oolite. *British Geological Survey Technical Report*, WH/93/185R.

COX, B M. 1994. Recent collecting from the Lias Group of 1:10 000 sheets SP 11 NE, SP 11 SE and SP 12 SE. *British Geological Survey Technical Report*, WH/94/212R.

COX, B M. 1994. An ammonite occurrence in the Middle Inferior Oolite of 1:10 000 Sheet SP 11 NW. *British Geological Survey Technical Report*, WH/94/220R.

COX, B M. 1994. An ammonite from the Great Oolite Group near Northleach, Gloucs. *British Geological Survey Technical Report*, WH/94/237R.

COX, B M. 1994. Recent collecting from 1:10 000 sheets SP 01 NE and SP 01 SE. *British Geological Survey Technical Report*, WH/94/241R.

COX, B M. 1994. Material from the Kellaways Formation of the ARC Lechlade Quarry. *British Geological Survey Technical Report*, WH/94/266R.

COX, B M. 1994. Recent collecting from the Lias Group of 1:10 000 sheets SP 11 NE and SP 21 NW. *British Geological Survey Technical Report*, WH/94/268R.

COX, B M. 1994. Inferior Oolite ammonites from Cassey Compton, Gloucestershire. *British Geological Survey Technical Report*, WH/94/283R.

COX, B M. 1994. An ammonite from the ?Witchellia Grit (Middle Inferior Oolite) of 1:10 000 Sheet SO 91 NE. *British Geological Survey Technical Report*, WH/94/221R.

Cox, B M. 1995. Recent collecting from the Inferior and Great Oolite groups of 1:10 000 sheets SP 01 NE and SP 01 SE. *British Geological Survey Technical Report* WH/95/077R.

Cox, B M. 1996. Notes on the BGS Northfield Farm Borehole, Withington, Gloucs. *British Geological Survey Technical Report*, WH/96/058R.

Ivimey-Cook, H C. 1984. Specimens collected in 1984 from sheets 235 and 236 for Cirencester project. *Palaeontological Department Report*, PD/84/51.

Ivimey-Cook, H C. 1985. Report on macrofossils from samples in Trial Pit 'A', Dowdeswell Reservoir, Gloucestershire. *Palaeontological Department Report*, PD/85/29.

Ivimey-Cook, H C. 1986. On specimens from the Great Oolite near Duntisbourne Abbots and from Foss Cross Quarry, Gloucestershire. *Palaeontological Department Report*, PD/86/57.

Ivimey-Cook, H C. 1988. Summary of Lower and Middle Jurassic fossils from localities on SP 21 SW Cirencester, Sheet 235. *British Geological Survey Technical Report*, WH/88/62R.

Ivimey-Cook, H C. 1988. Summary of Middle Jurassic fossils from localities on SP 00 NE Cirencester, Sheet 235. *British Geological Survey Technical Report*, WH/88/65R.

Ivimey-Cook, H C. 1988. Summary of Middle Jurassic fossils from localities on SP 00 SW Cirencester, Sheet 235. *British Geological Survey Technical Report*, WH/88/82R.

Ivimey-Cook, H C. 1993. The biostratigraphy of the Lower Jurassic of the Stowell Park Borehole. *British Geological Survey Technical Report*, WH/93/174R.

Ivimey-Cook, H C. 1993. The biostratigraphy of the Lower Jurassic in the Upton Borehole, Burford, Oxfordshire. *British Geological Survey Technical Report*, WH/93/175R.

Ivimey-Cook, H C. 1993. The Lower Jurassic of the Cirencester district (Sheet 235). *British Geological Survey Technical Report*, WH/93/176R.

Ivimey-Cook, H C. 1993. Further Jurassic fossils from 1:10 000 Sheet SO 91. *British Geological Survey Technical Report*, WH/93/259R.

Ivimey-Cook, H C. 1993. Lower and Middle Jurassic fossils in BGS collections from the northern half of the Cirencester Sheet and parts of adjacent sheets. *British Geological Survey Technical Report*, WH/93/306R.

Ivimey-Cook, H C. 1993. Further Middle Jurassic fossils from SP 01 SE. *British Geological Survey Technical Report*, WH/93/311R.

Ivimey-Cook, H C. 1993. The Penarth Group in the Stowell Park and Upton, Burford, boreholes, with other records in this vicinity. *British Geological Survey Technical Report*, WH/93/321R.

Ivimey-Cook, H C. 1994. Further Middle Jurassic fossils from 1:10 000 sheets SP 01, SP 02 and SP 11. *British Geological Survey Technical Report*, WH/94/89R.

Lott, G K. 1993. The petrology of the Middle Jurassic limestones in the Stowell Park Borehole, Gloucestershire, Cirencester Sheet (235). *British Geological Survey Technical Report*, WH/93/172R.

Lott, G K. 1994. A note on the clay mineralogy of six mudstone samples from the Fuller's Earth in the Daglingworth No. 3/94 borehole, Gloucestershire. *British Geological Survey Technical Report*, WH/94/210R

Lott, G K. 1995. Petrology of four limestone samples from the Lower and Middle Jurassic of the Gloucestershire area. *British Geological Survey Technical Report*, WH/95/93R.

Melville, R V. 1956. The stratigraphical palaeontology, ammonites excluded, of the Stowell Park Borehole. *Bulletin of the Geological Survey of Great Britain*, No. 11, 67–139.

Melville, R V. 1957. Great Oolite fossils from 1" Sheet 235. *Palaeontological Department Report*, PD/57/35.

Orbell, G. 1973. Palynology of the British Rhaeto-Liassic. *Bulletin of the Geological Survey of Great Britain*, No. 44. 1–44.

Penn, I E. 1970. Bibury Pumping Station bore: specimens received from Haydn Richards, 1962. *Palaeontological Department Report*, PD/70/28.

Penn, I E. 1970. Report on a borehole at Bibury Pumping Station. *Palaeontological Department Report*, PD/70/29.

Riding, J B. 1994. A palynological investigation of the BGS Stowell Park Borehole, Gloucestershire, from 114.15 m to 122.68 m. *British Geological Survey Technical Report*, WH/94/235R.

Spath, L F. 1956. The Liassic ammonite faunas of the Stowell Park Borehole. *Bulletin of the Geological Survey of Great Britain*, No. 11, 140–164.

Thomas, J E. 1985. The palynology of four samples from the 'Pea Grit' of Bibury Pumping Station Borehole, Cirencester Sheet. *Palaeontological Department Report*, PD/85/118.

Warrington, G. 1969. Stowell Park Borehole (Sheet 235): palynology of material from the Keuper Sandstone. *Palaeontological Department Report*, PDL/69/83. British Geological Survey.

Warrington, G. 1974. Palynology report: Keuper Marl and Keuper Sandstone. *Palaeontological Department Report*, PDL/74/313. British Geological Survey.

Warrington, G. 1974. Summary report: palynological investigations of the Triassic sequence of the Chipping Norton area with supplementary data from adjoining sheets. *Palaeontological Department Report*, PDL/74/314. British Geological Survey.

Warrington, G. 1993. The Permian (?) and Triassic of the Cirencester district. *British Geological Survey Technical Report*, WH/93/241C.

## DOCUMENTARY COLLECTIONS

### Borehole records

BGS holds the records of approximately 600 wells and boreholes for the Cirencester district. Most of these are descriptive, written logs but a proportion are downhole geophysical logs. The records are mainly stored on paper but can be accessed via a digital database containing index information. For further information contact the Records Officer at BGS Keyworth.

INDEX OF SELECTED BOREHOLES

An index of important boreholes in or close to the Cirencester district, including those boreholes cited in the text, is given below. Enquiries should be addressed to the Materials Collections Manager at BGS Keyworth.

* Indicates those boreholes from which core samples are retained in BGS collections.

| Borehole name | 1:50 000 Sheet | Borehole number | Grid reference | Depth (m) |
|---|---|---|---|---|
| Ablington Road | 235 | SP01NW/13 | SP 1109 0725 | 54 |
| Ampney Crucis | 235 | SP00SE/23 | SP 0595 0190 | 60.96 |
| Ampney St Mary | 235 | SP00SE/33 | SP 0894 0236 | 50.8 |
| Ampney St Peter (TWA) | 235 | SP00SE/24 | SP 0776 0120 | 54.86 |
| Apley Barn (BGS)* | 236 | SP31SW/3 | SP 2438 1066 | 1506.22 |
| Ashton Keynes STW (TWA) | 252 | SU09SE/17 | SU 0637 9318 | 136 |
| Barnsley Park | 235 | SP00NE/6 | SP 0821 0602 | 72.24 |
| Barton Mill, Cirencester | 235 | SP00SW/26 | SP 0173 0249 | 45.11 |
| Bathurst Sawmills | 235 | SO90SE/7 | SO 9697 0162 | 117 |
| Batsford (Lower Lemington)* | 217 | SP23SW/3 | SP 2158 3466 | 518.3 |
| Baunton PS AB No. 3 (TWA) | 235 | SP00SW/30 | SP 0191 0482 | 52 |
| Baunton Observation Bore (TWA) | 235 | SP00NW/1 | SP 0194 0505 | 67.06 |
| Bibury Pumping Station (TWA)* | 235 | SP10NW/1 | SP 1125 0710 | 57.91 |
| Bibury Pumping Station Old Well No. 1 (TWA) | 235 | SP10NW/7 | SP 1123 0712 | 45.11 |
| Bibury Trout Farm Observation Borehole (TWA) | 235 | SP10NW/8 | SP 1139 0702 | 55.47 |
| Bicester No. 1* | 219 | SP52SE/1 | SP 5878 2081 | 513.89 |
| Bisley (Nashend Farm) (BGS)* | 234 | SO90SW/1 | SO 9029 0491 | 72.95 |
| Broadfield Farm | 235 | SP11SW/13 | SP 1267 1116 | 60.96 |
| Carterton (Alvescot Road) (TWA) | 236 | SP20NE/49 | SP 2700 0832 | 65.84 |
| Chedworth Laines (BGS)* | 235 | SP01SW/4 | SP 0358 1179 | 29.65 |
| Cold Aston | 217 | SP11NW/6 | SP 1242 1991 | 78.33 |
| Coln St Aldwyns | 235 | SP10NW/12 | SP 1448 0665 | 50 |
| Colnpen Barn | 235 | SP00NE/12 | SP 0698 0806 | 92.96 |
| Cooles Farm No. 1* | 252 | SU09SW/52 | SU 0164 9214 | 3512.82 |
| Crickley Barrow | 235 | SP11SW/6 | SP 1021 1168 | 92.35 |
| Daglingworth 1/86* | 235 | SP00NW/24 | SP 0010 0597 | 23.58 |
| Daglingworth 3/94* | 235 | SP00NW/44 | SP 0002 0586 | 30.00 |
| Donkeywell Buildings (TWA) | 235 | SP10SW/23 | SP 1275 0342 | 97 |
| Down Ampney (TWA) | 252 | SU19NW/87 | SU 1041 9588 | 110.0 |
| Down Ampney DA2 (BGS)* | 252 | SU19NW/2 | SU 1180 9640 | 87.80 |
| Duntisbourne | 235 | SO90NE/5 | SO 9717 0807 | 88.39 |
| Elkstone (BGS)* | 235 | SO91SE/21 | SO 9675 1323 | 29 |
| Ewe Pens | 235 | SO90SE/5 | SO 9973 0279 | 106.68 |
| Fairford (TWA) | 235 | SP10SW/22 | SP 1434 0061 | 79 |
| Faringdon No. 1* | 253 | SU39SW/1 | SU 3244 9399 | 951.9 |
| Field Barn (TWA) | 235 | SP10SW/21 | SP 1188 0172 | 60 |
| Gas Council Borehole GCN10 | 235 | SP21NW/4 | SP 2301 1876 | 181.66 |
| Gas Council Borehole GCN37 | 235 | SP21NW/5 | SP 2371 1977 | 136.86 |
| Gas Council Borehole GS8A* | 217 | SP21NW/1 | SP 2150 1997 | 153.62 |
| Gas Council Borehole GS9 | 235 | SP11NE/1 | SP 1783 1967 | 143.56 |
| Gas Council Borehole GS13 | 236 | SP21NW/2 | SP 2445 1885 | 130.61 |
| Gas Council Borehole GS15* | 235 | SP21NW/3 | SP 2323 1723 | 172.82 |
| Gas Council Borehole GS16* | 235 | SP11NE/2 | SP 1928 1780 | 153.31 |
| Great Lemhill | 235 | SP20SW/62 | SP 2082 0199 | 42.67 |
| Guiting Power* | 217 | SP02SE/1 | SP 0855 2450 | 2185.42 |
| Harnhill (TWA)* | 252 | SP00SE/3 | SP 0682 0007 | 134 |
| Harwell HW3 (BGS)* | 253 | SU48NE/92 | SU 4680 8644 | 551.29 |
| Highworth No. 1* | 252 | SU19SE/7 | SU 1831 9153 | 1164.34 |
| Hill Barn Farm | 235 | SP01NE/5 | SP 0606 1626 | 91.44 |
| Hollow Fosse Farm | 235 | SP00NE/13 | SP 0576 0801 | 67.06 |
| Kempsey (BGS)* | 199 | SO84NE/2 | SO 8609 4933 | 3012.19 |
| Ladbarrow Farm | 235 | SP10NE/4 | SP 1735 0928 | 64.62 |
| Lechlade Waterworks | 235 | SP20SW/53 | SP 2143 0055 | 81.68 |
| Lewis Lane Pumping Station | 235 | SP00SW/21 | SP 0244 0170 | 83.82 |
| Lexham Lodge No. 2 | 235 | SO91NE/3 | SO 9670 1732 | 29.41 |
| Leygore Manor | 235 | SP11NW/3 | SP 1179 1648 | 81.69 |
| Little Lemhill Farm | 235 | SP20SW/54 | SP 2078 0117 | 38.71 |
| Lowerfield Farm | 235 | SP00SE/25 | SP 0842 0367 | 60.96 |
| Macaroni Downs | 235 | SP10NE/6 | SP 1828 0785 | 70.1 |
| Minchinhampton (Old Common) (BGS)* | 234 | SO80SE/4 | SO 8807 0098 | 78.69 |
| Meysey Hampton (TWA)* | 252 | SU19NW/36 | SU 1179 9903 | 126.49 |
| Netherton No. 1* | 200 | SO94SE/1 | SO 9982 4075 | 2320.82 |
| North Leigh (BGS)* | 236 | SP31SE/9 | SP 3829 1296 | 99.27 |
| Northfield Farm (BGS)* | 235 | SP01NW/3 | SP 0319 1718 | 29.3 |
| Northleach Grammar School | 235 | SP11SW/4 | SP 1182 1427 | 67.36 |
| Perrott's Brook | 235 | SP00NW/8 | SP 0195 0606 | 47.55 |
| Ready Token (TWA) | 235 | SP10SW/20 | SP 1139 0467 | 15.24 |
| Ready Token | 235 | SP10SW/14 | SP 1047 0440 | 77.72 |
| Rectory Farm | 235 | SO90NE/2 | SO 9709 0828 | 85.34 |
| Sandpool Farm (TWA)* | 252 | SU09SW/51 | SU 0122 9427 | 162.76 |
| Sheepbridge | 235 | SP10NE/1 | SP 1878 0696 | 50.5 |
| Sherborne No 1* | 235 | SP11SE/1 | SP 1562 1393 | 1946.15 |
| Shilton Road (TWA) | 236 | SP20NE/48 | SP 2712 0812 | 65.23 |
| Signet | 236 | SP21SW/2 | SP 2499 1003 | 429.46 |
| Southrop (RAF) | 235 | SP10SE/33 | SP 1801 0052 | 57.3 |
| Southrop (TWA) | 235 | SP10SE/41 | SP 1850 0234 | 105 |
| Stanford Hall | 235 | SP10SE/34 | SP 1909 0204 | 54.86 |
| Staverton No. 1* | 216 | SO82SE/49 | SO 8840 2290 | 1072.9 |
| Stowell Park (BGS)* | 235 | SP01SE/1 | SP 0835 1176 | 1372.51 |
| Stowell Park soakaway | 235 | SP01SE/23 | SP 0960 1418 | 39 |
| Tarlton Manor House | 252 | SO90SE/1 | SO 9573 0007 | 62.79 |
| Upton (BGS)* | 235 | SP21SW/1 | SP 2315 1313 | 1148.18 |
| Waiten Hill House | 252 | SP10SW/24 | SP 1304 0042 | 66 |
| Westwell No.1 | 235 | SP20NW/13 | SP 2075 0949 | 71.02 |

| Borehole name | 1:50 000 Sheet | Borehole number | Grid reference | Depth (m) |
|---|---|---|---|---|
| Westwell Manor | 235 | SP20NW/9 | SP 2231 0985 | 57.3 |
| Westwell Manor | 235 | SP20NW/7 | SP 206 091 | 121.92 |
| Windrush (RAF) | 235 | SP11SE/3 | SP 1873 1107 | 139.29 |
| Windyridge | 235 | SP01SE/4 | SP 0560 1154 | 53.95 |
| Winstone (Gaskill's Farm) (BGS)* | 235 | SO90NE/1 | SO 9510 0913 | 73.46 |
| Winstone (RAF) | 235 | SO91SE/1 | SO9644 1020 | 138.99 |
| Winterwell Farm | 235 | SP11SW/11 | SP 1062 1310 | 91.44 |
| The Woodhouse | 235 | SO90SE/8 | SO 9723 0320 | 43 |

## Hydrogeology

Data on water boreholes, wells and springs are held in the BGS (Hydrogeology Group) databases at BGS Wallingford. The hydrogeological databases include:

- A databank of all licensed wells, boreholes and springs, containing the permitted rates of abstraction (which may be confidential where they relate to individual industrial users) and the location, depth and diameter of the well or borehole.
- A databank of groundwater chemistry relating to all public water supply sources and selected industrial sources.
- Limited data on long-term changes in groundwater levels. Similar data are held by the Environment Agency.

## MATERIALS COLLECTIONS

### Geological Survey photographs

Copies of these photographs are deposited for reference in the library at BGS, Keyworth, Nottingham. Black and white prints can be supplied and, in addition, colour prints are available for the more recent photographs.

| Number | Date | Subject |
|---|---|---|
| A5756–5768 | 1929 | Sections exposed in quarries and railway cuttings, and landscapes; includes originals of plates used by Richardson (1933) |
| A8573–8576 | 1951 | Stowell Park Borehole site: drilling operations |
| A10527–10528 | 1966 | Foss Cross Quarry |
| A11023–11025 | 1967 | Sections exposed in Hailey Wood railway cutting [SO 962 012] |
| A12424–12425 | 1975 | Lee's Quarry, Taynton [SP 246 152] |
| A15415–15466 | 1995 | Sections and general views |
| GS533 | 1994 | Bourton Hill Quarry (Plate 5) |
| GS534 | 1993 | Farmington Quarry (Plate 7) |
| GS535 | 1995 | Thornhill Farm Quarry (Plate 11) |

### Petrological collection

About 300 hand specimens and companion thin sections comprise the petrological collection for the Cirencester district. Most of these were collected from the Survey's Stowell Park Borehole. Access to the collection is facilitated through a digital database, the *BGS Petmin Database*, which holds index data for England, Wales and Scotland. Further information can be obtained from the Curator, Petrography and Mineralogy Collections, BGS Keyworth.

### Biostratigraphy collections

Macrofossils and micropalaeontological residues for samples collected from exposures and boreholes in the Cirencester district are held in these collections. They cannot, at present, be accessed via a digital database but an indication of their holdings can be gained from scrutiny of the biostratigraphical reports listed above. Enquiries should be directed to the Curator, Biostratigraphy Collections, BGS Keyworth.

## MINERAL INDUSTRY OPERATORS (1994)

| Location | Operator | Mineral: geological unit |
|---|---|---|
| Daglingworth [SP 001 061] | ARC Southern | Limestone: White Limestone (and Hampen) Formation |
| Ampney Down [SP 048 070] | W E Berry | Limestone: Forest Marble Formation |
| Farmington [SP 131 169] | Farmington Stone Ltd | Limestone: Taynton Limestone Formation |
| Thornhill Farm [SP 181 005] | ARC Southern | Sand and gravel: River Terrace Deposits (Northmoor Member) |

## EARTH SCIENCE CONSERVATION

Earth science sites of Special Scientific Interest (SSSI) lying wholly or partly within the sheet are:

Foss Cross Quarry SSSI; Geological Conservation Review (GCR) site number 1541 [SP 0555 0927]

Leckhampton Hill and Charlton King's Common SSSI; GCR site number 168 [SO 946 183 to SO 952 187 to SO 951 179]

Stony Furlong railway cutting SSSI; GCR site number 2242 [SP 0605 1091 to SP 0635 1027].

Reports describing each of these sites are available from English Nature, the organisation which adminsters Sites of Special Scientific Interest, at Northminster House, Peterborough. PE1 1UA. Telephone 01733 455000. Fax (01733) 568834. The sites are also described by Cox and Sumbler (in prep.).

Chedworth Woods railway cuttings [SP 05 13] lie within a nature reserve managed by the Gloucestershire Trust for Wildlife Conservation.

The local record centre for the National Scheme for Geological Site Documentation is located at the Museum and Art Gallery, Queen's Road, Bristol, BS8 1RL.

### Addresses for data sources

BGS Hydrogeology Enquiry Service; wells, springs and water borehole records.
British Geological Survey, Hydrogeology Group
Maclean Building, Crowmarsh Gifford,
Wallingford, Oxfordshire, OX10 8BB
*Telephone*   01491 838800
*Fax*   01491 692345

London Information Office at the Natural History Museum
Earth Galleries
Exhibition Road, South Kensington
London SW7 2DE
*Telephone*   0171 589 4090
*Telex*   0171 938 9056/9057
*Fax*   0171 584 8270

British Geological Survey (Headquarters)
Keyworth, Nottingham NG12 5GG
*Telephone*   0115 936 3100
*Telex*   9378173 BGSKEY G
*Fax*   0115 936 3200
Web site *http://www.bgs.ac.uk.*

# REFERENCES

Most of the references listed below are held in the library of the British Geological Survey at Keyworth Nottingham. Copies of the references can be purchased subject to the current copyright legislation.

ADAMS, H F. 1963. The coal seams of the Upton borehole. Appendix A *in* The stratigraphy of the Geological Survey Upton Borehole, Oxfordshire. WORSSAM, B C. *Bulletin of the Geological Survey of Great Britain*, No. 20, 107–156.

AGER, D V. 1969. The Lower and Middle Jurassic rocks of the Cotswold escarpment and the Vale of Gloucester. *In* Excursion No. 2 Guide for north Somerset and Gloucestershire. International Field Symposium on the British Jurassic. University of Keele, B27–B43. TORRENS, H S (editor).

AGER, D V, DONOVAN, D T, KENNEDY, W J, McKERROW, W S, MUDGE, D C, and SELLWOOD, B W. 1973. The Cotswold Hills. *Geologists' Association Guide*, No. 36.

ALLEN, J R L, and KAYE, P. 1973. Sedimentary facies of the Forest Marble (Bathonian), Shipton-on-Cherwell Quarry, Oxfordshire. *Geological Magazine*, Vol. 110, 153–163.

ANON. 1972. *Natural Stone Directory* (2nd edition). (London: Park Lane Publications).

ANON. 1980a. Low rise buildings on shrinkable clay soil: Part 2. *Building Research Establishment, Watford, Digest*, No. 241.

ANON. 1980b. Low rise buildings on shrinkable clay soil: Part 3. *Building Research Establishment, Watford, Digest*, No. 242.

ANON. 1985. The influence of trees on house foundations in clay soils. *Building Research Establishment, Watford, Digest*, No. 298.

ANON. 1991. Sulphate and acid resistance of concrete in the ground. *Building Research Establishment, Watford, Digest*, No. 363.

ANON. 1993. Low rise buildings on shrinkable clay soil: Part 1. *Building Research Establishment, Watford, Digest*, No. 240.

ARKELL, W J. 1933a. *The Jurassic System in Great Britain.* (Oxford: Clarendon Press.)

ARKELL, W J. 1933b. The oysters of the Fuller's Earth; and on the evolution and nomenclature of the Upper Jurassic Catinulas and Gryphaeas. *Proceedings of the Cotteswold Naturalists' Field Club*, Vol. 25, 21–68.

ARKELL, W J. 1947a. *Oxford stone.* (London: Faber and Faber.)

ARKELL, W J. 1947b. *The geology of Oxford.* (Oxford: Clarendon Press.)

ARKELL, W J. 1951. A monograph of English Bathonian ammonites. Part 1. *Monograph of the Palaeontographical Society.*

ARKELL, W J. 1958. A monograph of English Bathonian ammonites. Part 8. *Monograph of the Palaeontographical Society.*

ARKELL, W J, and DONOVAN, D T. 1952. The Fuller's Earth of the Cotswolds and its relation to the Great Oolite. *Quarterly Journal of the Geological Society of London*, Vol. 107, 227–253.

BAKER, P G. 1974. The geology of Westington Hill Quarry, Gloucestershire. *Mercian Geologist*, Vol. 5, 133–142.

BAKER, P G. 1981. Interpretation of the Oolite Marl (Upper Aalenian, Lower Inferior Oolite) of the Cotswolds, England. *Proceedings of the Geologists' Association*, Vol. 92, 169–187.

BALLANTYNE C K, and HARRIS C. 1994. *The periglaciation of Great Britain.* (Cambridge: Cambridge University Press.)

BARCLAY, W J, AMBROSE, K, CHADWICK, R A, and PHARAOH, T C. 1997. Geology of the country around Worcester. *Memoir of the British Geological Survey*, Sheet 199 (England and Wales).

BARKER, M J. 1976. A stratigraphical, palaeoecological and biometrical study of some English Bathonian Gastropoda (especially Nerinacea). Unpublished PhD thesis, University of Keele.

BARKER, M J. 1994. The biostratigraphical potential of nerinacean gastropods — case studies from the Middle Jurassic of England and the Upper Jurassic of France. *Geobios*, Vol. 17, 93–101.

BARRON, A J M. 1986. Geological notes and local details for 1:10 000 sheets: SP 10 SE (Fairford). *British Geological Survey Technical Report*, WA/DM/86/12.

BARRON, A J M. 1995. *A preliminary study of the drift deposits of Gloucestershire, with special emphasis on potential resources of sand and gravel.* (Keyworth, Nottingham: British Geological Survey for Gloucestershire County Council.)

BARRON, A J M, SUMBLER, M G, and MORIGI, A N. 1997. A revised lithostratigraphy for the Inferior Oolite Group (Middle Jurassic) of the Cotswolds, England. *Proceedings of the Geologists' Association*, Vol. 108, 269–285.

BLAKE, J F. 1905. A monograph of the fauna of the Cornbrash. *Monograph of the Palaeontographical Society of London.*

BONEHAM, B F W, and WYATT, R J. 1993. The stratigraphical position of the Middle Jurassic (Bathonian) Stonesfield Slate of Stonesfield, Oxfordshire, U.K. *Proceedings of the Geologists' Association*, Vol. 104, 123–136.

BRADSHAW, M J. 1978. A facies analysis of the Bathonian of eastern England. Unpublished PhD thesis, University of Oxford.

BRIDGLAND, D R. 1994. *The Quaternary of the Thames. Geological Conservation Review Series*, Vol. 7. (London: Joint Nature Conservation Committee/Chapman and Hall.)

BRIGGS, D J. 1973. The Quaternary deposits of the Evenlode valley and adjacent areas. Unpublished PhD thesis, Bristol University.

BRIGGS, D J. 1975. Origin, depositional environment and age of the Cheltenham Sand and Gravel and related deposits. *Proceedings of the Geologists' Association*, Vol. 86, 333–348.

BRIGGS, D J, COOPE, G R, and GILBERTSON, D D. 1985. The chronology and environmental framework of early Man in the Upper Thames valley: a new model. *British Archaeological Report, British Series*, Vol. 137.

BRITISH GEOLOGICAL SURVEY. 1985. Pre-Permian geology of the UK (south). Maps 1 and 2. 1:100 000.

BRODIE, P B. 1850. On certain beds in the Inferior Oolite, near Cheltenham. *Quarterly Journal of the Geological Society of London*, Vol. 6, 239–251.

BROWN, R C, BRIGGS, D J, and GILBERTSON, D D. 1980. Depositional environment of late Pleistocene terrace gravels of the Vale of Bourton, Gloucestershire. *Mercian Geologist*, Vol. 7, 269–278.

BUCKLAND, W. 1818. Order of the superposition of strata. In *Outline of the geology of England and Wales*. Phillips, W. (London).

BUCKMAN, J. 1842. Sketch of the Oolite formation of the Cotteswold range of hills, near Cheltenham. *Geologist*, Vol. 1, 199–208.

BUCKMAN, J. 1843. Geological chart of the oolitic strata of the Cotswold Hills and the Lias of the Vale of Gloucester. (Cheltenham).

BUCKMAN, S S. 1860. On some fossil reptilian eggs from the Great Oolite of Cirencester. *Quarterly Journal of the Geological Society of London*, Vol. 16, 107–110.

BUCKMAN, S S. 1887. The Inferior Oolite between Andoversford and Bourton-on-the-Water. *Proceedings of the Cotteswold Naturalists' Field Club*, Vol. 9, 108–135.

BUCKMAN, S S. 1892. The sections exposed between Andoversford and Chedworth: a comparison with similar strata upon the Banbury Line. *Proceedings of the Cotteswold Naturalists' Field Club*, Vol. 10, 94–100.

BUCKMAN, S S. 1893. The Bajocian of the Sherborne district: its relation to subjacent and superjacent strata. *Quarterly Journal of the Geological Society of London*, Vol. 49, 479–522.

BUCKMAN, S S. 1895. The Bajocian of the mid-Cotteswolds. *Quarterly Journal of the Geological Society of London*, Vol. 51, 388–462.

BUCKMAN, S S. 1897. Deposits of the Bajocian age in the northern Cotteswolds: the Cleeve Hill Plateau. *Quarterly Journal of the Geological Society of London*, Vol. 53, 607–629.

BUCKMAN, S S. 1901. Bajocian and contiguous deposits in the north Cotteswolds: the main hill-mass. *Quarterly Journal of the Geological Society of London*, Vol. 57, 126–155.

BUCKMAN, S S. 1905a. A monograph of the ammonites of the 'Inferior Oolite Series'. *Monograph of the Palaeontographical Society*. Pt. 13, Supplement, pp. clxix-ccix.

BUCKMAN, S S. 1905b. On certain genera and species of Lycoteratidae. *Quarterly Journal of the Geological Society of London*, Vol. 61, 142–154.

BUCKMAN, S S. 1924–1925. *Type ammonites*. Vol. 5. (Thame and London.)

CALLAWAY, C. 1905. The occurrence of glacial clay on the Cotteswold Plateau. *Geological Magazine*, Vol. 2, 216–219.

CALLOMON, J H. 1995. Time from fossils: BUCKMAN S S, and Jurassic high-resolution geochronology. 85–112 in Milestones in geology. LE BAS, M J (editor). *Geological Society of London Memoir*, No. 16.

CALLOMON, J H, and CHANDLER, R B. 1990. A review of the ammonite horizons of the Aalenian–Bajocian stages in the Middle Jurassic of southern England. *Memorie descrittive della carta geologica d'Italia*, Vol. 40, 85–112.

CALLOMON, J H, and COPE, J C W. 1995. The Jurassic geology of Dorset. 51–103 in *Field geology of the British Jurassic*. TAYLOR, P D (editor). (London: Geological Society.)

CAVE, R. 1977. Geology of the Malmesbury District. *Memoir of the Geological Survey of Great Britain*, Sheet 251 (England and Wales).

CAVE, R, and COX, B M. 1975. The Kellaways Beds of the area between Chippenham and Malmesbury, Wiltshire. *Bulletin of the Geological Survey of Great Britain*, No. 54, 41–66.

CHADWICK, R A. 1985. Seismic reflection investigations into the stratigraphy and structural evolution of the Worcester Basin. *Journal of the Geological Society of London*, Vol. 142, 187–202.

CHADWICK, R A, and EVANS, D J. 1995. The timing and direction of Permo-Triassic extension in southern Britain. 161–192 In Permian and Triassic rifting in Northwest Europe. BOLDY, S A R (editor). *Special Publication of the Geological Society of London*, No. 91.

CHADWICK, R A, and SMITH, N J P. 1988. Evidence of negative structural inversion beneath central England from new seismic reflection data. *Journal of the Geological Society of London*, Vol. 145, 519–522.

CLIFTON-TAYLOR, A. 1972. *The pattern of English building*. (London: Faber and Faber.)

COPE, J C W (editor). 1980a. A correlation of Jurassic rocks in the British Isles. Part One: Introduction and Lower Jurassic. *Special Report of the Geological Society of London*, No. 14.

COPE, J C W (editor). 1980b. A correlation of Jurassic rocks in the British Isles. Part Two: Middle and Upper Jurassic. *Special Report of the Geological Society of London*, No. 15.

COX, B M, and SUMBLER, M G. in prep. *British Middle Jurassic stratigraphy*. Geological Conservation Review Series, Vol. 22. (Peterborough: Joint Nature Conservation Committee/Chapman and Hall.)

COX, B M, SUMBLER, M G, and MILNER, A C. 1999. Fossilized turtle eggs from Cirencester. *Proceedings of the Geologists' Association*, Vol. 110, 267–270.

COX, B M, SUMBLER, M G, and IVIMEY-COOK, H C. 1999. A formational framework for the Lower Jurassic of England and Wales (Onshore area). BGS Research Report No. RR/99/01.

DE RANCE, C E. 1878. On the Palaeozoic and secondary rocks of England as a source of water supply for towns and districts. *Transactions of the Manchester Geological Society*, Vol. 14.

DE RANCE, C E. 1879. Fourth report of the committee for investigating the circulation of the underground waters in the Jurassic, New Red Sandstone, and Permian formations of England. *Report of the British Association* for 1878 (Dublin). 382–419.

DEAN, W T, DONOVAN, D T, and HOWARTH, M K. 1961. The Liassic ammonite zones and subzones of the north-west European province. *Bulletin of the British Museum (Natural History)*, Vol. 4, 437–505.

DONOVAN, D T, HORTON, A, and IVIMEY-COOK, H C. 1979. The transgression of the Lower Lias over the northern flank of the London Platform. *Journal of the Geological Society of London*, Vol. 136, 165–173.

DOUGLAS, J A, and ARKELL, W J. 1928. The stratigraphical distribution of the Cornbrash. I The south-western area. *Quarterly Journal of the Geological Society of London*, Vol. 84, 117–178.

DOUGLAS, J A, and ARKELL, W J. 1932. The stratigraphical distribution of the Cornbrash. II The north-eastern area. *Quarterly Journal of the Geological Society of London*, Vol. 88, 112–170.

DUNHAM, K C, and POOLE, E G. 1974. The Oxfordshire Coalfield. *Journal of the Geological Society of London*, Vol. 130, 387–391.

FORSTER, A, CULSHAW, M G, and BELL, F G. 1995. Regional distribution of sulphate in rocks and soils of Britain. 95–104 in Engineering Geology of Construction. EDDLESTON, M, WALTHALL, S, CRIPPS, J C, and CULSHAW M G (editors). *Geological Society of London engineering geology Special Publication*, No. 10.

FOSTER, D, HOLLIDAY, D W, JONES, C M, OWENS, B, and WELSH, A. 1989. The concealed Upper Palaeozoic rocks of Berkshire and South Oxfordshire. *Proceedings of the Geologists' Association*, Vol. 100, 395–407.

GALLOIS, R W, and WORSSAM, B C. 1983. Stratigraphy of the Harwell boreholes. *Report of the Institute of Geological Sciences, FLPU*, No. 83–14.

GREEN, G W, and MELVILLE, R V. 1956. The stratigraphy of the Stowell Park Borehole (1949–1951). *Bulletin of the Geological Survey of Great Britain*, No. 11, 1–66.

HALLAM, A. 1964. Origin of the limestone–shale rhythm in the Blue Lias of England: a composite theory. *Journal of Geology*, Vol. 72, 157–169.

HARKER, A. 1884. On a remarkable exposure of Kellaways Rock in a recent cutting near Cirencester. *Proceedings of the Cotteswold Naturalists' Field Club*, Vol. 8, 176–187.

HARKER, A. 1890. On the sections in the Forest Marble and Great Oolite formations exposed by the new railway from Cirencester to Chedworth. *Proceedings of the Cotteswold Naturalists' Field Club*, Vol. 10, 82–94.

HARKER, A. 1891. On the geology of Cirencester Town, and a recent discovery of the Oxford Clay in a deep well boring at the Water Works. *Proceedings of the Cotteswold Naturalists' Field Club*, Vol. 10, 178–191.

HARLAND, T L, and TORRENS, H S. 1982. A redescription of the Bathonian red alga *Solenopora jurassica* from Gloucestershire, with remarks on its preservation. *Palaeontology*, Vol. 25, 905–912.

HAWKINS, A B, and PRIVETT K D. 1981. A building site on cambered ground at Radstock, Avon. *Quarterly Journal of Engineering Geology*, Vol. 14, 151–168.

HEY, R W. 1986. A re-examination of the Northern Drift of Oxfordshire. *Proceedings of the Geologists' Association*, Vol. 97, 291–302.

HIGGINBOTTOM, I E, and FOOKES, P G. 1971. Engineering aspects of periglacial features in Britain. *Quarterly Journal of Engineering Geology*, Vol. 3, 85–171.

HOLLINGWORTH, S E, TAYLOR, J H, and KELLAWAY, G A. 1944. Large scale superficial structures in the Northamptonshire Ironstone Field. *Quarterly Journal of the Geological Society*, Vol. 100, 1–44.

HOLLOWAY, S. 1983. The shell-detrital calcirudites of the Forest Marble Formation (Bathonian) of south-west England. *Proceedings of the Geologists' Association*, Vol. 94, 259–266.

HORSWILL, P, and HORTON, A. 1976. Cambering and valley bulging in the Gwash Valley at Empingham, Rutland. *Philosophical Transactions of the Royal Society of London*, A, Vol. 283, 427–451.

HORTON, A, AMBROSE, K, and COX, B M. 1989. Geological sequence at the Down Ampney Fault Research site, Gloucestershire, England. *British Geological Survey Technical Report*, WE/89/7.

HORTON, A, and POOLE, E G. 1977. The lithostratigraphy of three geophysical marker horizons in the Lower Lias of Oxfordshire. *Bulletin of the Geological Survey of Great Britain*, No. 62, 13–33.

HORTON, A, POOLE, E G, WILLIAMS, B J, ILLING, V C, and HOBSON, G D. 1987. Geology of the country around Chipping Norton. *Memoir of the British Geological Survey*, Sheet 218 (England and Wales).

HORTON, A, SUMBLER, M G, COX, B M, and AMBROSE, K. 1995. Geology of the country around Thame. *Memoir of the British Geological Survey*, Sheet 237 (England and Wales).

HOWARTH, M K. 1958. A monograph of the ammonites of the Liassic family Amaltheidae in Britain. Part 1. *Monograph of the Palaeontographical Society*.

HOWARTH, M K. 1980. The Toarcian age of the upper part of the Marlstone Rock Bed of England. *Palaeontology*, Vol. 23, 637–656.

HOWARTH, M K. 1992. The ammonite family Hildoceratidae in the Lower Jurassic of Britain. Part 1. *Monograph of the Palaeontographical Society*.

HULL, E. 1855. On the physical geography and Pleistocene phenomena of the Cotteswold Hills. *Quarterly Journal of the Geological Society of London*, Vol. 11, 475–496.

HULL, E. 1857. The geology of the country around Cheltenham. *Memoir of the Geological Survey of Great Britain*, (Old Series Sheet 44).

HUTCHINSON, J N. 1967. The free degradation of London Clay cliffs. *Proceedings of the Geotechnical Conference, Oslo*, Vol. 1, 113–118.

HUTCHINSON, J N. 1991. Periglacial and slope processes. 283–331 in Quaternary engineering geology. FORSTER, A, CULSHAW, M G, CRIPPS, J C, LITTLE, J A, and MOON, C F (editors). *Geological Society of London Engineering Geology Special Publication*, No. 7.

IVIMEY-COOK, H C, and DONOVAN, D T. 1983. The fauna of the Lower Jurassic. Appendix 3 in Geology of the country around Weston-super-Mare. WHITTAKER, A, and GREEN, G W. *Memoir of the Geological Survey*, Sheet 279 (England and Wales).

KELLAWAY, G A, and WELCH, F B A. 1993. Geology of the Bristol district. *Memoir of the British Geological Survey*.

KERSHAW, S, and SMITH, R. 1986. A Bathonian hardground at Foss Cross, near Cirencester. *Proceedings of the Cotteswold Naturalists' Field Club*, Vol. 39, 165–179.

LUCY, W C. 1872. The gravels of the Severn, Avon and Evenlode, and their extension over the Cotteswold Hills. *Proceedings of the Cotteswold Naturalists' Field Club*, Vol. 5, 71–125.

LUCY, W C. 1890. Notes on Jurassic rocks, at Crickley. *Proceedings of the Cotteswold Naturalists' Field Club*, Vol. 9, 289–299.

MELVILLE, R V. 1956. The stratigraphical palaeontology, ammonites excluded, of the Stowell Park Borehole. *Bulletin of the Geological Survey of Great Britain*, No. 11, 67–139.

MELVILLE, R V. 1963. Stratigraphical palaeontology of the Lias and Rhaetic beds in the Upton Borehole. *Bulletin of the Geological Survey of Great Britain*, No. 20, 163–175.

MERRIMAN, R J, PHARAOH, T C, WOODCOCK, N H, and DALY, P. 1993. The metamorphic history of the concealed Caledonides of eastern England and their foreland. *Geological Magazine*, Vol. 130, 613–620.

MOORLOCK, B S P, and HIGHLEY, D. 1991. An appraisal of fuller's earth resources in England and Wales. *British Geological Survey Technical Report*, WA/91/75.

MORGAN-JONES, M, and EGGBORO, M D. 1981. The hydrogeochemistry of the Jurassic limestones in Gloucestershire, England. *Quarterly Journal of Engineering Geology*, Vol. 14, 25–39.

MORIGI, A N. 1995a. Geological notes and local details for 1:10 000 Sheet SP 01 NW (Andoversford). *British Geological Survey Technical Report*, WA/95/107.

MORIGI, A N. 1995b. Geological notes and local details for 1:10 000 Sheet SP 01 SW (Colesbourne). *British Geological Survey Technical Report*, WA/95/106.

MUDGE, D C. 1978. Stratigraphy and sedimentation of the Lower Inferior Oolite of the Cotswolds. *Journal of the Geological Society of London*, Vol. 135, 611–627.

MURCHISON, R I. 1834. *Outline of the geology of the neighbourhood of Cheltenham.* (Davies: Cheltenham).

NEGUS, P E, and BEAUVAIS, L. 1975. The Fairford Coral Bed (English Bathonian) Gloucestershire. *Proceedings of the Geologists' Association*, Vol. 86, 183–204.

O'NEIL, H E, and SHOTTON, F W. 1974. Mammoth remains from gravel pits in the north Cotswolds. *Proceedings of the Cotteswold Naturalist's Field Club*, Vol. 36, 196–197.

OLD, R A, HAMBLIN, R J O, AMBROSE, K, and WARRINGTON, G. 1991. Geology of the country around Redditch. *Memoir of the British Geological Survey*, Sheet 183 (England and Wales).

ORBELL, G. 1973. Palynology of the British Rhaeto-Liassic. *Bulletin of the Geological Survey of Great Britain*, No. 44,1–44.

PAGE, K N. 1988. The stratigraphy and ammonites of the British Lower Callovian. Unpublished PhD thesis, University of London.

PAGE, K N. 1989. A stratigraphical revision for the English Lower Callovian. *Proceedings of the Geologists' Association*, Vol. 100, 363–382.

PAGE, K N. 1996. Observations on the succession of ammonite faunas in the Bathonian (Middle Jurassic) of south-west England and their correlation with a sub-Mediterranean 'Standard Zonation'. *Proceedings of the Ussher Society*, Vol. 9, 45–53.

PALMER, C P. 1971. The stratigraphy of the Stonehouse and Tuffley clay pits in Gloucestershire. *Proceedings of the Bristol Naturalists' Society*, Vol. 32, 58–68.

PALMER, C P. 1973. The palaeontology of the Liassic (Lower Jurassic) clay pits at Stonehouse and Tuffley in Gloucestershire. *Geological Magazine*, Vol. 110, 249–263.

PALMER, T J. 1979. The Hampen Marly and White Limestone Formations: Florida-type carbonate lagoons in the Jurassic of central England. *Palaeontology*, Vol. 22, 189–228.

PARKS, C D. 1991. A review of the possible mechanisms of cambering and valley bulging. 373–380 in *Quaternary engineering geology*. FORSTER, A, CULSHAW, M G, CRIPPS, J C, LITTLE, J A, and MOON, C F (editors). *Geological Society of London Engineering Geology Special Publication*, No. 7.

PARSONS, C F. 1976. Ammonite evidence for dating some Inferior Oolite sections in the North Cotswolds. *Proceedings of the Geologists' Association*, Vol. 87, 45–63.

PARSONS, C F. 1980. Aspects of the stratigraphy and ammonite faunas of the Aalenian–Bajocian stages in Great Britain. Unpublished PhD thesis, University of Keele.

PEACE, G R, and BESLEY, B M. 1997. End-Carboniferous fold-thrust structures, Oxfordshire, UK: implications for the structural evolution of the late Variscan foreland of south-central England. *Journal of the Geological Society of London*, Vol. 154, 225–237.

PENN, I E, and WYATT, R J. 1979. The stratigraphy and correlation of the Bathonian strata of the Bath–Frome area. *Report of the Institute of Geological Sciences*, No. 78/22, 23–88.

PHARAOH, T C, MERRIMAN, R J, EVANS, J A, BREWER, T S, WEBB, P C, and SMITH, N J P. 1991. Early Palaeozoic arc-related volcanism in the concealed Caledonides of southern Britain. *Annales de la Société Géologique de Belgique*, Vol. 114, 63–91.

PHELPS, M C. 1985. A refined ammonite stratigraphy for the Middle and Upper Carixian (*ibex* and *davoei* Zones, Lower Jurassic) in north-west Europe and stratigraphical details of the Carixian-Domerian boundary. *Geobios*, Vol. 18, 321–362.

POOLE, E G. 1969. The stratigraphy of the Geological Survey Apley Barn Borehole, Witney, Oxfordshire. *Bulletin of the Geological Survey of Great Britain*, No. 29, 1–103.

POOLE, E G. 1977. Stratigraphy of the Steeple Aston Borehole, Oxfordshire. *Bulletin of the Geological Survey of Great Britain*, No. 57.

POOLE, E G. 1978. Stratigraphy of the Withycombe Farm Borehole, near Banbury, Oxfordshire. *Bulletin of the Geological Survey of Great Britain*, No. 68.

RAMSAY, A C, AVELINE, W T, and HULL, E. 1858. Geology of parts of Wiltshire and Gloucestershire. *Memoir of the Geological Survey of Great Britain*. (Old Series Sheet 34).

RICHARDSON, L. 1904. *Handbook to the geology of Cheltenham and neighbourhood.* (Cheltenham: Norman, Sawyer and Co.)

RICHARDSON, L. 1906. Half-day excursion to Leckhampton Hill, Cheltenham. *Proceedings of the Cotteswold Naturalists' Field Club*, Vol. 15, 182–189.

RICHARDSON, L. 1907a. The Inferior Oolite and contiguous deposits of the district between the Rissingtons and Burford. *Quarterly Journal of the Geological Society of London*, Vol. 63, 437–444.

RICHARDSON, L. 1907b. Excursion to Bourton-on-the-Water and Burford. *Proceedings of the Cotteswold Naturalists' Field Club*, Vol. 16, 23–32.

RICHARDSON, L. 1910a. On two deep well-sinkings at Leckhampton Hill, Cheltenham. *Geological Magazine*, Dec. 5, Vol. 7, 101–104.

RICHARDSON, L. 1910b. The Inferior Oolite and contiguous deposits of the south Cotteswolds. *Proceedings of the Cotteswold Naturalists' Field Club*, Vol. 17, 63–136.

RICHARDSON, L. 1911. On the sections of the Forest Marble and Great Oolite on the railway between Cirencester and Chedworth, Gloucestershire. *Proceedings of the Geologists' Association*, Vol. 22, 95–115.

RICHARDSON, L. 1913. Memoir explanatory of a map of a part of Cheltenham and neighbourhood, showing the distribution of the sand, gravel and clay. *Proceedings of the Cotteswold Naturalists' Field Club*, Vol. 18, 125–136.

RICHARDSON, L. 1925. Excursion to Cirencester and district. *Proceedings of the Geologists' Association*, Vol. 36, 80–99.

RICHARDSON, L. 1927. Excursion to Rissington and Burford. *Proceedings of the Cotteswold Naturalists' Field Club*, Vol. 23, 12–13.

RICHARDSON, L. 1929. The country around Moreton in Marsh. *Memoir of the Geological Survey of Great Britain*. (Sheet 217, England and Wales).

RICHARDSON, L. 1930. Wells and springs of Gloucestershire. *Memoir of the Geological Survey of Great Britain*.

RICHARDSON, L. 1933. The country around Cirencester. *Memoir of the Geological Survey of Great Britain*. (Sheet 235, England and Wales).

RICHARDSON, L, and SANDFORD, K S. 1960. Great Chessels Gravel Pit near Bourton-on-the-Water, Glos., and the occurrence of mammalian remains. *Proceedings of the Geologists' Association*, Vol. 71, 40–46.

RICHARDSON, L, and SANDFORD, K S. 1961. Find of a mammoth tooth at Charlton Kings, Cheltenham. *Proceedings of the Cotteswold Naturalists' Field Club*, Vol. 33, 170–171.

ROBSON, P. 1975. The sand and gravel resources of the Thames Valley, the country around Cricklade, Wiltshire:

Description of 1:25 000 resource sheets SU 09/19 and parts of SP 00/10. *Mineral Assessment Report of the Institute of Geological Sciences*, No. 18.

ROBSON, P. 1976. The sand and gravel resources of the Thames Valley, the country between Lechlade and Standlake: Description of 1:25 000 sheet SP 30 and parts of SP 20, SU 29 and SU 39. *Mineral Assessment Report of the Institute of Geological Sciences*, No. 23.

ROE, D A (editor). 1976. *Field guide to the Oxford region.* (Oxford: Quaternary Research Association.)

SARJEANT, W A S. 1963. Dinoflagellates from upper Triassic sediments. *Nature, London*, Vol. 199, 353–354.

SAVAGE, R J G. 1961. The Witts collection of Stonesfield Slate fossils. *Proceedings of the Cotteswold Naturalists' Field Club*, Vol. 33, 177–182.

SELLWOOD, B W, and McKERROW, W S. 1974. Depositional environments in the lower part of the Great Oolite Group of Oxfordshire and north Gloucestershire. *Proceedings of the Geologists' Association*, Vol. 85, 189–210.

SIMMS, M J. 1990. Upper Pliensbachian stratigraphy in the Severn Basin area: evidence for anomalous structural controls in the Lower and Middle Jurassic. *Proceedings of the Geologists' Association*, Vol. 101, 131–144.

SMITH, N J P. 1987. The deep geology of central England: the prospectivity of the Palaeozoic rocks. 217–224 in *Petroleum geology of northwest Europe*. BROOKS, J, and GLENNIE, K W. (editors). (London: Graham and Trotman.)

SOIL SURVEY OF ENGLAND AND WALES. 1983. Soils of South West England: 1:250 000 scale.

SOIL SURVEY OF ENGLAND AND WALES. 1984. Soils and their use in South West England. *Soil Survey of England and Wales Bulletin*, No. 14.

SOPER, N J, WEBB, B C, and WOODCOCK, N J. 1987. Late Caledonian (Acadian) transpression in North West England: timings, geometry and geotectonic significance. *Proceedings of the Yorkshire Geological Society*, Vol. 46, 175–192.

SPATH, L F. 1938. *A catalogue of the ammonites of the Liassic family Liparoceratidae in the British Museum (Natural History).* (London: British Museum (Natural History).)

SPATH, L F. 1956. The Liassic ammonite faunas of the Stowell Park Borehole. *Bulletin of the Geological Survey of Great Britain*, No. 11, 140–164.

SUMBLER, M G. 1984. The stratigraphy of the Bathonian White Limestone and Forest Marble Formations of Oxfordshire. *Proceedings of the Geologists' Association*, Vol. 95, 51–64.

SUMBLER, M G. 1991. The Fairford Coral Bed: new data on the White Limestone Formation (Bathonian) of the Gloucestershire Cotswolds. *Proceedings of the Geologists' Association*, Vol. 102, 55–62.

SUMBLER, M G. 1994a. Geological notes and local details for 1:10 000 Sheet SP 11 SE (Sherborne). *British Geological Survey Technical Report*, WA/94/26.

SUMBLER, M G. 1994b. Geological notes and local details for 1:10 000 Sheet SP 21 SW (The Barringtons). *British Geological Survey Technical Report*, WA/94/92.

SUMBLER, M G. 1995a. Geological notes and local details for 1:10 000 Sheet SP 11 NE (The Rissingtons). *British Geological Survey Technical Report*, WA/95/17.

SUMBLER, M G. 1995b. Geological notes and local details for 1:10 000 Sheet SP 11 NW (Farmington). *British Geological Survey Technical Report*, WA/95/3.

SUMBLER, M G. 1995c. Geological notes and local details for 1:10 000 Sheet SP 00 NE (Barnsley, Gloucestershire). *British Geological Survey Technical Report*, WA/95/66.

SUMBLER, M G. 1995d. The terraces of the rivers Thame and Thames and their bearing on the chronology of glaciation in central and eastern England. *Proceedings of the Geologists' Association*, Vol. 106, 93–106.

SUMBLER, M G. 1996. *British regional geology: London and the Thames valley.* 4th edition. (London: HMSO for the British Geological Survey.)

SUMBLER, M G. 1999. Correlation of the Bathonian (Middle Jurassic) succession in the Minchinhampton-Burford district. *Proceedings of the Geologists' Association*, Vol. 110, 53–64.

SUMBLER, M G, and BARRON, A J M. 1995. Geological notes and local details for 1:10 000 Sheet SP 01 SE (Chedworth). *British Geological Survey Technical Report*, WA/95/73.

SUMBLER, M G, and BARRON, A J M. 1996. The type section of the Hampen Formation (Middle Jurassic, Great Oolite Group) at Hampen Cutting, Gloucestershire. *Proceedings of the Cotteswold Naturalists' Field Club*, Vol. 40, 118–128.

SUMBLER, M G, and WILLIAMSON, I T. 1999. Lee's Quarry Taynton: a type locality for the Taynton Limestone Formation (Middle Jurassic, Great Oolite Group). *Proceedings of the Cotteswold Naturalists' Field Club*. Vol. 41, 222–229.

TIDDEMAN, R H. 1910. The water supply of Oxfordshire. *Memoir of the Geological Survey of Great Britain*.

TOMES, R F. 1886. On some new or imperfectly known madreporaria from the Inferior Oolite of Oxfordshire, Gloucestershire and Dorsetshire. *Geological Magazine*, Vol. 23, 385–398; 443–452.

TOMLINSON, M E. 1940. Pleistocene gravels of the Cotswold subedge plain from Mickleton to the Frome valley. *Quarterly Journal of the Geological Society of London*, Vol. 96, 385–421.

TORRENS, H S. 1969. The stratigraphical distribution of Bathonian ammonites in central England. *Geological Magazine*, Vol. 106, 63–76.

TORRENS, H S. 1974. Standard zones of the Bathonian. *Mémoire du Bureau des Recherches Géologiques et Minières*, Vol. 75, 581–604.

VEREY, D. 1979. *Buildings of England: Gloucestershire, the Cotswolds.* (Penguin.)

WARRINGTON, G. 1970. The stratigraphy and palaeontology of the 'Keuper' Series of the central Midlands of England. *Quarterly Journal of the Geological Society of London*, Vol. 126, 183–223.

WARRINGTON, G, AUDLEY-CHARLES, M G, ELLIOTT, R E, EVANS, W B, IVIMEY-COOK, H C, KENT, P E, ROBINSON, P L, SHOTTON, F W, and TAYLOR, F M. 1980. A correlation of Triassic rocks in the British Isles. *Special Report of the Geological Society of London*, No. 13.

WETHERED, E. 1891. The Inferior Oolite of the Cotteswold Hills, with special reference to its microscopical structure. *Quarterly Journal of the Geological Society of London*, Vol. 47, 550–570.

WHITEMAN, C A, and ROSE, J. 1992. Thames river sediments of the British Early and Middle Pleistocene. *Quaternary Science Reviews*, Vol. 11, 363–375.

WHITTAKER, A (editor). 1985. *Atlas of onshore sedimentary basins in England and Wales.* (Glasgow: Blackie and Sons Ltd.)

WILLIAMSON, I T. 1995. Geological notes and local details for 1:10 000 Sheet SP 21 NW (Fifield). *British Geological Survey Technical Report*, WA/95/79.

WILLS, L J. 1970.   The Triassic succession in the central Midlands in its regional setting.   *Quarterly Journal of the Geological Society of London*, Vol. 225–285.

WILLS, L J. 1976.   The Trias of Worcestershire and Warwickshire.   *Report of the Institute of Geological Sciences.* No. 76/2.

WOODWARD, H B. 1893.   The Jurassic rocks of Britain. Vol. 3. The Lias of England and Wales (Yorkshire excepted).   *Memoir of the Geological Survey of the United Kingdom.*

WOODWARD, H B. 1894.   The Jurassic rocks of Britain; Vol. 4. The Lower Oolitic Rocks of Britain (Yorkshire excepted).   *Memoir of the Geological Survey of the United Kingdom.*

WOODWARD, H B. 1895.   The Jurassic rocks of Britain. Vol. 5. The Middle and Upper Oolitic rocks of England (Yorkshire excepted).   *Memoir of the Geological Survey of the United Kingdom.*

WORSSAM, B C. 1963.   The stratigraphy of the Geological Survey Upton Borehole, Oxfordshire.   *Bulletin of the Geological Survey of Great Britain*, No. 20, 107–156.

WORSSAM, B C. 1987.   Constitution of Northern Drift at a Cotswold site.   *Proceedings of the Geologists' Association*, Vol. 98, 269–270.

WORSSAM, B C, and BISSON, G. 1961.   The geology of the country between Sherborne, Gloucestershire and Burford, Oxfordshire.   *Bulletin of the Geological Survey of Great Britain*, No. 17, 75–115.

WORSSAM, B C, ELLISON, R A, and MOORLOCK, B S P. 1989.   Geology of the country around Tewkesbury.   *Memoir of the British Geological Survey*, Sheet 216 (England and Wales).

WRIGHT, T. 1856.   On the palaeontological and stratigraphical relations of the so-called 'Sands of the Inferior Oolite'.   *Quarterly Journal of the Geological Society of London*, Vol. 12, 292–325.

WRIGHT, T. 1860.   On the subdivisions of the Inferior Oolite of the south of England, compared with the equivalent beds of that formation on the Yorkshire coast.   *Quarterly Journal of the Geological Society of London*, Vol. 16, 1–48.

WYATT, R J. 1996.   A correlation of the Bathonian (Middle Jurassic) succession between Bath and Burford, and its relation to that near Oxford.   *Proceedings of the Geologists' Association*, Vol. 107, 299–322.

# AUTHOR CITATIONS FOR FOSSIL SPECIES

To satisfy the rules and recommendations of the international codes of botanical and zoological nomenclature, authors of cited species are listed below.

## Chapter 3    (Basement geology)

*Atreta* [*Dimyopsis*] *intusstriata* (Emmrich, 1853)
*Eotrapezium concentricum* (Moore, 1861)
*Eotrapezium germari* (Dunker, 1846)
*Meleagrinella fallax* (Pflücker, 1868)
*Modiolus hillanoides* (Chapuis and Dewalque, 1855)
*Modiolus langportensis* (Richardson and Tutcher, 1914)
*Naiadita lanceolata* J Buckman, 1850
*Protocardia rhaetica* (Merian, 1853)
*Rhaetavicula contorta* (Portlock, 1843)

## Chapter 4    (Lias Group)

*Aegoceras capricornus* (Schlotheim, 1820)
*Amaltheus subnodosus* (Young and Bird, 1828)
*Cleviceras exaratum* (Young and Bird, 1828)
*Dactylioceras holandrei* (d'Orbigny, 1845)
*Dactylioceras mucronatum* (d'Orbigny, 1844)
*Dactylioceras semicelatum* (Simpson, 1843)
*Dumortieria levesquei* (d'Orbigny, 1844)
*Eleganticeras elegantulum* (Young and Bird, 1822)
*Gibbirhynchia micra* Ager, 1954
*Gibbirhynchia tiltonensis* Ager, 1954
*Harpoceras falciferum* (J Sowerby, 1820)
*Harpoceras serpentinum* (Schlotheim, 1813)
*Haugia grandis* S S Buckman, 1898

*Lobothyris edwardsi* (Davidson, 1851)
*Lobothyris punctata* (J Sowerby, 1813)
*Lytoceras sublineatum* (Oppel, 1856)
*Nannirhynchia pygmaea* (Morris, 1847)
*Oistoceras curvicorne* (Schloenbach, 1863)
*Phymatoceras lilli* (von Hauer, 1856)
*Pleuroceras hawskerense* (Young and Bird, 1828)
*Pleuroceras solare* (Phillips, 1829)
*Pseudopecten equivalvis* (J Sowerby, 1816)
*Tetrarhynchia tetrahedra* (J Sowerby, 1812)
*Tiltoniceras antiquum* (Wright, 1882)

## Chapter 5    (Inferior Oolite)

*Acanthothyris spinosa* (Linnaeus, 1767)
*Aulacothyris meriani* (Oppel, 1857)
*Clypeus ploti* Salter, 1857
*Entolium corneolum* (Young and Bird, 1828)
*Gervillella acuta* (J de C Sowerby, 1826)
*Gryphaea bilobata* J de C Sowerby, 1816
*Lobothyris buckmani* (Davidson, 1851)
*Pachylytoceras phylloceratiodes* S S Buckman, 1905
*Plectoidothyris plicata* (J Buckman, 1844)
*Plectothyris fimbria* (J Sowerby, 1822)
*Propeamussium pumilum* (Lamarck, 1819)
*Stiphrothyris tumida* (Davidson, 1878)
*Terebratula globata* J de C Sowerby, 1823
*Trigonia costata* Parkinson, 1811
*Witchellia laeviuscula* (J de C Sowerby, 1824)
*Witchellia platymorpha* S S Buckman, 1925

## Chapter 6    (Great Oolite)

*Aphanoptyxis bladonensis* (Arkell, 1931)
*Aphanoptyxis excavata* Barker M S, 1976
*Aphanoptyxis langrunensis* (d'Orbigny, 1850)
*Bakevellia waltoni* (Lycett, 1863)
*Cererithyris intermedia* (J Sowerby, 1812)
*Chomatoseris porpites* (Wm Smith, 1816)
*Clydoniceras discus* (J Sowerby, 1813)
*Clydoniceras discus* var. *hochstetteri* (Oppel, 1857)
*Clypeus muelleri* Wright, 1859

*Digonella digonoides* S S Buckman, 1913
*Epithyris oxonica* Arkell, 1931
*Isastraea limitata* (Lamouroux, 1849)
*Meleagrinella echinata* (Wm Smith, 1817)
*Microthyridina lagenalis* (Schlotheim, 1820)
*Microthyridina siddingtonensis* (Walker, 1878)
*Modiolus imbricatus* (J Sowerby, 1818)
*Morrisiceras comma* (S S Buckman, 1921)
*Obovothyris obovata* (J Sowerby, 1812)
*Ostrea sowerbyi* Morris and Lycett, 1853
*Plagiostoma subcardiiformis* (Greppin, 1867)
*Praeexogyra acuminata* (J Sowerby, 1816)
*Praeexogyra hebridica* (Forbes, 1851)
*Procerites imitator* (S S Buckman, 1922)
*Procerites progracilis* (Cox and Arkell, 1950)
*Procerites quercinus* (Terquem and Jourdy, 1869)
*Procerites mirabilis* Arkell, 1958
*Procerites tmetolobus* S S Buckman, 1923
*Solenopora jurassica* Brown, 1894
*Stylina babeana* d'Orbigny, 1850
*Thamnasteria lyelli* (Edwards and Haime, 1851)
*Tulites mustela* Arkell, 1954

## Chapter 7    (Kellaways and Oxford Clay formations)

*Ammonites macrocephalus* Schlotheim, 1813
*Anisocardia tenera* (J Sowerby, 1821)
*Nicaniella phillis* (d'Orbigny, 1850)
*Pleuromya alduini* (Brongniart, 1821)
*Rollierella minima* (J Sowerby, 1821)

## Chapter 8    (Quaternary)

*Coelodonta antiquitatis* (Blumenbach, 1799)
*Mammuthus primigenius* (Blumenbach, 1799)

# INDEX

**BRITISH GEOLOGICAL SURVEY**

Keyworth, Nottingham NG12 5GG
0115 936 3100

Murchison House, West Mains Road, Edinburgh EH9 3LA
0131 667 1000

London Information Office, Natural History Museum
Earth Galleries, Exhibition Road, London SW7 2DE
020 7589 4090

The full range of Survey publications is available through the
Sales Desks at Keyworth and at Murchison House, Edinburgh,
and in the BGS London Information Office in the Natural
History Museum (Earth Galleries). The adjacent bookshop
stocks the more popular books for sale over the counter. Most
BGS books and reports can be bought from The Stationery
Office and through Stationery Office agents and retailers.
Maps are listed in the BGS Map Catalogue, and can be bought
together with books and reports through BGS-approved
stockists and agents as well as direct from BGS.

*The British Geological Survey carries out the geological survey of Great
Britain and Northern Ireland (the latter as an agency service for the
government of Northern Ireland), and of the surrounding continental
shelf, as well as its basic research projects. It also undertakes
programmes of British technical aid in geology in developing countries
as arranged by the Department for International Development and
other agencies.*

*The British Geological Survey is a component body of the Natural
Environment Research Council.*

Published by The Stationery Office and available from:

**The Publications Centre**
(mail, telephone and fax orders only)
PO Box 276, London SW8 5DT
Telephone orders/General enquiries 0870 600 5522
Fax orders 0870 600 5533

www.tso-online.co.uk

**The Stationery Office Bookshops**
123 Kingsway, London WC2B 6PQ
020 7242 6393  Fax 020 7242 6412
68–69 Bull Street, Birmingham B4 6AD
0121 236 9696  Fax 0121 236 9699
33 Wine Street, Bristol BS1 2BQ
0117 926 4306  Fax 0117 929 4515
9–21 Princess Street, Manchester M60 8AS
0161 834 7201  Fax 0161 833 0634
16 Arthur Street, Belfast BT1 4GD
028 9023 8451  Fax 028 9023 5401
The Stationery Office Oriel Bookshop
18–19 High Street, Cardiff CF1 2BZ
029 2039 5548  Fax 029 2038 4347
71 Lothian Road, Edinburgh EH3 9AZ
0870 606 5566  Fax 0870 606 5588

**The Stationery Office's Accredited Agents**
(see Yellow Pages)

*and through good booksellers*